Re-Presenting the Good Society

Studies in Contemporary German Social Thought (partial listing)
Thomas McCarthy, general editor

Re-Presenting the Good Society

Maeve Cooke

The MIT Press
Cambridge, Massachusetts
London, England

MIT Press books may be purchased at special quantity discounts for business or sales promotional use. For information, please email special_sales@mitpress.mit.edu or write to Special Sales Department, The MIT Press, 55 Hayward Street, Cambridge, MA 02142.

This book was set in Baskerville by SNP Bestset Typesetter Ltd., Hong Kong, and was printed and bound in the United States of America.

Library of Congress Cataloging-in-Publication Data

Cooke, Maeve.
Re-presenting the good society / Maeve Cooke.
    p.   cm.—(Studies in contemporary German social thought.)
Includes bibliographical references and index.
ISBN 0-262-03347-X (hc : alk. paper)
1. Critical theory. 2. Sociology—Philosophy. 3. Social sciences—Philosophy. I. Title. II. Series.

HM585.C663   2006
301.01—dc22
                                                                    2005054456

10 9 8 7 6 5 4 3 2 1

For Martin

Contents

Acknowledgments

This book was made possible through a number of research fellowships that freed me from my teaching and administrative duties to spend time in a variety of exciting academic environments. I would like to express my gratitude to the agencies and institutions concerned for their generous assistance. Thanks are due, in particular, to the Irish Research Council for the Humanities and Social Sciences, who awarded me a government of Ireland senior research fellowship for twelve months from 2002 to 2003, to University College Dublin, who awarded me a president's fellowship for twelve months from 1999 to 2000, and to the Alexander von Humboldt Stiftung who granted me a research fellowship from 1994 to 1996, allowing me to spend eighteen months at the Otto Suhr Institut für Politikwissenschaft, Freie Universität Berlin, and a further research fellowship in 2001, that allowed me to spend nine months at the Institut für Philosophie, Johann Wolfgang Goethe Universität, Frankfurt am Main. My sponsor on these last two occasions was Professor Axel Honneth, and I am deeply grateful to him and his colleagues for their hospitality. While in Berlin I was also made welcome by Professor Albrecht Wellmer and his colleagues at the Institut für Philosophie, Freie Universität Berlin, for which, too, I am most grateful.

I benefited on many occasions from the stimulating discussions that followed the presentation of my work at research seminars and conferences. The lively debates, both informal and formal, at the annual meetings of the Philosophy and the Social Sciences Conference in Prague deserve particular mention here.

I would like to express my thanks to Kevin Ryan for commenting on an earlier draft of chapter 4, to Martin Löw-Beer for commenting on a paper that grew into chapter 6, and to Axel Honneth and Alessandro Ferrara for commenting on much earlier versions of chapter 7. Sincere thanks are also due to the anonymous readers whose engaged and constructive reports proved very helpful when making my final revisions. Finally I would like to thank Martin Sauter, who read many versions of many chapters and, in the end, the entire manuscript; without his critical yet encouraging comments this book could not have been written.

Re-Presenting the Good Society

Introduction

"Man is born free; and everywhere he is in chains."[1] Thus, Rousseau, writing at a time of immense intellectual and social change in Europe, sowed the seeds of a mode of ethically oriented, critical thinking that can be given the name of *critical social theory*. His seminal contribution was to suggest that certain kinds of social arrangements may prevent human beings from realizing their potentials as human beings. Underlying this suggestion was a view of human nature as malleable. In contrast to the ethical views that had prevailed up to then, Rousseau saw human nature not as essentially fixed and given but as open to the formative influences of the social arrangements in which human beings are involved in their everyday lives. Crucially, moreover, he maintained that these social arrangements were the result of human activity. Again in contrast to the hitherto dominant traditions, he rejected the view that certain kinds of social relations, structures, or institutions are naturally necessary, divinely ordained, or historically inevitable, holding that human beings themselves could establish alternative, more beneficial ones. Since Rousseau, critical social theory has been guided by this insight.[2]

Critical social theory has also focused on *individual* human flourishing. To be sure, this aspect, though central, should not be overinflated; critical social thinking is not individualist in the sense of asserting the priority of individual goals at the expense of communal and social values or in the sense of conceiving of human beings atomistically, as self-contained centers of ethical value. Indeed, critical social thinkers often appeal to an idea of social solidarity and understand ethical value in intersubjective terms.

Nonetheless, critical social theory is individualist in two important senses: first, in the sense that it prioritizes the individual's well-being as opposed to that of the collective; second, in the sense that it stresses the need for the individual herself to be able freely to accept a given conception of human flourishing as the best—most attractive and most rationally compelling—one. Its individualist dimension is often expressed in terms of an ethical idea of autonomous agency: according to this idea, the individual must be able to see her actions and projects as expressions of her freedom and reason, and be prepared to take responsibility for their ethical validity.

Rousseau's emphasis on *historically contingent, social* impediments to *individual* human flourishing marks him out as a child of modernity. Indeed, his critical social thinking, like that of his successors, relies on a cluster of normative assumptions that are constitutive, in particular, for Western, modern self-understanding.[3] These include the assumptions that historical time is progressive as opposed to cyclical; that political authority is neither divinely ordained, nor naturally given, but a matter of cooperation among human beings for their mutual benefit; that there are no authoritative standards independent of history and sociocultural context that could adjudicate rival claims to validity, especially in the areas of science, law, politics, morality, and art; that human knowledge is contestable, in the sense of being open to revision on the basis of good reasons; and that human beings are essentially equal by virtue of a capacity such as reason, or freedom, or moral judgment, and are entitled to respect on grounds of that capacity.

These and related normative assumptions constitute key elements of the evaluative horizon of Western modernity in the sense that they now unavoidably shape the identities, institutions, proposals, and practices of its inhabitants. They reflect the intellectual shifts that took place in the Western world from around the fifteenth century onwards, giving rise to new ideas about history and nature, about authority and knowledge, and about human beings and their interrelationships. They share in common an antiauthoritarian impulse that, once again, can be expressed by the idea of autonomous agency: by the idea that human beings must have reasons for the validity of their perceptions, interpretations, and evaluations, and for subjecting themselves to laws and political regimes, that they are able to *call their own*.[4] Ideas of this kind are constitutive in the sense that they are formative of individual and collective identities, both constraining and enabling thought and behavior. This is not to say that inhabitants of Western modernity must accept the validity of such formative ideas. Famously, Nietzsche rejected a conception of historical time as progressive as well as the idea that all human beings are equal.[5] The point is that if such formative ideas are rejected, those who reject them must take on the task of reorienting self-interpretations so that the normative assumptions in question no longer seem convincing. Nietzsche, of course, took on precisely this task.

A further central assumption underlying critical social theory is evident in Rousseau's writings—the thesis that the social arrangements preventing human beings from realizing their potentials may be accompanied by, or even themselves give rise to, faulty perceptions of needs and interests. As a result, social change for the better is not simply a matter of changing social arrangements to establish better modes of living together in a better organized and regulated society; it may also involve changing perceptions. From Rousseau onwards critical social theories have generally acknowledged that the human beings who suffer under certain kinds of social arrangements may not be aware of the harmful effects of those arrangements, and may even resist the social critic's attempts to bring them to their attention. Consequently, critical social theories address the question of transformation in a double respect: they seek to identify possibilities for changes in social arrangements, while recognizing that this may require changes in prevailing perceptions of needs and interests.

In calling for social and cognitive transformation, critical social theories are guided by an idea of the good society in which the identified social obstacles to human flourishing would once and for all have been overcome. This idea may be articulated more or less explicitly; indeed, frequently, it is presented negatively and must be extrapolated from the critical social theorist's descriptions of what is wrong with social arrangements in the society in question. Nonetheless, without some, more or less determinate, guiding idea of the good society, critical social thinking would be inconceivable: it would lack an ethical basis for its critical diagnoses and its endeavor to stimulate social and cognitive transformation would have no ethical point.

The possibility of faulty perceptions of needs and interests means that the validity of these guiding ideas of the good society must have some independence of the ideas of the good society that are dominant in the social order in question. Traditionally, this independence has been interpreted as a context-transcending one: the validity of a particular idea of the good society was held to extend beyond the assignments of meaning and value in a historically specific, sociocultural context—it was deemed valid for everyone, everywhere, irrespective of sociocultural context and historical epoch.

Today, the concept of context-transcending validity is not easy to defend. Whereas Rousseau could still appeal unselfconsciously to normative assumptions about the nature of human beings, contemporary critical social theories have to address the question of how to justify the ideas of the good society that guide their critical analyses. Important shifts in the Western social imaginary over the past one hundred and fifty years have led to a serious problem of justification.[6] The "linguistic turn" of Western philosophy means that there is now a widespread acceptance that ideas of knowledge and validity are always mediated linguistically, and that language is conditioned by history and context; the influence of Nietzsche means that, today, the subjectivity and partiality of ethical judgments seems incontrovertible; Foucault's descriptions of epistemological and ethical orders as instruments of repressive power raises suspicion that claims to context-transcending validity, by obscuring their own origins in particular epistemological and ethical orders, collude in the dissemination and perpetuation of social repression.

As a consequence of these shifts, contemporary critical social theories have to confront the question of how to justify the claims to validity they make for the ideas of the good society guiding their critical diagnoses and emancipatory projections. On the one hand, they must endeavor to proceed in a nonauthoritarian manner by taking account of the historicity of knowledge and validity claims, recognizing the subjectivity and partiality of ethical judgments, and acknowledging the possibility that claims to context-transcending validity are perhaps yet one more means of exercising repressive social power. On the other hand, they must seek to uphold ideas of the good society that raise claims to validity that are not reducible to the contingent preferences of the inhabitants of historically specific, sociocultural contexts. We might say, the justificatory dilemma facing contemporary critical social theories is how to maintain an idea of context-transcending, ethical validity without violating their own antiauthoritarian impulses. A principal aim of the following discussion is to find a way of dealing with this dilemma. Since the tension between an antiauthoritarian impulse and a guiding idea of context-transcending validity is today an integral part of critical social theory, I argue that it should be negotiated rather than eliminated.

In chapter 1 I highlight the transformative dimension of critical social theory, using the difference in the respective views on the status of claims regarding change for the better to set up the debate between "radically contextualist" and "context-transcending" approaches to critical social theory. This debate structures much of the discussion in the book. In accordance with the antiauthoritarian impulses that can be expressed in the concept of situated rationality, both approaches, as I present them, take the deep-seated, normative intuitions and expectations of the inhabitants of a particular social order as the normative reference point for their social criticism. They diverge, however, in their interpretations of the status of these deep-seated intuitions and expectations: radically contextualist approaches deny them any rationality or purpose beyond the social order in question; context-transcending approaches attribute to them presumptive universal validity and regard them as open in principle to interrogation on the basis of good reasons. Each approach has certain strengths and weaknesses. I conclude that critical social theories cannot do without the idea of context-transcending validity, but that the difficulties they face in attempting to maintain such an idea are serious.

In chapter 2, I discuss the radically contextualist position of Richard Rorty, contending that it not only leads to unacceptably restricted models of critical social thinking and democratic politics, it also proves impossible to sustain consistently.

In chapter 3, I examine the attempts of Jürgen Habermas and Axel Honneth to maintain a reference to context-transcending validity while avoiding epistemological and ethical authoritarianism. The foundationalist—authoritarian—residues I discern in their theories can be overcome, I suggest, by adopting an approach to context-transcending validity, and a corresponding model of practical rationality, along lines I propose in chapters 5 to 7.

Before turning to that approach to context-transcending validity, however, I look at the poststructuralist critical social thinking of Judith Butler and Ernesto Laclau. In chapter 4 I argue that their radical democratic concerns require them, too, to engage with the question of context-transcending validity, despite their antipathy to justificatory issues.

In chapter 5 I confront the question of how to conceive of ethical validity in a context-transcending sense. The challenge is find a nonauthoritarian way of construing the relation between the idea of the good society guiding a particular critical social theory and the good society itself. I show how Laclau's account of the universal as a transcendent ethical object that is incarnated in particular, constitutively inadequate, political representations, can help to find a way of meeting that challenge. With this, I arrive at my core thesis. My central claim is that we should conceive of the good society as *re-presented* in particular representations that are constitutively inadequate to it: such particular re-presentations seek to *present* the transcendent ethical object ("the good society") powerfully; however, they always fail to capture it completely. I suggest that Habermas's idea of the ideal speech situation can be seen as a particular re-presentation of this kind. In elaborating my conception I characterize particular re-presentations of the good society as regulative ideas that have an imaginary, fictive character; crucially, however, I equip these regulative ideas with claims to validity that are open to intersubjective interrogation in public processes of argumentation.

In chapter 6 I make the case for the connection between context-transcending validity and argumentation, drawing attention to the central importance of the ethical idea of autonomous agency. This leads me to outline a model of autonomy that would fit well with the aims of contemporary critical social theories, while taking on board the valid objections of poststructuralist, communitarian, and feminist critiques of autonomy. I then propose a nonauthoritarian model of practical rationality that would allow for a rationally backed evaluation of competing ideas of the good society.

In chapter 7 I elucidate the implications of my reflections on the idea of context-transcending validity for the utopian dimension of critical social theory, showing how the approach I advocate enables it to avoid the problems of "bad utopianism" and "finalism" that have plagued it traditionally. In critical engagement with Albrecht Wellmer, who argues for a context-transcending perspective on truth that dispenses with regulative ideas, I defend the need for *re-presentations* of the good society. I also show that Habermas's model of moral deliberation projects the idea of a communicative utopia whose static, closed character is out of tune with the dynamic approach to validity that I have advocated, and I call upon him to bring it into line with his revised account of truth.

In chapter 8 I draw attention to the authoritarian implications of critical social theories that disconnect *theory* from *praxis*, and I make the case for maintaining a close connection between the two terms. I argue, however, that the relation between them requires rearticulation, for the traditional understanding leads to an authoritarian conception of praxis. Furthermore, using as illustration a recent debate between Nancy Fraser and Axel Honneth, I call for a reconsideration of the explanatory component of critical social thinking, proposing that contemporary critical social theories eschew grand theories that purport to explain the causes of the social evils they identify, and concentrate instead on investigating the multiple and multifaceted ways in which these social evils are disseminated and perpetuated.

Throughout the book I use the term "critical social theory" in a general sense. Although the name is often used to designate the particular tradition of critical social thinking associated with Max Horkheimer, Herbert Marcuse, Theodor Adorno, and other members of the Frankfurt School, I use it to refer to any mode of ethically oriented reflection that looks critically at social arrangements from the point of view of the obstacles they pose for individual human flourishing, or that reflects on what it means to do so. If Rousseau is a seminal figure in the history of such thinking, the seeds he sows are multiple and various. In the nineteenth century they bear fruit above all in the philosophical writings of Hegel, Marx, and Nietzsche. From the turn of the twentieth century, critical social thinking receives an added impetus from the newly emerging discipline of sociology—Max Weber, Émile Durkheim, and Georg Simmel are the prominent figures here. It is also increasingly influenced by psychoanalysis, especially the work of Sigmund Freud. These strands are integrated in the interdisciplinary and empirically oriented approach advocated by the critical social thinkers of the Frankfurt School. Today, theorists such as Habermas and Honneth still affiliate themselves with this tradition but, increasingly, the distinctiveness of its line of thinking is becoming blurred. Although interdisciplinarity and empirical underpinning were once particular hallmarks of the Frankfurt School tradition, today they can be found in other approaches to social criticism, in particular, those inspired by the work of Michel Foucault. As a result it is no longer possible to draw a sharp distinction between the Frankfurt School approach and other approaches. Furthermore, it seems unnecessarily restrictive to exclude contemporary writers from the enterprise of critical social theory on grounds of their primarily philosophical interventions—thinkers such as Richard Rorty, Judith Butler, and Charles Taylor come to mind here. For these reasons, I have opted for a looser definition of critical social theory. On my understanding, it embraces all contemporary thinkers who engage in social criticism guided by an idea of the good society in which the salient obstacles to human flourishing would once and for all have been removed, or who reflect on what it means to engage in such criticism.

The term "ethical," too, is used in a general sense to refer to modes of thinking and acting that are guided by a concern for the good. It may be noted, however, that I construe the concern for the good as a concern for a transcendent object that always exceeds its particular representations, thus giving the category of the ethical a context-transcending quality that it lacks, for example, in Habermas's work. Habermas bases his distinction between ethical questions and moral questions on the allegedly context-specific character of the former and the allegedly context-transcending character of the latter.[7] Evidently, in making the case for a conception of ethical validity that is inherently context transcending, I reject Habermas's basis for this distinction. This does not mean that I reject the distinction between the domains of the ethical and the moral. In my view, a plausible basis for distinguishing the two domains would be the difference between the kinds of ideas of the transcendent object that orient ethical thinking and acting on the one hand, and moral thinking and acting on the other. I do not explore this question, however, since, for the most part, the distinction between ethical questions and moral questions has no bearing on my discussion.

1

Change for the Better

As a mode of reflection that looks critically at social arrangements from the point of view of the obstacles they pose for individual human flourishing, critical social theory has a built-in emancipatory perspective. Recalling the words of Rousseau, we might say that it seeks to liberate human beings from the social chains that bind them by showing how certain, historically contingent, social arrangements prevent them from fulfilling their potentials as human beings; its critical diagnoses and emancipatory projections are guided by an idea of the good society in which the salient social obstacles to human flourishing would once and for all have been overcome.

Transformation is therefore a key concept in critical social theory. Its centrality follows from a view of the social obstacles to human flourishing as being *contingent*: that is, the social arrangements that produce such obstacles are held to be neither divinely ordained, naturally necessary, nor historically inevitable and are therefore replaceable by other, more beneficial arrangements. Insofar as they posit a connection between theory and praxis, critical social theories interpret this as a call for transformative action: human beings themselves, by way of concrete struggles and interventions, must seek to transform the social arrangements that impede human flourishing. To do so, they must want to do so—they must be motivated to change the social arrangements in question; this implies, at a minimum, that they see such arrangements as impediments. To see them as such may require the transformation of perceptions of needs and interests.

The possibility of such a transformation is crucial because critical social theories rely on the distinction between the particular ideas of the good society orienting their critical diagnoses and emancipatory projections, on the one hand, and the ideas of the good society dominant in the social order that is the object of their critique, on the other. However, as we shall see, if critical social theories are to avoid epistemological and ethical authoritarianism, they must suppose that their guiding ideas of the good society are able, potentially, to connect with the deep-seated, normative intuitions and expectations that are formative of the identities of the human beings they address: the inhabitants of the social order in question must be able, potentially, to recognize these intuitions and expectations as ethically valid, even though they may currently be lost, obscured, suppressed, or articulated in normatively deficient ways. In other words, on a nonauthoritarian understanding, the normative ideas guiding critical social theories, although not simply reducible to those prevailing in a particular social order, are nonetheless ideas with which the aforementioned inhabitants are in a sense already familiar; moreover, they are capable of being recognized as such when recovered, recalled, or presented in an illuminating way.

The distinction between their own guiding ideas of the good society and those dominant in the criticized social order allows critical social theories to regard the prevailing perceptions of needs and interests as possibly faulty: insofar as the inhabitants of the social order in question are guided by faulty views of the good society, they will hold correspondingly faulty views of human flourishing in general and of their own needs and interests in particular. In such cases, the transformation of prevailing social arrangements calls for a prior cognitive transformation.

To be sure, there are significant differences among critical social theories as to how faulty perceptions of the good society, of human flourishing, and of needs and interests should be rectified. Some theories propose therapeutic processes of recovery (Hegel);[1] some, poetic processes of world disclosure (Adorno);[2] some, reconstructive theories (Habermas).[3] Other theories propose hermeneutic processes of retrieval (Charles Taylor)[4] and others still, subversive bodily performances (Judith Butler).[5] Moreover, rectifying faulty perceptions of needs and interests may be understood as a task that either can be completed finally or can never, in principle, be concluded. Notwithstanding such differences, however, critical social theorists are united in the view that rectifying faulty perceptions is part of the critical enterprise itself.

A complication arises in critical social theories in which faulty perceptions are traced back to the social system and explained as an effect of that system's interest in its own self-preservation.[6] This is the classical view of ideology as "false consciousness." In such cases, the problem is twofold: not only are the human beings who suffer from the negative effects of certain kinds of social arrangements unaware of these negative effects, there are structural obstacles to bringing them to their attention.

In the classical view, made famous by Marx, Lukács, Adorno, and others, ideology is systemically induced—that is, necessary—false consciousness.[7] Ideology in this sense refers to a general blindness of human beings to their real needs or interests that is induced by a given social or economic system for the purposes of its own reproduction. This idea is already anticipated in the work of Rousseau. With his criticism of *amour propre* as a corrupt form of self-love that develops only when human beings enter into association with one another, Rousseau makes the crucial link between false consciousness and life in certain social structures.[8] Marx takes the further step required for the idea of systemically induced false consciousness. He combines the view that false consciousness is socially produced with a view that it is produced in the interests of a self-maintaining socioeconomic system.[9]

However, this conception of ideology has fallen into disrepute for a number of reasons. To begin with, the notion of ideology as necessary false consciousness raises the questions of who is in a position to engage in ideology critique and from what vantage point it is possible for them to do so. The critique of ideology as necessary false consciousness seems to presuppose a vantage point outside of the otherwise closed ideological circle that is accessible only to some privileged individuals or groups within the social order in question, denying the other inhabitants of the social order the ability to themselves know what is good for them. This opens such a critique to the accusation of epistemological and ethical authoritarianism (I return to this point below).

A further reason for rejecting the thesis of necessary false consciousness is that it is anachronistic: it no longer seems to fit the reality of complex modern societies. The thesis of necessary false consciousness relies on a picture of the socioeconomic system as a self-interested, self-maintaining organism that is (at best) out of date. In this picture, the socioeconomic system itself is held responsible for bringing about a condition of general false consciousness and is accused of doing so for the sake of its own interests as opposed to the interests of the human beings it is supposed to serve.[10] The socioeconomic system is thus assigned the attributes of a human agent with rational and moral powers; it is seen as a rational agent with interests of its own and as a moral agent who is responsible for its actions and against whom moral claims can be made. This kind of personification of the social or economic system has become increasingly implausible in modern societies, which are not only complex internally but connected with a multitude of other societies in complicated ways. Consequently, the notion of ideology as *necessary* false consciousness appears outdated.

Jürgen Habermas draws attention to yet another way in which the concept of ideology is anachronistic. Initially, Habermas upheld the legacy of Marx, Lukács, and Adorno by according a central place to the idea of ideology as necessary false consciousness.[11] He gradually moved away from the notion of ideology critique, however, and now seems to have distanced himself completely from it.[12] His present position seems to be that the concept of ideology no longer fits the forms of consciousness characteristic of late capitalist societies. For Habermas, all ideologies take the form of totalizing conceptions of order, imposing a socially integrative interpretation of society as a meaningful whole. Their effectiveness requires a realm of belief and action that is perceived as "sacred," in the sense of being immune to the corrosive effects of rational scrutiny. However, the process of cultural rationalization characteristic of modernity is a process of desacralization, which entails the subjection of ever more areas of social life to critical scrutiny. As a result, global interpretations that bestow meaning on society as a whole are no longer sustainable. As Habermas puts it: "the communicative practice of everyday life no longer affords any niches for the structural violence of ideologies."[13] In his view, the fragmentation of consciousness has now replaced ideological thought forms as their functional equivalent. Thus, for Habermas, in the desacralized societies of late capitalism, blindness to real needs and interests is no longer due to the acceptance of a deceptive interpretation of society as a meaningful whole; rather blindness, which for him, as we shall see in chapter 3, means blindness to the colonization of communicative rationality by the functionalist rationality of the economic and administrative systems, is the result of a fragmented consciousness that blocks the correct view of things by preventing interpretations of the whole from coming about in the first place.[14]

For reasons such as these, the concept of ideology as necessary false consciousness has lost favor among many contemporary critical social theorists, most noticeably among those in the Frankfurt School tradition.[15] It rarely features in their analyses of social evils and, when it does, it tends to fall prey to the kinds of epistemological, ethical, and social-theoretical difficulties alluded to above. To be sure, the sociotheoretical difficulties could be avoided by giving up the thesis of necessary false consciousness. Moreover, the epistemological and ethical difficulties could be alleviated by moving to an account of ideology that gives up any claim to an epistemically privileged vantage point and that focuses on the forms ideological distortion takes rather than on the content of false consciousness. On such an account of ideology, the object of critique would not be the falsity of certain propositional contents but, for example, the ideological closure involved when certain ethical or political contents are removed from the realm of public interrogation (I come back to this idea of ideological closure in chapter 5 below).

I have suggested that, in seeking to bring about changes in social arrangements, critical social theories recognize that cognitive transformation may be a prerequisite of social transformation. Those of us who, in the eyes of a particular theorist, lack a proper perception of the social obstacles to human flourishing, are called upon to revise our views of the prevailing social arrangements, to reconsider our views of the good society, and to rethink our views of our needs and interests. Evidently, cognitive transformation is not sought for its own sake but for the sake of the superior perceptions of society and human flourishing in which it is supposed to result. Thus, it is not a good in itself but a means of achieving one. The crucial concept, therefore, is not cognitive transformation but beneficial cognitive transformation: what is sought is not just a change in the way we see things but a shift in perception that constitutes a change for the better. This holds also for transformative action that is directed at existing social arrangements. Here, too, transformation is to be understood as bringing about improvement, as a step forward that can be described as learning or progress.

We may say, therefore, that progress is a central concern of critical social theory—progress on the level of social order and, where necessary, on the level of perceptions.[16] Clearly, progress is an evaluative term; it implies the availability of an evaluative perspective from which changes can be assessed as for the better or for the worse. In the case of critical social theories, it is their guiding ideas of the good society that provide the required evaluative perspective: the vantage point from which changes in perceptions of needs and interests, or changes in existing social arrangements, can be seen as changes for the better or for the worse. The crucial question for our present purposes concerns the status of these guiding ideas of the good society, and the status of the forms of cognitive and social transformation for which they call. Four broad positions with regard to their status can be distinguished; however, not all of them fit well with the self-understanding and concerns of contemporary critical social theories.

• The first position appeals to the normative ideas expressed in the *Sittlichkeit* ("ethical life") of the society in question. Changes in perceptions of needs and interests are deemed changes for the better because they bring us closer to how things should be as determined by certain (linguistically mediated) social conventions, practices, and codes of behavior. This position asserts a difference between the normative ideas held by some inhabitants of a particular social order and those held by the inhabitants in general. Appeals to "how we do things here" are typical of this position. Candidates for beneficial transformation tend to be those who have not yet been adequately socialized into the social practices of the context in question, for example, children, foreigners, or the psychologically disturbed. I call this the *conventionalist* position.

• The second position appeals to normative ideas implicit but not fully realized within a given sociocultural context. The changes in question are deemed changes for the better because they bring us closer to how things would be, if only we were able to realize our own deepest hopes and aspirations. This position asserts a difference between the normative ideas that orient the everyday lives of the inhabitants of a particular sociocultural context and the ideas that would orient their lives, if only they were able to become more like themselves at their best (for example, more consistent or more strong willed or more open to the interpretations of human flourishing proposed by others). In contrast to the first position, therefore, it appeals to deep-seated, normative intuitions and expectations that, at any given time, may not be appropriately articulated or realized; accordingly, its guiding ideas of the good society may diverge from those articulated in the dominant ethical practices and codes of behavior. Similarly, it posits a difference between the social arrangements that prevail in a given sociocultural context and those that would prevail if these social arrangements were to fully express the deep-seated, normative intuitions and expectations that are formative of their inhabitants' identities. The crucial feature of this position is that the normative ideas guiding criticism are purely internal to the codes of behavior and practices of the inhabitants of a particular sociocultural context; they have no purpose or rationality beyond this context. To be sure, the ideas in question may have to be retrieved from obscurity or articulated more clearly or convincingly, and much effort may be needed in order to bring existing behavior and practices into line with them. The important point is that there is no vantage point external to a particular sociocultural context that would provide a basis for assessing the validity of the normative ideas held by its inhabitants. I call this the *radically contextualist* position.

• The third position appeals to normative ideas that are at once immanent to the sociocultural context in question and transcend it. As in the case of the second position, the ideas appealed to are context immanent in the sense that they are implicit within a particular sociocultural context, although possibly obscured, or forgotten, or not yet properly articulated. In contrast to the second position, however, these normative ideas are attributed with a rationality or purpose beyond that particular context. They are not merely expressions of *our* deepest hopes and aspirations (although they are that too); they represent hopes and aspirations that everyone, everywhere should have if they are to be able to fulfill their potentials as human beings. This position sees changes in the perceptions of needs and interests, or changes in the prevailing social arrangements, as changes for the better not only because they bring us closer to our own, historically and contextually specific ideals, but because they are steps forward for humankind in general. I call this the *context-transcending* position.

• The fourth position appeals to a transcendent, final authority. The changes in question are deemed changes for the better because they bring us closer to how things should be as determined by some transcendent power or idea whose authority is unquestionable. This position asserts a difference between the normative ideas that prevail in a given sociocultural context and those that would prevail if its inhabitants were to see their needs and interests in the ethically valid light. Similarly, it posits a difference between the social arrangements prevailing in a particular social order and those that would prevail if its inhabitants were to hold the correct view of the good society. The crucial feature of this position, which sets it off from the preceding one, is that correct perception entails the acceptance of the unquestionable authority of some transcendent power or idea. Thus, appeals to the authority of a divine will, or to natural necessity, or to the logic of history, are typical. I call this the *authoritarian* position.

Of these four, only two—the radically contextualist and the context-transcending positions—are congruent with the self-understanding and concerns found in contemporary critical social theories. The inappropriateness of the first and fourth positions is due to their assertion of an ethical standpoint that is unquestionable, immune to any kind of critical interrogation. With this assertion, they imply that ethical validity is accessible; moreover, that it can be established independently of the ethical reasoning of concrete human agents. By construing ethical validity as unquestionable, they invite accusations of epistemological authoritarianism; by disconnecting ethical validity from the reasoning of concrete human agents, they invite accusations of ethical authoritarianism. This brings them into conflict with the antiauthoritarian impulses of contemporary critical social theories.

In the introductory chapter, I situated critical social theory as an enterprise within the normative horizon of modernity, specifically, Western modernity. I also drew attention to certain important shifts that have taken place within this social imaginary; these shifts have undermined the view that unmediated access to reality or truth is possible, have led to widespread acceptance of the view that ethical judgments are subjective and partial, and have fostered suspicion of context-transcending validity claims as possible instruments of repressive social power. In consequence of these and related shifts, contemporary critical social theories are driven by an antiauthoritarian impulse, which can be expressed by the concept of *situated rationality*.

To begin with, situated rationality entails the view that the social theorist's critical perspective is inescapably conditioned by historical, cultural, social, and subjective factors: her perspective is not—and cannot be—neutral. In addition, it entails the view that the social theorist's critical perspective expresses normative intuitions and expectations that are formative of the identities of the inhabitants of the sociocultural context that is the object of her critique—her perspective is internal to that context.

The first aspect of situated rationality is primarily epistemological. It articulates a conception of knowledge that has gained currency within the normative horizon of Western modernity, particularly since the latter part of the nineteenth century. According to this conception, human knowledge is temporal, subjective, and partial: our perceptions of the ways things are, or of how they should be, are unavoidably influenced by the historically specific, sociocultural context in which we live our lives as embodied, finite human beings. All access to reality, or to validity in a context-transcending sense, is mediated by history, context, and embodied subjectivity. The widespread acceptance of this view of knowledge is often associated with the "linguistic turn" of twentieth-century philosophy. When understood in a general way, this turn stands for a shift in how human knowledge is construed. Wittgenstein, Heidegger, and Dewey are key figures in this regard, calling on us to dispense with the notion of knowledge as accurate representation and to adopt instead a pragmatic conception of knowledge as mediated by social conventions and practices.[17]

The second aspect is primarily ethical. It entails the view that critical social theory should be guided by the deep-seated, normative intuitions and expectations of the inhabitants of the social order in question. It articulates the ethical idea of autonomous agency, understood as the individual human being's freedom to form and pursue her conceptions of the good on the basis of reasons she is able to call her own. In chapter 6 I propose an interpretation of the idea of autonomy that connects it with the ethical norm of rational accountability, according to which the autonomous agent takes on a responsibility to support her views with reasons, if need be. The ethical idea of autonomous agency, with its emphasis on rational accountability, requires those who accept the validity of a particular critical perspective or emancipatory projection to have good reasons for doing so. From the point of view of autonomous agency, having good reasons implies, among other things, that the human subjects concerned make them their own good reasons—reasons that make sense to them in the context of their intuitions, expectations, commitments, convictions, and experiences as a whole. In other words, to see something as a good reason, human subjects must be capable of integrating it into the affectively imbued constellations of reasons that are formative of their identities. Failure to establish a connection with the most stable elements in these constellations would result in a lack of coherence; jettisoning all the other elements in order to make room for it would result in a lack of depth.[18] A similar need for integration holds on a collective level. If the inhabitants of a historically and culturally specific social order are to have good reasons for approving of a particular idea of the good society, these reasons must connect with the most stable elements in the affectively imbued constellations of reasons that shape their collective identity. Thus, it is in large measure due to a respect for autonomous agency that contemporary social theorists take already existing, deep-seated, normative intuitions and expectations as a fundamental point of orientation in their appeal to ideas of the good society.

Typically, these normative intuitions and expectations are sedimented in a multiplicity of social practices, norms, and institutions and may not be readily apparent. Sometimes, they will have been forgotten or obscured: in such cases, processes of hermeneutic retrieval, or aesthetic shock techniques, may be necessary before their validity can be recognized. Sometimes they will have been suppressed: in such cases, a process of therapy or, again, aesthetic shock techniques, may be required to recover them. Sometimes, they may lack the appropriate theoretical form: in such cases, they must be reconstructed appropriately by the theorist. At other times, some of these ideas and expectations may be highly visible, constituting the explicit issues motivating concrete social struggles and movements. However, contemporary critical social theorists tend to be wary of attaching too much importance to the demands and expectations *expressed* in social struggles and movements. This is because the deep-seated, normative intuitions and expectations implicit in every social order are rarely fully articulated, informing social struggles and movements indirectly rather than directly. Furthermore, the demands and expectations voiced in certain social struggles and movements may be incompatible with the deep-seated, normative intuitions and expectations shared by most other inhabitants of the sociocultural context in question. Here we may consider how the claims to racial supremacy expressed in neo-Nazi movements clash with deep-seated commitments to equal respect for the dignity of all human beings. (This raises the questions of who decides what "our" deepest hopes and aspirations are, and on what basis. My discussion in chapters 5 to 7 suggests that it is a matter for practical deliberation among all concerned.) Indeed, the demands and expectations articulated in some social struggles and movements may clash with those articulated in other ones, where both parties claim to express our deepest hopes and aspirations. Here we may think of the demands of equality voiced by proponents of positive discrimination in favor of women, and the demands of merit or desert voiced by their opponents. (This raises the questions of who decides which principle should have priority in a given situation, and on what basis. Again, my discussion will suggest that it is a matter for practical deliberation among all concerned.) Notwithstanding these and related difficulties, contemporary critical social theories agree that the most appropriate reference point, at least initially, for assessing whether cognitive and social change is change for the better is the set of normative intuitions and expectations that shape our identities as individuals and citizens within a historically specific, sociocultural context.

This position is also found in poststructuralist versions of social criticism. Although they possess a number of distinctive features that mark them off, in particular, from hermeneutic, therapeutic, and reconstructive approaches, poststructuralist social theories share with these an orientation toward already existing normative intuitions and expectations as their reference point for criticism. Poststructuralist social critics stress the ways in which every actualization of our deep-seated, normative intuitions and expectations produces its own "outside," denying some aspect of these intuitions and expectations. The point is also about the incompleteness of identity: every articulation of normative intuitions or expectations is held to open a gap between what it affirms and what it denies. For poststructuralist social critics, this gap is a space of historical possibility for beneficial cognitive, bodily, and social transformation; what is excluded can be made politically salient and activated with a view to bringing about various kinds of changes for the better. Accordingly, poststructuralist social criticism is concerned less with the retrieval of forgotten, obscured, or suppressed normative intuitions and expectations, or with reconstructing them in the appropriate theoretical form, than with the subversive and innovative rearticulation of them.

Here, it is important to recognize the multiple forms such rearticulation may take. Whereas hermeneutic retrieval, therapeutic recovery, and reconstructive theory are primarily linguistic modes of articulating normative intuitions and expectations, relying on narratives, conversations, or argumentation, poststructuralists also draw attention to the nonlinguistic ways in which deep-seated, normative intuitions and expectations may be rearticulated or reenacted. They often attach importance to anomalous and disruptive bodily practices, in which a given vocabulary is pushed to its limits so that new conceptual possibilities can emerge. Notwithstanding such differences in emphasis, however, poststructuralist critical social thinking shares with other contemporary approaches an insistence on the unavailability of an ethical vantage point beyond the influences of history and context, as well as a perception that the social critic must take her orientation from already existing, deep-seated, normative intuitions and expectations. Thus, although their concern with nonargumentative—and often, nonverbal—modes of critical interrogation may make them hostile to the term "situated rationality," poststructuralist critical social theories fully endorse the antiauthoritarian impulse it expresses.

Within the Left-Hegelian tradition of critical social thinking,[19] the idea of situated rationality has a further dimension. Here, too, critical social theories appeal to normative intuitions and expectations that are already embedded within the criticized social order; however, in seeking a reference point for criticism that is immanent to the context in question, their concern traditionally was not to avoid ethical authoritarianism but to uncover rational potentials within the process of history itself. The potentials in question were deemed rational in the sense that, historically, they represent a gain in rationality: they are expressions of the movement of reason in history (this is the Hegelian legacy). On this view of history, reason is thought to be sedimented in social practices and in deep-seated, normative intuitions and expectations; consequently, these are deemed to have rational potentials that can be released under favorable conditions.[20] The difficulty facing contemporary critical social theo-rists in this tradition, however, is that, by setting up history as a final authority, an immanent approach of the Hegelian kind seems at odds with the non-authoritarian impulse expressed by the idea of situated rationality. In chapter 3 I discuss Jürgen Habermas's and Axel Honneth's attempts to defend the immanence of criticism in a modified Hegelian sense without succumbing to epistemological and ethical authoritarianism.

The antiauthoritarian impulse that I attribute to contemporary critical social theory explains my use of the term "context-transcending" to character-ize those approaches that claim universal validity for their critical perspectives and emancipatory projections. I call approaches of this kind "context-tran-scending" rather than "universalist" to underscore the importance of a dynamic interpretation of the universality that they claim. This dynamic quality can be contrasted with the static quality of claims to universal validity that posit the possibility of an end point of reason. When construed statically, claims to universal validity allege that the realization of reason in the historical world is possible: they allege, for example, that a world in which each human subject would be granted the full respect that is due to him, or in which human subjects would live in perfect harmony with each other, or in which human subjects would live in perfect harmony with nature is an attainable condition for human beings. In positing the attainability of a fully rational world, however, they deny the finitude of human knowledge and understanding, the contingency of human life and history, and the creativity of human free will (I return to this point in chapter 7 below). Moreover, they invite the accusation of epistemological authoritarianism since, by positing the possibility of the realization of reason in the historical world, they sets limits to the contestability of knowledge and validity. On a dynamic understanding of claims to universal validity, by contrast, no such limits are laid down. Although claims are raised for the validity of certain ethical ideas across sociocultural contexts and historical epochs, there is an accompanying aware-ness that there is an ineliminable gap between the aspiration of universal validity and all actual claims to instantiate it. The idea of universality, in other words, is itself construed as context transcending: it is held never to be com-mensurate with its historically specific articulations. Clearly, a dynamic inter-pretation of the idea of universality fits well with the antiauthoritarian impulse I attribute to contemporary critical social theories. It is for this reason that I use the term "context-transcending" to refer to contemporary theories that claim universal validity for the ideas of the good society that guide them.

Of the four positions identified, I have claimed that only the radically contextualist and the context-transcending views of ethical validity are congruent with the self-understanding and concerns of contemporary critical social theory. From this common basis, however, the radically contextualist and context-transcending positions move off in different directions. Since the debate as to which direction is the best one structures my discussion in the following chapters, it is worth emphasizing the antiauthoritarian impulse uniting both positions.[21] Both positions concur in the view that no unmediated and no privileged access to reality or to ethical validity is available; they also agree that ethical validity must be recognizable as such to autonomous human agents. The point on which they diverge is the importance of ideas of context-transcending validity in critical social thinking.

Advocates of a context-transcending approach claim that critical social theories cannot do without a reference to context-transcending validity. The core argument is that without such a reference, the critical interrogation of social life would be unacceptably limited in scope. An additional argument is that giving up this reference is simply not sustainable. Advocates of a radically contextualist approach dispute both arguments. They contend that effective social criticism does not require any kind of reference to context-transcending validity; moreover, that appeal to validity in this sense is not unavoidable.

The debate between the context-transcending and radically contextualist positions can also be cast in terms of the concept of ethical progress. Our question has been the status of the particular ideas of ethical validity through reference to which changes in social arrangements, or changes in perceptions of needs and interests, are deemed changes for the better. In contemporary critical social theory, as we have seen, both the radically contextualist and context-transcending approaches respond to this question by pointing toward the deep-seated, normative intuitions and expectations of the inhabitants of the social order being subjected to criticism. They diverge, however, regarding the status of these deep-seated intuitions and expectations. Whereas radically contextualist approaches deny them any rationality or purpose beyond the social order in which they play a formative role, context-transcending approaches attribute to them presumptive universal validity and regard them as open in principle to interrogation on the basis of good reasons. Thus, for radically contextualist social critics, our deepest hopes and aspirations are utterly contingent. Although we, as inhabitants of a particular social order may attach great importance to them, and although they form our identities and shape our institutions and practices, there is no standpoint from which they could be deemed rationally superior to the deep-seated hopes and aspirations that are formative of identities in historically earlier or culturally different social orders. Context-transcending social critics, by contrast, regard our deepest hopes and aspirations as presumptively rational. They presume that there is a rational basis for seeing them as improvements over earlier hopes and aspirations, or as superior to conflicting ones, and that, if not, they should be abandoned or modified. These diverging views regarding the status of deep-seated, normative intuitions and expectations are connected with diverging conceptions of ethical progress.

On the radically contextualist view, the notion of ethical progress has no purchase beyond a historically specific, sociocultural context. This is because the normative intuitions and expectations embedded in a particular social order are regarded as normatively arbitrary: since there is no universal context of which they are part, there are no rational grounds for extending them to all human beings everywhere. Accordingly, the concept of progress is restricted to changes for the better *within* a historically specific, sociocultural context. Progress occurs, for example, when we, as inhabitants of Western modernity, pass laws that increase democratic accountability or develop educational institutions that are more inclusive and open. It is inapplicable, however, to changes in those deep-seated, normative intuitions and expectations through reference to which democratic accountability, inclusiveness, and openness are regarded as valuable goals for human beings. On the radically contextualist view, accordingly, the kinds of change that, following the work of Thomas Kuhn, have come to be known as "paradigm shifts" are regarded as random and arational—as purely arbitrary from a rational point of view.[22]

On the context-transcending view, by contrast, the concept of ethical progress can be applied *across* historical and social contexts. Since our deepest normative hopes and aspirations are accorded a presumptive rationality, they are presumed to constitute progress—change for the better—in relation to earlier hopes and aspirations and to be superior to culturally different ones. As such, they are ascribed a presumptive universal validity—they are presumed to be valid for everyone, everywhere, irrespective of sociocultural context, until challenged on the basis of good reasons. Accordingly, on the context-transcending view, the concept of progress can be used to describe historical changes that affect deep-seated, normative intuitions and expectations (i.e., paradigm shifts); in other words, it can be used in relation to ethically significant changes that result from intercultural encounters, engagement with the historical past, technological innovations, ecological developments, new life situations, and the like.

Each of these views gives rise to different problems. The main problem arising from radically contextualist approaches is that they are unacceptably restricted in scope: they are unable to offer a critical perspective *across* socio-cultural or historical contexts and must confine their critical observations to the immediate contexts in which they are situated. Their contextually restricted conceptions of progress mean that they lack the conceptual resources required for the critical interrogation of *new* ethical ideas that emerge as the result of intercultural encounters, engagement with the historical past, technological innovations, changing life situations, ecological developments, and so on; for the same reason, they lack the conceptual resources necessary for the critical interrogation of their own guiding ideas vis-à-vis the ones that have preceded them or currently challenge them.

We might also say that radically contextualist approaches lack the conceptual resources necessary to conceive of challenges to the deep-seated, normative intuitions and expectations, which are formative of identities in a particular social order, as *rational* disputes. Since they deny to such formative intuitions and expectations any rationality or truth value in an overarching, universal sense, the only nonauthoritarian basis on which, ultimately, they could be defended, rejected, or rearticulated, is arbitrary preference or strategic interest. Accordingly, responses to new ethical ideas, or to ethical paradigm changes, become, ultimately, a matter of arbitrary preference or strategic interest. This disadvantage is particularly evident under conditions of globalization in which cultures with diverging or conflicting, deep-seated, normative intuitions and expectations come into increasing contact with one another. Radically contextualist approaches lack the conceptual resources required in order to characterize intercultural exchanges as (mutual) learning processes; consequently, they are unable to describe any new ethical ideas that emerge from such encounters as ethical gains or losses. Their inability to provide a critical perspective affects the motivation of parties with significantly different or conflicting cultural views to enter into intercultural dialogue: if deliberation regarding new ethical ideas lacks any rational basis, the motivation for participating in processes of intercultural exchange cannot be the hope (on both sides) of cognitive or social change for the better; motivation can only be a matter of subjective desire or strategic interest; this implies that it would be incoherent to attempt to convince anyone of the nonsubjective or nonstrategic value of engaging in such intercultural encounters.[23] A similar point can be made with regard to critical reflection on new ethical ideas that emerge in the wake of technological innovations, ecological developments, intercultural encounters, and so on. Although biotechnological innovations such as cloning, or ecological changes such as global warming, may give rise to new ethical ideas, radically contextualist approaches lack the conceptual resources necessary to interrogate them critically. Evidently, the same difficulty holds for their own guiding ethical ideas. Lacking an idea of context-transcending validity, radically contextualist critical social theories lack the conceptual resources required to engage in argument concerning their guiding hopes and aspirations and to attempt to defend them as improvements vis-à-vis earlier or conflicting ones.[24]

But context-transcending approaches have their own difficulties. Their strength is their ability to extend a critical perspective to the ethically significant social changes that emerge from intercultural exchanges, technological innovations, and the like, as well as to their own guiding normative intuitions and expectations. This extended scope gives them the advantage over radically contextualist approaches, particularly under conditions of globalization and in periods of rapid social, technological, and ecological change. However, they are faced with the challenging task of reconciling their reference to context-transcending validity with the claims of situated rationality or, as I prefer to formulate it, the challenge of maintaining a productive tension between the two.

This challenge gains in urgency if the radically contextualist position proves seriously inadequate. In the next chapter, I demonstrate its inadequacies. I do so by considering one of the most forceful contemporary proposals for a radically contextualist approach to social criticism: the pragmatist approach proposed by Richard Rorty. Rorty makes a vigorous—and, at times, ingenious—case for a purely internal, or immanent, perspective. The discussion shows, however, that his radically contextualist approach, if adhered to consistently, is limited in the ways indicated above. Interestingly, it also reveals that Rorty is consistently unable to sustain a radically contextualist position. Such contextualism, it seems, is inherently unstable.

2

The Instability of Radical Contextualism

One of the most cogent presentations of the radically contextualist position is offered by Richard Rorty. For Rorty, the evaluative vocabulary employed in discussing the validity of normative ideas has no purchase outside of the particular sociocultural context in which that discussion takes place.[1] This does not imply uncritical acceptance of the normative ideas predominant in a given sociocultural context; such ideas can certainly be subjected to critical interrogation once we accept that the reference point for criticism cannot be some notion of context-transcending validity. On Rorty's account, the only useful evaluative standards for assessing the validity of normative ideas are valid exclusively for "us." They have their basis in the deep-seated, normative intuitions and expectations of the inhabitants of the sociocultural context in question. These intuitions and expectations are conceived as purely pragmatic needs and preferences. On this basis, Rorty distances himself from the attempts of Habermas and others to defend notions of universal validity based on context-transcending idealizations (for example, conceptions of truth as idealized rational acceptability or conceptions of justice as the outcome of an idealized discursive procedure for assessing the universalizability of norms). Against such projections of context-transcending validity, Rorty insists that normative ideas such as the ideal speech situation or ideal conversational community are no more than "picture[s] of 'us' as we should like to be." He elaborates: "Nor can I see what 'us' can mean here except: us educated, sophisticated, tolerant, wet liberals, the people who are always willing to hear the other side, to think out all the implications, etc."[2] He allows that, from the perspectives of the inhabitants themselves, the evaluative standards operative in a given sociocultural context are open to criticism and can be reformed on the basis of good reasons; what he disputes is the usefulness of ideas of context-transcending validity in such processes of criticism and reform.[3]

In his confrontations over the years with Habermas, Rorty has taken pains to emphasize that their approaches to social criticism share much in common.[4] He claims that the only point on which he differs from Habermas concerns the utility of the notion of "universal validity";[5] furthermore, he finds this difference between himself and Habermas "unimportant, when compared with the overlap between our views."[6] In chapter 1, however, I identified precisely this difference as the core of a dispute that divides contemporary critical social theory. On my presentation of the dispute, radically contextualist approaches seek to eliminate any reference to context-transcending validity on the grounds that it cannot be reconciled with the claims of situated rationality and is, moreover, unnecessary for the purposes of effective social criticism. Context-transcending approaches, by contrast, seek to uphold a reference to context-transcending validity in a way that does not compromise their commitment to situated rationality, contending that without such a reference, social criticism would be unacceptably restricted in scope: it would be unable to offer a critical perspective on new normative ideas that emerge from intercultural encounters, engagement with the historical past, technological innovations, ecological changes, new life situations, and so on; moreover, it would lack the conceptual resources necessary in order to defend its own guiding normative intuitions and expectations as improvements vis-à-vis earlier or conflicting ones. An additional argument against radically contextualist approaches to critical social thinking is that their proponents fail to maintain it consistently: as a rule they end up smuggling in some kind of reference to context-transcending validity. These arguments suggest that the difference between Habermas and Rorty is not so unimportant. Rather than downplaying their disagreement, therefore, I will attempt to bring it more clearly into view. In this chapter, I examine Rorty's rejection of context-transcending validity. In the next chapter, I consider Habermas's (and Honneth's) endeavor to defend it.

For Rorty, ideas of context-transcending validity cannot be made relevant to the public realm of deliberation concerning common purposes or policies. The standards of rationality employed in public processes of deliberation are always specific to a particular, local context and it is pointless to presuppose some bird's-eye viewpoint from which they would be seen as valid for all actual and possible contexts. He holds that this kind of presupposition is not only futile, it is arrogant, unhealthy, and immature. In order to see this, he invites us to look at our practices of rational deliberation from the perspective of those who reject their guiding norms. What we describe as participation in rational deliberation appears to our opponents as a struggle for power; as an exertion, not of the discriminating force of reason, but of the sheer force of will. He claims, moreover, that the longing for context-transcending standards is unwholesome and a symptom of immaturity—the yearning for the unconditioned and absolute is unhealthy[7] and indicates a merely transitional stage of moral development.[8] Rorty does not object to the vocabulary of learning, progress, and improvement, so long as we face up to the contingency of our own most central beliefs and desires and so long as we do not succumb to the illusion that we are getting closer to how things are in themselves, or how they should be.[9] He urges us to accept that progress is not a matter of getting closer to truth or to justice, in the sense of getting closer to the intrinsic character of reality or to morality. To help avoid this illusion he recommends substituting metaphors of evolutionary development for metaphors of progressively less distorted perception.[10]

Rorty refers approvingly to Dewey's pragmatic view of why societies evolve into other societies: "Societies evolve into other societies by finding that the moral language they have been using brings with it consequences they do not like. . . . To say that moral progress occurs is to say that later societies are more complex, more developed, more articulate, and above all, more flexible than their predecessors."[11] He warns, however, against being misled by this kind of evaluative language. As he interprets Dewey, these attributes have no value in themselves; they merely express the pragmatic needs of the inhabitants of a particular social context. Thus, it is futile to ask, "why flexibility, articulation, variety, and interestingness are worthy ends to pursue—why they are morally relevant ends for individuals or societies."[12] Again following Dewey, Rorty maintains that it is as pointless for us to ask whether we are going in the right direction as it would have been for squirrels to ask whether their evolution from shrews had been going in the right direction. In short, we should abandon the idea that ethical progress is rationally defensible in some context-transcending sense. Social criticism has no purchase outside of its own, historically contingent sociocultural context; we might say, it is completely immanent to this context.

It is important to see that Rorty's neo-Darwinian–pragmatist conception[13] is able to accommodate innovation and creativity. He can argue, for example, that the need to create new and better modes of social relations, and new and better sorts of human beings, is simply part of the natural history of the human species;[14] accordingly, it is as useless to query it as it is to query why squirrels

have the need to gather nuts.[15] He could say that creativity is an interest
"rooted in fundamental features of our embodiment and activities as social
creatures [that] transcend[s] more parochial features of our vocabularies."[16]

Such claims are not implausible. A study of human history shows human
beings to have certain general needs that are relatively invariant. Arguably, the
need to invent or create is one of these general needs, on a par with needs
relating to food, drink, and shelter.[17] Support for this claim could be provided
by the findings of empirically based research—biological, historical, anthropological, psychological, sociological, and so on. Over and above this, no
foundation is available; to request one would be futile.

Thus, a case could be made that creativity has emerged as a human need
in the course of the evolution of the species. However, the ability to account
for the need for creativity is insufficient for the purposes of critical social theory.
From its point of view, the main question is not why human beings need to be
creative, but what they see as important goals for their creativity. Human
beings, as Rorty acknowledges, are not neutral about such goals but describe
them in evaluative terms (for instance, as creating new and better modes of
social relations). Moreover, they distinguish purposes that should be pursued
from those that should be rejected. From the point of view of human beings
themselves, therefore, it is not pointless to ask what constitutes new and better
social structures or new and better ideas relating to human flourishing, and
why we should prefer one set of ideas to another.[18] Indeed, *pace* Rorty, this
evaluative orientation, too, could be seen as a natural fact about human beings
that is bound up with their creative impulses. Proponents of such a view might
observe that, in the history of the human species, creativity appears to have
been valued less for its own sake than for the sake of what has resulted from
it; indeed, even in contexts in which there has been a cult of genius, emphasizing creativity, evaluative questions concerning the ends toward which creativity
is directed have usually been considered relevant. Nietzsche, for example,
valued not creativity as such but creativity that produces new, noble, forms of
being. It could be argued, therefore, that an orientation toward evaluative
standards is already built into the human interest in creativity. If this is accepted,
Rorty's remarks require qualification. It is not creativity tout court that is a
human interest, but creativity directed toward a purpose that is held to be
worthwhile.[19]

Furthermore, within the sociocultural context of Western modernity, human
beings who ask which manifestations of creativity are good and which are not
good, commonly see themselves as seeking truth or justice. Moreover, they

conceive of truth and justice in context-transcending terms: they may think of truth as correspondence to an independently existing reality and of justice as a condition of perfect mutual understanding or perfect equality; in addition, as Rorty himself suggests, they may see themselves as implicitly claiming to be able to justify their assertions to *all* audiences, actual and possible.[20] Unlike many pragmatists, however, Rorty, is unwilling to accept these common intuitions. He does not want to leave the language of common sense as it is;[21] rather, he sees himself as part of a pragmatist tradition of "contributing to world-historical change in humanity's self-image."[22] His aim is to encourage us to revise our intellectual and ethical intuitions, thereby contributing to a long, slow process of sociocultural change that would result in new vocabularies of evolutionary development in the domains of truth and justice.[23] In other words, he aims to educate human beings to give up their arrogant, unhealthy, and immature reliance on ideas of context-transcending validity.

Rorty's aim to bring about cultural change is, of course, consistent with his emphasis on human creativity. But what could motivate us to endorse the particular kind of change he aims for—the relinquishing of ideas of context-transcending validity? Since, the kind of sociocultural change he aims for challenges fundamental elements of the modern vocabulary, it seems no rational motivation is conceivable. This is because, on Rorty's radically contexualist view, there is no perspective from which the rationality of fundamental shifts in vocabulary could be assessed. Presumably, therefore, his efforts to get us to revise our normative intuitions and expectations should be seen as poetic rather than political, as appealing to our imaginative as opposed to rational capacities (I come back to this point below).[24] Nonetheless, Rorty does offer one major reason, and a number of subsidiary ones, for why we should dispense with ideas of context-transcending validity—or, as he puts it, projections of the unconditioned and absolute—in favor of a neo-Darwinian–pragmatist position. As already indicated, the main reason he gives is that such ideas are pointless, claiming in addition that they are unhealthy and a sign of arrogance and immaturity. His argument here is epistemological.

Rorty argues that no *knowledge* regarding the intrinsic nature of reality or morality is available and that, consequently, truth is not serviceable as a goal of enquiry. This is because "a goal is something you can *know* that you are getting closer to, or farther away from;[25] there is no way to know our distance from truth, nor even whether we are closer to it than our ancestors were."[26] The point can also be made in terms of a distinction between the unrecognizable and the recognizable: "The grounding premise of my argument is that you cannot aim at something, cannot work to get it, unless you can recognize it once you have got it. One difference between truth and justification is that between the unrecognizable and the recognizable."[27]

Few contemporary proponents of context-transcending social criticism would dispute his claim that we have no unmediated access to reality or to morality as they are "in themselves." As we saw in earlier chapters, in common with all who have embraced the "linguistic turn" of post-nineteenth-century thinking, contemporary critical social theorists acknowledge the mediating influences of language, history, context, and embodied subjectivity on our perceptions. They do not claim that there are description-independent perceptions of reality or of human needs and interests. However, it is one thing to accept Rorty's point about the mediated nature of perception; it is another to agree that this rules out notions of the unconditioned and absolute as useful goals of enquiry.

When Rorty contends that a goal is "something that you can know that you are getting closer to," he seems to mean "know" in the sense of propositional knowledge: knowing *that* as opposed to the practical and usually tacit knowledge involved in knowing *how*. However, even if we confine ourselves to those human purposes in connection with which propositional knowledge is sought, his contention is dubious. Many of the goals that guide us in our everyday behavior are defined only vaguely (for example, the goal of a healthy lifestyle); in such cases, an important part of the process of reaching the goal is becoming clearer as to what the goal really is; knowledge as to where you stand with regard to attaining the goal is often not the issue.

More significantly, Rorty dismisses too hastily the imaginative dimension to our pursuit of the unconditioned and absolute. These are goals not in a literal but in a figurative sense. In chapters 5 to 7 below I argue in more detail that, as inhabitants of a reflexive modernity, we are able to recognize our particular ideas of context-transcending validity (truth, justice, and so on) as imaginative projections of an "impossible" transcendent object. On my account, such projections do not provide criteria. Their purpose is not to provide critical standards that would allow us to adjudicate between true and false perceptions or between better and worse forms of social life. Instead, they serve purposes of ethical disclosure and orientation. The important point in the present context is that those who appeal to particular representations of truth or justice recognize them as imaginative projections of a transcendent object that are constitutively inadequate to that object. In addition, they recognize that neither truth and justice qua transcendent objects nor their particular representations can provide criteria for adjudicating the correctness of our perceptions of reality or the rightness of our perceptions of human flourishing. Finally, they regard a particular representation's claim to offer ethical orientation, together with its claim to disclose the ethical object powerfully, as a contestable validity claim and, as such, always open to interrogation on the basis of good reasons. When they engage in the pursuit of truth and justice, therefore, they adopt a double perspective. On the one side, they are guided by particular representations of the unconditioned and absolute. On the other side, they acknowledge these representations as imaginative projections of a transcendent object that can never be captured completely by human representations.

For the inhabitants of a reflexive modernity, it seems possible to hold such a double perspective in their thinking about truth and justice. Rorty, however, rules this out. He presents the issue dichotomously: *either* language, logical space, and the realm of possibility are open-ended *or* the aim of thought is the attainment of a bird's-eye view.[28] Holding both positions does not seem to be an option. This dichotomy is closely linked to a second: the dichotomy between the private realm of the imagination, on the one hand, and the public realm of democratic politics, on the other. The former is the domain of creativity— of poetry—and is "necessarily private, unshared, unsuited to argument."[29] The latter is the domain of justice—for Rorty, better described as solidarity—and is "necessarily public and shared, a medium for argumentative exchange."[30] Ideas of the unconditioned and absolute belong to the private realm of the imagination—more specifically, the realm of the sublime—and simply "cannot be made relevant to democratic politics."[31] It seems that, in Rorty's view, the democratic imagination is more restricted than the creative, poetic one; to imagine myself defending my assertion to any possible audience (as Karl Otto Apel, Jürgen Habermas, Hilary Putnam, and others invite us to do) would be to exceed its limits.[32] The dichotomy between the private realm of the imagination and the public realm of democratic politics is connected with a further one: the dichotomy between argument (in a strong sense), and education or persuasion.[33]

Rorty uses the concept of argument both in a weaker and in a stronger sense, corresponding to a distinction he makes between "reason" and "Reason." On the stronger understanding, the concept of argument refers to attempts to convince others of the truth of a position through appeal to Reason, which is conceived as some kind of neutral ground. This sense is evident in his dismissal of attempts to rationally defend a view of human flourishing whose basic premises are not already implicitly accepted in the sociocultural context in question. Thus, Heidegger's rejection of the project of the French Revolution, and Dewey's acceptance of it, are held to be "tacit and unarguable."[34] Here, Rorty appears to exclude the possibility of rational argument on the grounds that it presupposes the availability of some neutral philosophical standpoint, which would supply it with premises.[35] On the weaker understanding, by contrast, the concept of argument refers to the exchange of reasons within a horizon of values that we all share. This sense is evident in his references to argumentative exchanges in the public realm of democratic politics; it is also evident in his own practice of argument: for example, in his attempts to convince us of the pointlessness of the concept of truth in the political realm.[36] Rorty claims that argument in this weaker sense is better described as "education," pointing out that the strategies deployed in educating are multiple. Furthermore, at least from an external perspective, there is no significant difference between offering reasons, on the one hand, and "wheedling,"[37] "strategic sensitivity training"[38]—or even reaching for a gun[39]—on the other. Once again, the issue is presented dichotomously: either we suppose the availability of some neutral ground of Reason, which supplies objectively valid premises for our arguments and criteria for assessing the outcomes of our deliberations; or we accept that there is no difference in principle between offering good reasons in support of a position and persuasion by various strategic means.

A relationship of mutual dependency exists between these dichotomies and Rorty's thesis that ideas of context-transcending validity are pointless. Ultimately, it is this thesis that makes sense of the dichotomies; in turn, the dichotomies serve to reinforce the thesis. Clearly, therefore, a great deal turns on whether the dichotomies can be sustained. Rorty's own work suggests at least two reasons for doubting their sustainability. First, there are tensions in his writings that threaten to undermine his sharp distinction between the private realm of the creative imagination and the public realm of democratic politics. Second, by revising his view that paradigm shifts are normatively arbitrary, he has undermined his clear distinction between argument (in a strong sense) and education-persuasion.

On a number of occasions, Rorty blurs his distinction between the private realm of the creative imagination and the public realm of democratic politics. In an essay on feminism and pragmatism, for example, he evokes the image of "a pragmatist feminist [who sees] herself as helping to create women rather than attempting to describe them more accurately."[40] Pragmatist feminists are characterized as "utopians," practicing critique from the point of view of a real or imagined alternative community whose linguistic practices are different from our own. He sees them as aiming to invent new languages, new beings, and new social structures that are better than the ones presently available.[41] In attributing this utopian aim to pragmatist feminists, however, Rorty implies that poetic discourse—discourse that aims to create new descriptions and self-descriptions—does have a place in the domain of justice.

A further example is his attribution of the American Revolution to the powerful creative imaginations of Thomas Jefferson and friends. Citing Cornelius Castoriadis's notion of instituting the social imaginary, Rorty emphasizes the role of the Founding Fathers' imagination in creating what we now think of as "the American people."[42] Once again, the creative imagination is not relegated to the purely private realm but shown to open up new possibilities in the realm of democratic politics.

Yet another example is his characterization of philosophers as messengers of hope. Rorty recommends that, instead of trying to ground democratic politics on principles, philosophers should get to work substituting hope of "the fully-fledged democracy which is yet to come" for accurate and final knowledge.[43] Significantly, Rorty endorses Robert Brandom's suggestion that the point of this fully fledged democracy "should be to ensure that a hundred private flowers blossom, and a hundred novel schools of thought contend."[44] In other words, the utopian vision motivating democratic politics is not just one of increased solidarity but one of unfettered creativity, of a "specifically human life: a life in which there is a chance to compose one's own variations on old themes, to put one's own twist on old words, to change a vocabulary by using it."[45] Once again, the dichotomy between private creativity and public solidarity is set in motion here. Indeed, Rorty now accepts Brandom's "friendly amendment" to the effect that creativity—the private dimension of language—is a feature of all uses of language, public as well as private.[46] If he accepts this, however, he is obliged to accept that his own sharp distinction between the private realm of the creative imagination and the realm of democratic politics is no longer tenable.

With the collapse of this dichotomy, the door is opened for a reflexive perspective on truth and justice that allows us to combine the idealizing, context-transcending moments inherent in the common understanding of these concepts with a self-conscious awareness that the unconditioned and absolute are not attainable by finite human beings. By conceding that the creative imagination cannot be confined to a self-contained, private sphere of human action, and by acknowledging its important contributions in the realm of democratic politics, Rorty makes room for a less restricted understanding of the democratic imagination that would allow it to envision conditions that are not in fact realizable by human beings, but nonetheless serve important functions of ethical disclosure and orientation.

The instability of his sharp distinction between argument in a strong sense and education-persuasion, and the corresponding distinction between Reason and reason, is equally significant. Here, too, collapse of the dichotomy opens the door for an alternative conception, in this case, a conception of rationality that is neither purely immanent to the social context in question nor completely transcendent of it. (In chapters 5 and 6 below I outline the principal features of such a conception, which is an integral part of the account of context-transcending validity that I propose.) It is noteworthy that Rorty, too, makes use of an alternative, nondichotomous conception, supporting my contention that radical contextualists themselves find a purely immanent approach inadequate and smuggle in ideas of context-transcending validity such as truth. Both the instability of the Reason–reason dichotomy, and Rorty's own use of an alternative conception of rationality, are evident in his recent response to Habermas.

Habermas objects to Rorty's picture of the progress of knowledge as a contingent succession of incommensurable paradigms, claiming that intellectual paradigms form a dialectical relationship as opposed to an arbitrary sequence.[47] His point can be extended to paradigms in general, understood as the set of implicitly normative discursive practices that constitute a historically specific, scientific, philosophical, or ethical vocabulary. In his earlier work, Rorty insisted that such paradigms succeed one another randomly.[48] (Indeed, as we saw in chapter 1, this is the only position consistent with a radically contextualist position.) Now, however, he concedes that paradigm change is not arbitrary: intellectual and ethical paradigms replace their predecessors to resolve difficulties that could no longer be made sense of within the earlier framework. He accepts that paradigm shifts are learning experiences, not "leaps in the dark"; they succeed one another as a result of the need for new ways of thinking that are necessary to make sense of accumulated anomalies.[49]

Of course, in describing paradigm changes as learning experiences as opposed to leaps in the dark, Rorty's very choice of metaphor negatively evokes an image of enlightenment, suggesting that we should see such changes as measured steps toward the light. Given that he repeatedly warns us not to be misled by this kind of evaluative language, however, the image presumably expresses the internal perspective of the inhabitants of a particular, local context (from a perspective external to this context, paradigm change would have to appear as random). But this way of construing it is not available to Rorty. As we know, his radically contextualist position commits him to a dichotomous view of reason: *either* reason is reduced to what counts as reason in the justificatory practices operative in a given context (and is better described as education-persuasion); *or* it must be exposed as Reason, as an arrogant, unhealthy, and immature projection of a neutral ground, which is irrelevant for all practical purposes. In the present instance, the difficulty arises because the weaker, context-bound conception of rationality cannot be applied in the case of paradigm shifts. This is due to the kind of learning that is characteristic of paradigm change. As we saw in our discussion in chapter 1, change of this kind calls into question the very standards of rationality that, in the preceding period of epistemic stability, determined what should count as rational—what should be regarded as "light" and "darkness." The notion of a paradigm shift refers to situations in which fundamental elements of a given vocabulary are shaken up and lose their cogency; in such situations, consequently, justificatory practices are problematized: what counts as a good reason becomes a matter of dispute.[50] Since, on the radically contextualist view, reason is simply what counts as a good reason, the concept of rationality cannot be applied to such disputes; although they may produce new premises for (what counts as) rational argument they are not themselves describable in terms of reason, for the concept has no application here. Thus, consistency requires Rorty to describe such disputes as arational. Although he could, for example, regard them as manifestations of strategic will, of subjective preference, or of poetic creativity, he cannot consistently regard them as rational deliberations, even from the perspectives of the participants themselves. (This is why, as I emphasized in chapter 1, a radically contextualist position excludes the possibility of rational deliberation on *new* ethical ideas.) If disputes concerning fundamental elements of our vocabularies cannot be described in rational terms, the same holds for the shifts in perception that result from such disputes: they, too, are arational. In other words, changes in vocabulary, although they may constitute new standards of cogency in argument, are themselves purely arbitrary, even from the internal perspective of those whose perceptions undergo such changes. Thus, Rorty's radical contextualism denies him any perspective from which paradigm shifts could be construed as nonarbitrary. To see them as such would be to hold a view of reason as context transcending—to grant it some purchase outside of historically specific, local practices of justification.[51] In conceding this point to Habermas, therefore, Rorty seems to concede the need for an alternative, nondichotomous conception of rationality that would combine sensitivity to history and context with a context-transcending perspective. By doing so, of course, he also concedes the usefulness of ideas of context-transcending validity and, accordingly, the limitations of the radically contextualist position.

This chapter has considered Rorty's presentation of the radically contextualist position, one of the most forceful and brilliant presentations to be found in contemporary critical social thinking. Rorty's unequivocal rejection of ideas of context-transcending validity is what marks him off from contemporary critical social thinkers who share his view that unmediated knowledge of reality is impossible and that the exercise of human rationality is always subject to the influences of history and context. Our discussion has shown, however, that Rorty is unable to sustain his radically contextualist standpoint. Although this position, it seems, is inherently unstable, as of yet the alternatives are unclear. In the following chapters, I discuss the tensions between contextualism and context transcendence as they appear in the critical social thinking of Habermas and Honneth, Butler and Laclau, Taylor, Wellmer, and Benhabib.[52] These tensions, I have suggested, must be negotiated rather than eliminated. What is required is a model of justification in which critical interrogation of normative ideas is guided by an idea of context-transcending validity that is congruent with the antiauthoritarian impulses of contempory critical social theories. As we shall see, none of the thinkers whose work I discuss quite succeed in satisfying this requirement. Nevertheless, in each case, a consideration of the strengths and weaknesses of their position casts light on the steps that must be taken to do so. In the next chapter, I look at the writings of two contemporary representatives of the Frankfurt School tradition of critical social thinking in which the tension between contextualism and context transcendence is formulated in terms of a dialectics of immanence and transcendence.

3
Dialectics of Immanence and Transcendence

Our discussion of Rorty suggests that critical social theories must endeavor to avoid radical contextualism by identifying potentials for social change for the better within the existing social order that are held to possess a rationality extending beyond the boundaries of that or any other historically specific, social order. This raises questions concerning the rational assessment of their critical diagnoses and emancipatory projections; I refer to these as questions of *justification*. On the assumption that change for the better is not an automatic process that takes place behind the backs of the agents concerned,[1] questions of justification are intimately connected with questions concerning the feelings, emotions, and reasons that move human beings to accept the validity claims raised for particular critical diagnoses and emancipatory projections; I refer to these as questions of *motivation*.

Questions of justification and motivation are linked by the ethical idea of autonomous agency. In chapter 6 I make a proposal for a conception of autonomy that would fit well with the concerns of contemporary critical social theory. The central intuition on which it rests is that autonomy consists in the freedom of human beings to form and pursue their conceptions of the good on the basis of reasons that they can call their own. From chapter 1 we have already gained some sense of what it means to be able to call reasons one's own (in chapter 6 I offer a more detailed interpretation): if human subjects are to be able to see the reasons offered in support of the ethical content of a particular idea of the good society as their own reasons, these reasons must connect with the constellations of reasons shaping their particular identities. It is clear from this that the autonomous agent's motivation to act must have a rational basis, which means that it must be capable of being supported by subjectively persuasive reasons whose validity is not purely subjective. Thus, on the premise that critical social theory is guided by a fundamental concern with individual autonomy, questions of justification and motivation are closely related and, for the most part, can be treated as two sides of the same problem.

The question of motivation does have one significant aspect that takes it beyond the question of justification: its connection with transformative social action. Critical social theories, as we know, draw attention to the ways in which the prevailing social arrangements create social conditions that hinder individual human flourishing. Moreover, they reject the view that the arrangements in question are divinely ordained, naturally necessary, or historically predetermined, endeavoring to show that they are contingent on human activity and capable of being changed by way of it. In the Left-Hegelian tradition of critical social theory,[2] this has been taken to mean that critical social theories cannot rest content with providing good reasons in support of their critical diagnoses and emancipatory perspectives; they must, in addition, motivate their addressees to engage in thought and action aimed at overcoming the social obstacles to human flourishing that they identify. This requires them to provide a convincing account of the ways in which the criticized social arrangements produce obstacles to human flourishing. In other words, on the traditional Left-Hegelian understanding, the transformative dimension of critical social theory requires the theorist to explain the causes of the social evils (social oppression, social injustice, social harm, social domination, and the like) that she identifies. On this understanding, motivation is not just the psychological side of the question of justification, it is also a question of enlightening explanations of the causes of particular social evils; these explanations are supposed to set in train social action directed toward beneficially transforming the social conditions that produce the identified evils. In chapter 8 I show the need to rearticulate the relation between theory and praxis as traditionally understood, and to query the traditional emphasis on providing an explanation of the *causes* of social evils. My discussion suggests, among other things, that the motivating power of critical social theories does not depend in the first instance on their explanatory capacities, but on the power of their emancipatory projections and corresponding social-theoretical descriptions to win the affectively imbued, rational approval of human subjects to whom autonomy is imputed. For this reason, my discussion below of questions of motivation focuses on its psychological rather than explanatory aspect.

For contemporary critical social theorists, the challenge as I have presented it is to find a way of negotiating the tensions between the idea of context-transcending validity, on the one side, and their own antiauthoritarian impulses, on the other. The challenge could also be described in terms of negotiating the tensions between objectivism and contextualism.[3] Within the Frankfurt School tradition of critical social thinking, represented today by theorists such as Jürgen Habermas and Axel Honneth, it is usually formulated as a dialectics of immanence and transcendence.

The endeavor to sustain a dialectical relationship between immanence and transcendence plays a central role in the Frankfurt School—or more generally, Left-Hegelian—tradition of critical social theory. The theorist's critical perspective is supposed to be at once context transcending, in the sense of extending to human beings in general irrespective of history and context, and immanent, in the sense of being anchored in ethically significant, subjective experiences within the existing social reality, whereby the focus is often on negative experiences. By means of this dialectics, Left-Hegelian critical social theory endeavors to maintain an emancipatory perspective, which, though transhistorical and cross-cultural in reach, derives a motivating power from its embodiment in particular subjective experiences.[4] However, the challenge facing contemporary critical social theorists is not just a matter of finding ways to sustain a dialectics of immanence and transcendence. As we have seen, a crucial additional requirement is to avoid the pitfalls of epistemological and ethical authoritarianism. Accordingly, the notions of immanence and transcendence must be construed in ways that take account of the epistemological and ethical demands of situated rationality. For much of the history of this tradition, from Karl Marx through György Lukács up to Max Horkheimer and Theodor W. Adorno, the conformity of the dialectics with the demands of situated rationality was simply not an issue. The immanent aspect raised no problems for these thinkers, since it was taken for granted that critical social theory's emancipatory perspective was anchored in the proletariat's experiences of alienated labor. The context-transcending aspect seemed equally straightforward, since it was taken for granted that the universal validity of the proletariat's experiences was underwritten by the progress of history, to which an inherent rationality was attributed. Today, however, neither assumption can be regarded as self-evident.

Both assumptions sit uneasily with the demands of situated rationality; they are philosophically out of tune with the antiauthoritarian orientation of the conceptions of knowledge, validity, and human agency associated with it. By epistemically privileging one particular social group (the proletariat) and setting it up as an authority on the true nature of social reality, the first assumption is open to the ethical objection that it is exclusive and antidemocratic—that it denies the universality of the capacity for rational agency. By designating one particular social group's experiences as an unshakeable foundation for valid knowledge, the second assumption is open to the epistemological objection that it is finalist and ahistorical—that it denies the finitude of human reason and the influences of history and context on knowledge.

In the history of Left-Hegelian thinking, initial worries concerning these guiding assumptions did not take the form of epistemological or ethical objections, but rather empirical ones. Already by the first part of the twentieth century, there were clear empirical grounds for querying them. The location of emancipatory potentials in the negative experiences of the proletariat was called into question by the development of capitalism; empirical studies indicated that the progress of capitalism did not, as had been expected, result in the elimination of alienated labor due to its own internal contradictions; instead it produced a general willingness to accept the shortcomings of the system in return for improved working and living conditions. Similarly, the historical events of the twentieth century provided empirical reasons for doubting the logic of rational progression at the center of the Left-Hegelian philosophy of history: the widespread manifestations of irrationality in Europe in various forms of totalitarianism seriously undermined any claims to discern such a logic.

As has been well-documented, Horkheimer and Adorno's *Dialectic of Enlightenment* marks a significant break in the development of this tradition of critical social theory.[5] From the point of view of our present concerns, it could be said that the book abandons a *dialectics* of immanence and transcendence, asserting the second pole at the expense of the first one. Its pessimistic view of twentieth-century capitalist social orders as saturated by an all-pervasive, repressive, instrumental rationality suppresses the immanent component of critical social thinking. If, as the authors contend, the development of capitalism has enabled instrumental rationality to extend deep into the consciousness of each human being, a reservoir of emancipatory intuitions and expectations is no longer available within the capitalist social order. Accordingly, critical social theory can no longer base its context-transcending critical diagnoses and emancipatory projections on intuitions and expectations that are already contained within the existing social order. To begin with, this gives rise to a problem of motivation. With their thesis that instrumental rationality has now penetrated into every aspect of human consciousness, the authors eliminate the possibility of any kind of human reflection on, or conscious human resistance to, its oppressive, dehumanizing effects. *Dialectic of Enlightenment* finds itself in the unwelcome situation of offering a critical diagnosis of twentieth-century capitalism that can neither be accepted on the basis of good reasons nor acted upon intentionally by anyone who hears it. Since their diagnosis is unable to connect with the constellations of reasons shaping individual subjectivities, these subjugated subjectivities can have no reasons to be moved by the diagnosis to think and act in appropriate ways. Evidently, therefore, Horkheimer and Adorno's critique of instrumental rationality represents a dead end for critical social theory. By suppressing its immanent component, it denies the possibility of rationally motivated thought and action that aim to overcome the social obstacles to human flourishing identified by the theory.[6]

This problem of motivation is accompanied by a corresponding problem of justification. Since critical social theory can no longer offer reasons for its emancipatory perspective that the human agents in question see (or could come to see) as their own, the validity of its guiding idea of the good society is not open to critical interrogation and is supported only by the unquestionable authority of the social critic. Although these authoritarian tendencies are especially visible in *Dialectic of Enlightenment*, they are already apparent in earlier Left-Hegelian attempts to anchor the theory's critical perspective in the negative experiences of the proletariat. As we have seen, justificatory strategies of this kind are open to the charge of being antidemocratic and exclusive, since they restrict insight into the truth of their critical diagnoses and emancipatory projections to an epistemically privileged social group. But Horkheimer and Adorno are even more restrictive: they limit access to the truth about human beings and society to the epistemically privileged social critic. By offering a critical diagnosis and an emancipatory perspective to which no one (except themselves or like-minded social critics) can have epistemic access, they intensify the authoritarian tendencies of their predecessors in the Left-Hegelian tradition.

One beneficial result of the additional authoritarian step taken by Horkheimer and Adorno is that it draws attention to these tendencies. Most theorists today who position themselves within the Left-Hegelian tradition acknowledge its leanings toward authoritarianism, recognizing that *Dialectic of Enlightenment* merely intensifies problems of justification and motivation that have accompanied the dialectics of immanence and transcendence from the outset. They accept that there are not just empirical grounds but also epistemological and ethical reasons for why the proletariat's experiences of alienated labor can no longer provide a rational basis for the validity of the theory's critical perspective. Although they attempt to restart the dialectics of immanence and transcendence by finding some alternative foothold within social reality, they also aim to avoid the authoritarianism that is an inherent danger of this tradition of thinking. This endeavor links them to all other strands of contemporary critical social theory that attempt to negotiate the tensions between contextualism and context-transcending validity—between immanence and transcendence—in conformity with the demands of situated rationality.

It is sometimes maintained that Left-Hegelian critical social theory has distinctive features that, even today, set it apart from other approaches and that renouncing these features would constitute a significant loss for critical social thinking. Honneth, for example, has argued this position in a number of articles. He contends that Left-Hegelian theory's adoption of a critical method that proceeds by way of a dialectics of immanence and transcendence sets it off from other methods of critical social investigation and is, accordingly, an "unrenounceable premise of the old tradition."[7] On the assumption that a context-transcending perspective, too, is an indispensable premise, Honneth focuses on the immanent component as the decisive characteristic of the Left-Hegelian approach.[8] He insists that critical social theory must be able to rediscover an element of its own critical viewpoint within social reality in the form of an emancipatory "pretheoretical resource" (*vorwissenschaftliche Instanz*). In the wake of *Dialectic of Enlightenment*'s suppression of the immanent component, he calls for the reestablishment of theoretical access to the social sphere in which an interest in emancipation can be anchored pretheoretically.[9]

Over the last decade, Honneth has refined his thesis that critical social theory must find a pretheoretical anchor within the existing social order for its emancipatory perspective. In his recent writings, he draws attention to the influence of Freud on Left-Hegelian thinking, showing how Freudian theory enables the Frankfurt School critical theorists to tie the human subject's interest in emancipation to her socially induced suffering.[10] He argues that, in different ways, Horkheimer, Adorno, Marcuse, and the early Habermas make use of the Freudian idea that psychological suffering and the desire to escape it are inseparable. In the context of critical social theory, this means that those who suffer from the negative effects of capitalism have an automatic desire to be released from this suffering. Although they may lack a consciousness of their socially induced, psychological suffering, which may manifest itself only as a bodily symptom, they have a latent interest in release from it that can be tapped into by the critical social theorist. Of course, the situation is more complicated when the desire to be released from suffering manifests itself only in the form of a bodily symptom. This is Adorno's position, for example: since the expansion of instrumental rationality impedes conscious resistance to the oppressive effects of the capitalist social order, resistance is now purely somatic.[11] Notwithstanding such complications, however, the thesis of a latent subjective interest in emancipation has evident advantages. Two of these advantages are particularly clear: if the critical social theorist can reckon with a latent interest in emancipation, the problems of justification and motivation are resolved. The critical social theorist does not have to subject her diagnoses of social pathologies to critical interrogation, since the experiential basis of her claims is indisputable. Nor does she have to concern herself with the reasons human subjects could have for finding her imaginative projections of the good society persuasive, for the desire for the projected society is pregiven.

The difficulties with such a thesis are also evident, however. The critical theorists of the Frankfurt School could point to a latent subjective interest in emancipation that resolved the problems of justification and motivation—if not the problem of conscious, rational motivation—because they assumed that the objective validity of their critical viewpoint was secured by the rationality of the historical process itself. The latent desire to be released from suffering could be seen as a rational desire, because the rationality of the critical social theorist's viewpoint was not in doubt. As soon as the rationality of the theorist's critical perspective becomes a matter of dispute, however, the problems of justification and motivation reemerge. When this happens, the theorist can no longer point to certain symptoms as indisputable evidence of an interest in emancipation; rather, she now has to justify her critical diagnosis by providing reasons for her claim that the manifestations in question are symptoms of certain kinds of socially induced suffering. For this reason, the Freud-inspired attempts by Frankfurt School critical social theorists to identify a latent subjective interest in emancipation within social reality does not resolve the problem of the dialectical relationship between immanence and transcendence; it merely highlights some of the greatest difficulties connected with it. Moreover, it cannot be considered a radically new direction within Left-Hegelianism; it merely takes a different route in the same direction of locating a pretheoretical resource within the existing social order for its emancipatory perspective.

It is not at all clear why the emphasis on the need to find a subjective foothold for critique within existing social reality should continue to demarcate Left-Hegelian theory from other modes of critical social thinking. Although historically this may have constituted a real point of difference, contemporary critical social theories are more or less unanimous in accepting the need to take their orienting ideas of the good society from the deep-seated, normative intuitions and expectations embedded in the social order that is the object of their critique. In chapter 1 I accounted for this by way of the ethical component of the idea of situated rationality. This calls upon critical social theory to offer an emancipatory perspective that its addressees can accept, or come to accept, for their own good reasons: reasons that have a psychological basis in their particular subjectivities. To this extent, respect for the ethical demands of situated rationality now connects other contemporary approaches to critical social thinking with its Left-Hegelian versions.

Nor can it be the particular interpretation of immanence offered by Left-Hegelian theory that distinguishes it from other approaches. Traditionally, as we have seen, Left-Hegelianism secured a foothold for critique in the social experiences of the proletariat. Today, however, theorists such as Honneth who position themselves within this tradition reject that particular strategy as misguided. Moreover, they tend to agree that it is not just a matter of identifying some other social group whose negative experiences could anchor critique in actual, historical reality, but a matter of rethinking the traditional Left-Hegelian strategy. Honneth himself is clearly aware of this. Thus, in this respect, too, contemporary Left-Hegelian critical social thinking is in agreement with contemporary critical social theory more generally. In view of these important points of connection, there seems little to gain from separating contemporary theorists who position themselves within the Left-Hegelian tradition from other critical social theorists on grounds of an allegedly distinctive approach.

It is more helpful, I suggest, to see contemporary context-transcending approaches to critical social theory as united in all salient respects. Even those who do not affiliate themselves with the Left-Hegelian tradition can be said to share a concern to sustain a dialectics of immanence and transcendence, while avoiding epistemological and ethical authoritarianism. As I see it, all contemporary critical social theories face the challenge of how to find a foothold for context-transcending social criticism within the existing social order, in a way that is congruent with the demands of situated rationality. They must avoid epistemological authoritarianism by allowing for open-ended, fair, inclusive, and public processes of interrogation of their critical diagnoses, and of the idea of the good society guiding these diagnoses. Equally, they must avoid ethical authoritarianism by acknowledging the human capacity for autonomous agency. This requires them to offer critical diagnoses, and corresponding ideas of the good society, that could be accepted on the basis of their own good reasons by their addressees. In order to meet this ethical requirement, they must extend the circle of rational deliberators to *all* who are affected negatively by the social order in question, and offer reasons for their views that find, or could find, resonance psychologically in the subjectivities of their addressees.

Although I have argued that it is difficult to discern any significant theoretical differences in contemporary critical social theory between Left-Hegelian and other approaches, my discussion in the remainder of this chapter focuses on two theorists who affiliate themselves with the Left-Hegelian tradition. This is because its longstanding concern with sustaining a dialectics of immanence and transcendence has sensitized theorists who have emerged from within this tradition to the difficulties posed by the task. Habermas and Honneth are two such theorists; each explicitly confronts the question of how to restore and rethink the immanent component of critical social theory, with a view to restarting a dialectics of immanence and transcendence.[12] In different ways, each attempts to revitalize the Left-Hegelian tradition by securing their theory's emancipatory perspective in existing social practices or experiences, while avoiding the multiple problems that result from locating it in the social experiences of the proletariat.

Habermas's major contribution is to have recognized the need for a fundamental paradigm shift. In his view, most of the theoretical problems of classical Left-Hegelian theory are connected with a subject-object model of cognition and action. According to this model, knowledge and action are conceived instrumentally as the imposition of will by a solitary human subject on an object distinct from him. Habermas advocates a complete break with this model:[13] he argues that the critique of instrumental rationality—developed most fully in *Dialectic of Enlightenment* but central to the entire tradition of Left-Hegelian theory—is not a fruitful direction for critical social thinking since it relies on a model of cognition and action that fails to allow for a nonrepressive relationship between the knowing and acting subject and the object of her thought and action. Instead he proposes a switch to an intersubjective framework. This intersubjective framework, presented most systematically in his *The Theory of Communicative Action*, enables him to develop a normative conception of cognition in terms of intersubjective processes of reaching understanding, as well as a normative conception of communicative action as a nonrepressive mode of social integration.[14] Furthermore, the theory of communicative rationality and action is supposed to provide normative standards for a critique of the pathologies of modern social life. In contrast to the diagnosis offered by Horkheimer and Adorno, these pathologies are described not as the result of the extension of instrumental rationality but as the result of the colonization of intersubjective ("communicative") rationality by the forces of systems ("functionalist") rationality.

Honneth welcomes Habermas's shift in paradigm, while expressing certain reservations concerning his theory of communicative action.[15] He applauds the move to an intersubjective framework, agreeing that the move away from a subject-object model helps to avoid the theoretical difficulties besetting the Left-Hegelian tradition and opens up fruitful new possibilities for critical social theory. He disagrees, however, with the particular intersubjective interpretation of the conditions of human flourishing that Habermas offers. Whereas Habermas projects a vision of the good society in which human beings would have achieved a state of perfect communication, Honneth evokes the idea of a social condition in which human beings would have achieved a state of perfect mutual recognition of each individual's needs, rights, and distinctive contributions to society. These different normative conceptions of the good society result in different conceptions of what constitutes a social obstacle to human flourishing. Habermas is concerned with social impediments to the development of communicative relations based on practices of reason giving; he argues that, currently, the functionalist rationality of the economic and administrative systems pose the greatest threat to such communicative relations. Honneth, by contrast, is concerned with social impediments to the development of an ethical personality, construed as a plural conception that comprises three irreducible elements; these impediments take the form of institutional arrangements that deny the individual human being full social recognition of her needs, rights, and distinctive contributions to society.

Thus, Habermas and Honneth agree on the merits of an intersubjective approach to critical social theory, disagreeing as to which idea of the good society should guide the theory and, hence, what constitutes a social obstacle to human flourishing. In the following sections I take a closer look at the theories proposed by Habermas and Honneth, focusing on the ability of each to sustain a dialectics of immanence and transcendence without relapsing into epistemological or ethical authoritarianism.

The linchpin of Habermas's critical social theory is his theory of communicative action.[16] This sets out to show that a potential for emancipation can be extracted from everyday practices of communication. The emancipatory potential takes the form of a rational potential that Habermas discerns in communicative action; by this he means everyday modes of action that are oriented toward mutual understanding (*Verständigung*). In its simplest terms, communicative action is a form of linguistic interaction that involves raising and responding to validity claims. It establishes a relationship between speaker and hearer that is based on a number of normative expectations and obligations; the speaker takes on an obligation to support her claim with reasons, if challenged, and the hearer takes on a similar obligation to provide reasons for his "yes" or "no." This implies that communicative action is conceptually tied to—more or less rudimentary—practices of argumentation. Habermas maintains that the validity claims raised in everyday practices of communicative action have a context-transcending, critical force that derives from idealizations built into the concept of argumentation.[17] One set of idealizations refers to the *procedure* of argumentation: to the normative promise contained in the general understanding of how argumentation should be conducted. Examples here are the idealizing presuppositions that all participants are motivated by a concern to find the single right answer, that no force is exerted except that of the better argument, and that all relevant arguments are considered. Another set refers to the *outcome* of argumentation: to the normative promise contained in the general understanding of the point of argumentation. An example here is the presupposition that a universal consensus reached under the conditions of an idealized procedure of argumentation constitutes the validity of claims to moral validity. In both cases, the tension between the normative promise contained in these idealizations and what happens in everyday communicative practices provides a basis for criticism: in the one case, they permit criticism of the ways in which the outcomes of argumentation are reached; in the other case, they permit criticism of the outcomes from the point of view of moral validity.[18] The critical power of communicative action—Habermas's name for this is "communicative rationality"—resides primarily in the tension between an idealized procedure of argumentation and what happens in actual empirical practices.

It is important to note that this critical power is not purely immanent to a particular sociocultural context. Since it is grounded in universal features of language use, it expresses a critical perspective with context-transcending force, in the sense that its validity would have to be accepted by everyone, everywhere, irrespective of sociocultural context and historical epoch.

There is a further respect in which the idea of communicative rationality has a context-transcending, critical force. Habermas suggests that the regulation of social interaction by way of communicative rationality is a crucial precondition of any good society. We might say: the theory of communicative action projects the idea of a good society in which communicative rationality would regulate what Habermas calls the "lifeworld"[19] in the three domains of cultural reproduction, social integration, and personal identity formation. In the first domain, the theory of communicative action evokes the idea of a social condition in which cultural interpretations and practices would be subjected to ongoing critical scrutiny in public processes of cognitively construed, intersubjective deliberation. In the second domain, it evokes the idea of a social condition in which valid moral norms, political principles, laws, and public policies would be the outcome of public processes of cognitively construed, intersubjective deliberation. In the third domain, it evokes the idea of a social condition in which human beings would develop as autonomous agents for whom no aspect of their own subjectivity was in principle immune from rational criticism, understood, once again, as a cognitively construed, intersubjective process of deliberation. The idea of the good society projected by the theory of communicative action provides a basis for criticizing processes of social development that inhibit the realization of communicative rationality in these three domains.[20]

In *The Theory of Communicative Action*, Habermas criticizes processes of social development in contemporary capitalist societies on precisely these grounds. He argues that the social conditions necessary for human flourishing are impaired by the colonization of the communicatively regulated domains of social life by the forces of functionalist reason.[21] The concept of functionalist reason refers to the imperatives of self-regulating economic and administrative systems.[22] In contrast to communicative reason, which, as we have seen, operates by way of intersubjective processes of raising and responding to validity claims, it operates by way of the functional interconnection of action consequences.[23] Moreover, whereas communicative reason—like strategic action—is dependent on the conscious intentions of human agents, functionalist reason bypasses the intentions of human agents entirely.[24] Habermas does not reject functionalist imperatives; indeed, he maintains that the development of functionalist reason, too, is an indispensable condition of human flourishing; what he criticizes is the current imbalance between the demands of functionalist and communicative reason and the trend toward the progressive domination of the former at the expense of the latter.[25]

Thus, in addition to the critical power it derives from the discrepancy between an idealized notion of argumentation and actual communicative practices, the theory of communicative action derives critical power from its vision of a communicatively rationalized social order. Moreover, this critical power, too, is universal in reach; the idea of communicative rationalization expresses the hope of a better social order that, according to Habermas, is implicit in communicative practices everywhere; consequently, mechanisms of social reproduction that inhibit the realization of this hope would have to be recognized as impediments to human flourishing by everyone, irrespective of sociocultural context and historical epoch.

In these ways, the theory of communicative action provides a critical perspective that is at once context transcending and immanent to everyday contexts of interaction. Furthermore, this critical perspective is construed in a nonauthoritarian way—Habermas's word for this is "postmetaphysical."[26] Although the requirements of postmetaphysical thinking are not identical to those of situated reason, for our immediate purposes, the differences are unimportant.[27]

As a postmetaphysical conception of reason, communicative rationality seeks to take account of the ethical and epistemological demands of situated reason in a number of ways. It responds to the ethical demands of situated reason by making emancipation contingent on the thinking and acting of autonomous human agents. Clearly distancing himself from the Hegelian-Marxist philosophy of history, Habermas rejects the notion of a naturally or necessary dynamics of history pushing us inexorably toward the fulfillment of the promise of communicative reason.[28] He stresses that communicative rationality is a nonteleological conception of reason: its realization is contingent on the thinking and acting of concrete human beings. Accordingly, communicative rationality does not refer to the progressive unfolding of an abstractly conceived reason, but to a potential that may or may not be realized by way of the thinking and acting of particular human agents (or groups of agents) in particular sociocultural contexts.[29] In keeping with his commitment to the normative horizon of modernity, Habermas makes the idea of autonomous human agency the normative core of his theory;[30] thus, the kind of thinking and acting he envisages is that of autonomous agents. Autonomous agency is construed in terms of rational accountability.[31] Autonomous agents must have reasons for their judgments and actions for which they are rationally accountable—that they could defend, if need be, in intersubjective processes of rational deliberation. In chapter 6 below I suggest that rational account-ability is a nonauthoritarian interpretation of the idea of owning one's reasons: of having reasons for one's judgments and actions that one can call one's own. Thus, by making emancipation dependent on the thinking and acting of rationally accountable agents, Habermas interprets it in a way that is congru-ent with the ethical component of the idea of situated rationality.[32]

Thanks to his shift from a subject-object model of cognition and action to an intersubjective one, Habermas is also well placed to give an account of emancipation that is epistemologically nonauthoritarian. With regard to the motivation to think and act in emancipatory ways, he is able to avoid a position that roots motivation in invariant psychological structures that are immune to the influences of history and context. On his intersubjective view, rational motivation can be construed as a psychological structure acquired by the indi-vidual subject by way of socialization into practices of communicative action. The main focus of his theory, however, is on the question of justification: on the normative grounding of his emancipatory perspective. The concept of communicative rationality responds to the epistemological demands of situ-ated reason by pursuing a nonfoundationalist justificatory strategy. Foundation-alism is the attempt to establish the absolute, universal validity of some kind of knowledge or action. Habermas rejects the view that philosophy can ascer-tain the foundations of valid knowledge once and for all; indeed, he demotes philosophy from its Kantian position as the supreme epistemic authority, calling on it instead to enter into a cooperative relationship with empirically oriented, reconstructive sciences.[32] Examples of the latter include Chomsky's generative grammar, Piaget's theory of cognitive development, and Kohlberg's account of moral development, all of which set out to reconstruct the pretheo-retical, implicit knowledge and competences of acting and speaking subjects. Habermas stresses that the knowledge produced by such sciences is hypotheti-cal, not absolute; it is subject to empirical testing and often relies on indirect substantiation through a coherence with the findings of other empirical theo-ries. In addition, the reconstructive sciences understand the validity of the knowledge they produce fallibilistically. A fallibilist understanding of validity takes into account that claims to validity are raised in actual, sociocultural contexts that do not remain invariable but are subject to change; also that no one can predict whether changes in context will have an effect on what is accepted here and now as sufficient justification in support of a given validity claim. On a fallibilist understanding, therefore, knowledge is conceived as always subject to modification in light of technological innovations, intercultural encounters, ecological developments, new life situations, and the like.

Habermas endeavors to provide this kind of nonfoundationalist justification for his emancipatory perspective. This is why communicative rationality expresses an emancipatory potential that is held to be grounded in the pretheoretical, intuitive, communicative competences of socialized human beings. He maintains that these can be rationally reconstructed by way of a linguistic investigation into the pragmatic dimensions of everyday language use that remains on a formal level.[33] What he calls formal-pragmatic investigations reveal that communicatively competent social agents know (pretheoretically, intuitively) that successful communicative action involves reciprocal normative expectations and obligations. The obligations generate a binding force that is a source of social cohesion; the normative expectations take the form of idealizing presuppositions that, as we have seen, pertain either to the outcome of communicative action or to the way in which it is conducted. The important point for our present purposes is that formal pragmatics is a reconstructive science and, as such, is open to empirical objections, for instance, of a sociological, historical, psychological, or neurological kind. Like Chomsky's, Piaget's, or Kohlberg's theories, therefore, Habermas's thesis of an implicit emancipatory potential can be challenged by empirical counterevidence.[34]

One kind of objection has, in fact, been empirically based. This objection casts doubt on the universality of the idealizing presuppositions in which the concept of communicative rationality is rooted. Critics doubt that there is empirical evidence to substantiate Habermas's claim that the idealizations he identifies are a feature of language use in general; historical and cross-cultural studies suggest that certain of these idealizations orient communicative practices only in certain sociocultural contexts, as a result of certain historical developments.[35] For example, Habermas's "discourse ethics" relies on the thesis that a conception of moral validity defined in terms of argumentatively achieved agreement as to the generalizability of interests can be extracted from formal-pragmatic investigations into the presuppositions of moral argumentation.[36] Here it can be objected that such a conception of moral validity presupposes a conception of moral argumentation that emerges only in sociocultural contexts in which knowledge has been desacralized, in which authority has been secularized, and in which the principle of universal moral respect has been internalized—in other words, under conditions of modernity. Some of the idealizations pertaining to the conduct of argumentation, too, express moral ideas that have become established only under conditions of modernity.

Whereas some of the idealizations identified by Habermas may indeed be genuinely universal features of communicative action—possible candidates include the ideas that participants in validity-related discussions are guided by a common concern for the single right answer and that only the force of the better argument prevails—others are clearly socioculturally specific. Most worryingly for Habermas, normative expectations concerning social inclusiveness and equality appear to belong to the latter category.[37]

Thus, the idealizing presupposition that no one will be excluded from participation in discussion on the basis of race, gender, social class, ideology, intellectual capacity, and so on seems to be specific to modern societies, indeed, even to certain kinds of modern societies. The same holds for the idealizing supposition that the contributions of all parties to the discussion carry equal weight. Since the critical force of his concept of communicative rationality depends to a considerable degree on precisely these normative expectations, Habermas cannot simply disregard them.[38] It is the discrepancy between idealizing presuppositions relating to inclusiveness and what happens in actual social practices that permits the criticism of democratic arrangements that exclude certain human beings on grounds of race, gender, and so on. Similarly, it is the discrepancy between idealizing presuppositions relating to equality and what happens in actual social practices that permits the criticism of democratic arrangements that grant disproportionate weight to the arguments raised by economically powerful or socially privileged groups and individuals. If Habermas were to disregard normative expectations relating to social inclusiveness and equality, the critical purchase of the concept of communicative rationality would be very weak indeed.

For this reason, the empirically based objection that some of the idealizing presuppositions underpinning the critical power of the idea of communicative action are socioculturally specific presents Habermas with the following problem. If he wants to maintain an empirical basis for his critical perspective on forms of social exclusion and inequality, he must acknowledge the sociocultural specificity of that perspective; but by doing so, he threatens to lose the conceptual resources necessary for the purposes of cross-cultural and transhistorical social criticism. If the empirical objection holds, therefore, Habermas has to reconsider his answer to the question of how to maintain a context-transcending, critical perspective, while avoiding the limitations of the radically contextualist position.

Just as empirical doubts as to the universality of the normative expectations identified by Habermas threaten the critical force of the concept of communicative action, they also threaten the critical power of his utopian vision of a communicatively rationalized social order. The validity of this normative picture depends on the validity of normative ideas such as rational accountability, transparency of communication, social inclusiveness, social equality, and the contestability of human knowledge. If empirical studies cast doubt on the universality of these and related normative ideas, they also cast doubt on the universal reach of his utopian vision. Just as the empirical objection, if sustainable, requires him to acknowledge the context specificity of his critical perspective on forms of social exclusion and inequality, it also requires him to acknowledge the context specificity of the idea of the good society projected by his theory of communicative action. Once again, Habermas's theory is faced with the threat of radical contextualism and, once again, it must find some way of avoiding it.

The colonization thesis adds yet another complication. Although the critical power of the colonization thesis is closely tied to the idea of a communicatively rationalized social order, it has a further dimension that results from Habermas's normative vision of a harmonious, nonselective pattern of social development. Habermas, as we know, does not reject the demands of functionalist rationality out of hand; what he rejects is the ever-increasing encroachment of functionalist rationality into the communicatively regulated domains of cultural reproduction, social integration, and personal identity formation. Criticizing this as colonization, he calls instead for a balanced relationship between processes of functionalist rationalization and processes of communicative rationalization. However, the normative basis for this idea of a balanced relationship is quite unclear. To be sure, he repeatedly expresses the notion of a nonselective pattern of rationalization in terms of the harmonious interplay of the three cultural value spheres identified by Max Weber: the cognitive-instrumental (science), the moral-practical (law and morality), and the aesthetic-expressive (art and literature).[39] For Habermas, this idea of free and harmonious interplay between the three cultural value spheres expresses the idea of the unity of reason under conditions of modernity. Rejecting logocentric and substantive notions, he proposes a multidimensional conception of reason in which three separate moments of rationality (the cognitive-instrumental, the moral-practical, and the aesthetic-expressive) would be joined in a formal unity.[40]

Here, too, Habermas draws on the reconstructive program of formal pragmatics. The ideas of formal unity and free interplay of distinct dimensions of validity are underpinned formal-pragmatically by the thesis that, in everyday communication, the speaker with every speech act makes reference to three mutually irreducible dimensions of validity simultaneously: the cognitive-instrumental, the moral-practical, and the aesthetic-expressive. The difficulty is not that this underpinning is unstable—indeed, the substance of the thesis seems to be justified.[41] The problem is that the ideas of the unity of reason under conditions of modernity and of the free interplay of the three cultural value spheres, however good their formal-pragmatic underpinning, cannot be correlated with the idea of a balanced relationship between functionalist and communicative rationalization processes.

The explanation for this is simple. Both ideas—that of the formal unity of a multidimensional reason as well as that of the free interplay of the cultural value spheres—refer to a relationship between the *cognitive-instrumental*, moral-practical, and aesthetic-expressive dimensions. Since *The Theory of Communicative Action*, however, Habermas has insisted that functionalist rationality is not the same as cognitive-instrumental rationality. In identifying functionalist rationality (as opposed to instrumental reason) as the mode of rationality that is characteristic of the economic and administrative subsystems, Habermas sees himself as breaking decisively with earlier generations of critical theorists, above all with Horkheimer and Adorno—and, indeed, with his own earlier writings.[42] Irrespective of the merits of this shift in perspective from instrumental to functionalist rationality, the point remains that the two are different modes of social integration and reproduction.[43] Instrumental rationality, like communicative rationality, operates by way of the conscious intentions of social agents (in instrumental action, social agents instrumentalize each other as a means for the success of their respective actions; in communicative action, they enter into reciprocal relationships of obligation). Functionalist rationality, by contrast, bypasses the conscious intentions of social agents entirely: the economic and administrative systems themselves act as the transmitter of the system-maintaining imperatives.

Such a significant difference between functionalist and instrumental rationality means that Habermas's idea of a balanced pattern of social development cannot be supported by the formal-pragmatic thesis just mentioned. Indeed, it is hard to see how it could be supported by any other formal-pragmatic thesis, for formal pragmatics reconstructs the pretheoretical, intuitive knowledge of participants in communicative action and has nothing to say about functionalist rationality. Formal pragmatics cannot tell us whether functionalist rationalization is necessary at all in order to achieve the good society or, if it is, how much is needed. For this reason, if Habermas wishes to uphold the critical force of his colonization thesis, he will have to look for some other kind of justificatory strategy.

The above considerations suggest that formal pragmatics is at times inadequate and at times unsuitable for the purposes of justifying the critical force of Habermas's emancipatory perspective. Formal pragmatics fails to yield an idea of communicative action sufficiently robust for his critical purposes; nor can it be used to ground the idea of a balanced relationship between functionalist and communicative rationality. I want to suggest, however, that Habermas does not have to abandon his formal-pragmatic strategy; instead he should historicize it, acknowledging that his linguistic reflections cast light only on the communicative practices of the inhabitants of modern societies. If historicized in this way, Habermas can no longer justify the strong idealizations that he requires for the purposes of his critical perspective—in particular, the idealizations relating to the inclusivity, fairness, and openness of argumentation—through reference to universal presuppositions of linguistic communication; he must justify them, instead, through reference to the deep-seated, normative intuitions and expectations that are formative of the identities of the inhabitants of modernity. The difficulty is that this seems to leave him with the same problems as Rorty.

In order to avoid a radically contextualist position, therefore, Habermas must supplement his historicized formal-pragmatic justificatory strategy; as the discussion in the following chapters endeavors to make clear, what he requires, in addition, is a justificatory strategy that allows him to assert the context-transcending validity of the deep-seated, normative intuitions and expectations from which the critical force of the idea of communicative action is extracted. This additional level of justification is necessary to avoid the problems connected with radical contextualism. On the first, context-immanent, level, Habermas would show, by way of a rational reconstruction of normative intuitions and expectations, that his emancipatory perspective fits well with the deep-seated, normative intuitions and expectations of the inhabitants of modernity;[44] on the second, context-transcending, level, he would justify the context-transcending validity of these intuitions and expectations—or, at least, offer an account of what it means to do so.[45]

A justificatory strategy that proceeds in two steps, from the context-immanent to the context-transcending level of justification, would also allow Habermas to give a more adequate account of motivation. Although, as we have seen, his intersubjectivist paradigm allows him to give a nonauthoritarian interpretation of motivation qua psychological structure, he rarely engages directly with this question. When he does, it tends to be in the context of his account of moral validity (i.e., discourse ethics).[46] Here he acknowledges that discourse ethics throws little light on the motivation to obey moral norms, but claims that this is not the task of postmetaphysical philosophy. Philosophy guided by a postmetaphysical impulse can merely explicate the moral point of view, which Habermas, drawing once more on formal pragmatics, reconstructs as a principle of universalizabiliy. It cannot explain why we should follow our moral insights or, indeed, be moral at all.[47] On some occasions, Habermas acknowledges this as a problem;[48] on other occasions, he appears to wish to deflate the issue by remarking that such questions are primarily questions of socialization.[49]

There are reasons internal to Habermas's theory as a whole that account for his neglect of the problem of motivation. These reasons are closely connected with his formal-pragmatic justificatory strategy. Formal pragmatics is supposed to provide support for the concept of communicative rationality by reconstructing pretheoretical, intuitive knowledge of what participation in communicative action entails. Similarly, it is supposed to underpin the concept of moral validity by reconstructing pretheoretical, intuitive knowledge of what participation in moral argumentation entails. As we have seen, the idealizing presuppositions uncovered by such reconstructions are allegedly universal: Habermas claims that they guide communicative practices in all historical and sociocultural contexts. Although his focus is on its implications for the question of justification, the universality thesis also affects the question of motivation. If, as Habermas contends, the presuppositions in question are features of all forms of communicative action, then the question of why we should be guided by them no longer refers to the psychology of particular human subjects in particular sociocultural contexts but moves onto an abstract, general level. The question, now, is not what it means for particular human subjects in particular sociocultural contexts to endorse the idea of communicative rationality; the question, instead, is what it means for human beings in general to endorse this idea.

Habermas's answer (to this second question) is that motivation is pregiven: since communicative action is a fundamental, indispensable mode of social reproduction and integration, every human being has a pregiven interest in ensuring that its built-in normative content is realized to the best possible degree (and also that it is not subsumed by functionalist rationality). In other words, by underpinning the context-transcending, critical power of his social theory with a formal-pragmatic reconstruction of universal features of communicative language use, Habermas can downplay the importance of the question of motivation since, for such language users, motivation is held to be pregiven. Not surprisingly, therefore, the comments he makes regarding motivation remain on a highly abstract level: reiterating his claim that all forms of sociocultural life depend for their reproduction on processes of communicative action, he maintains that withdrawing completely from communicative action is possible only at the cost of schizophrenia or suicide.[50]

This answer may be adequate so long as the idealizing presuppositions in question are genuinely universal. The situation changes, however, as soon as the historicity of the idealizing presuppositions underpinning the idea of communicative rationality is accepted. In that case, the motivation to endorse the idea of communicative rationality, and to think and act in accordance with it, must also be historicized. If he gives up his strong universality thesis, therefore, Habermas has to offer an account of the motivation for endorsing his emancipatory perspective that refers to the inhabitants of *modern* sociocultural contexts and shows how his idea of communicative rationality resonates with their deep-seated, normative intuitions and expectations. This is only the first step, however. If that account is to avoid the pitfalls of radical contextualism without falling prey to epistemological or ethical authoritarianism, it must allow for the context-transcending validity of these deep-seated, normative intuitions and expectations. Clearly, therefore, the question of motivation, too, calls for an account of what it means to assert the context-transcending validity of deep-seated—formative—intuitions and expectations.

Habermas has not confronted this issue satisfactorily. To be sure, in his writings subsequent to *The Theory of Communicative Action* there is some evidence that he is prepared to accept that formal pragmatics provides only limited support for his concept of communicative rationality. Although he continues to affirm the importance of formal pragmatics as a justificatory strategy, he seems prepared to admit that, on its own, formal pragmatics cannot justify the emancipatory perspective offered by his critical social theory.[51] On occasion, for instance, he acknowledges the need for an accompanying theory of modernity, perhaps even for a theory of moral learning processes.[52]

What Habermas in fact requires, as our discussion in chapters 5 to 7 will show, is an account of what it means to see modernity as the result of an ethically significant learning process. My qualification here is important since Habermas has already outlined a theory of moral learning,[53] and has offered an account of modernity.[54] However, his theory of moral learning, which relies heavily on the work of Lawrence Kohlberg, is open to the same kind of empirically based criticism that was brought to bear against his formal pragmatics: it invites the objection that its reconstructions of moral competence have application only for the inhabitants of particular sociocultural contexts.[55] His account of modernity is more promising. This takes the form of twelve lectures that engage critically with some of the most prominent critics of the emancipatory promise of modernity from Nietzsche onward, examining among other things Heidegger's critique of metaphysics, the poststructuralist theories of Foucault and Derrida, and the systems theory of Luhmann. Insofar as he successfully exposes the confusions and contradictions of these rival accounts of modernity, Habermas could be said to make the case for his own emancipatory account in a critical-hermeneutic manner that is more in tune with the idea of situated rationality than the universalist claims of formal pragmatics. However, a hermeneutic approach of this kind has the same limitations as the historicized version of formal pragmatics that I advocated as the first step of an appropriate justificatory strategy. Just as that historicized version has to leave open the question of the context-transcending validity of the deep-seated, normative intuitions and expectations on which it relies for its critical perspective, Habermas's hermeneutic strategy has to leave open the question of the context-transcending validity of the idea of communicative rationality that informs his critical perspective on the rival accounts of modernity.

The same limitation characterizes the normative model of the legitimacy conditions of modern legal and political orders offered by Habermas in *Between Fact and Norms*, his major work of the 1990s. Although in this book he does, at times, endorse a formal-pragmatic justificatory strategy,[56] for the most part, he employs a reconstructive method that leaves open the question of whether or not he assigns context-transcending claims to the results of his reconstructions. On the one hand, it is clear that the intention behind his reconstructions of the normative intuitions and expectations of the inhabitants of modern legal and political orders is to establish a basis for a critical perspective on law and politics in contemporary democracies. On the other hand, he pays little attention to the question of whether this critical perspective has context-transcending force. Instead, he concentrates on the question of how normative political theory can be made empirically relevant—how the critical perspective offered by normative theory can be articulated and implemented in the democratic orders of contemporary constitutional states.[57] One negative consequence of this lack of attention to the question of context-transcending validity is that it leads to ambiguities in his account of democratic legitimacy: Habermas seems at one and the same time to assert that the force of the normative claims to validity raised by legal-political norms and principles is confined to specific sociocultural contexts *and* to attribute to them a context-transcending force.[58] A further negative consequence is that it blurs the differences between Habermas's approach to law and validity and, to use an example other than Rorty, the constructivist strategy adopted by John Rawls in *Political Liberalism*.[59] Since one of Habermas's principal objections to the strategy Rawls pursues in that book is that it purchases "the neutrality of his conception of justice at the cost of forsaking its cognitive validity claim,"[60] he cannot lightly dismiss this problem.

In his normative account of modern liberal democratic societies Rawls offers a justification of the principles on which a modern society must be constituted if it is to ensure the fair cooperation of its citizens as free and equal persons. The justification is constructivist in the sense that the validity of the normative principles underpinning the basic structure of a society is *constructed* by citizens by way of the exercise of public reason.[61] The idea of public reason is a normative concept that requires citizens to consider the kinds of reasons they may reasonably give one another when fundamental political questions are at stake (by this he means questions relating to constitutional essentials and basic matters of justice).[62] The important point for our present purposes is that Rawls's justificatory approach professes agnosticism concerning the *truth* of the deep-seated intuitions and expectations that constitute what he calls our "individual comprehensive doctrines" and with which objectively valid political principles must be compatible.[63] Accordingly, the standard of correctness to which Rawls's idea of political reason appeals is not moral truth but *reasonableness*.[64] "To say that a political conviction is objective is to say that there are reasons, specified by a reasonable and mutually recognizable political conception . . . sufficient to convince all reasonable persons that it is reasonable."[65] Political constructivism neither affirms nor denies the concept of truth, it simply does without it.[66] It sees the question of the truth of political convictions as a matter not for political discussion but for the individual's nonpublic deliberations that he may engage in only when he exchanges his citizen's cap for the one he wears as a member of a family, church, or professional group—or any other of the many associations of civil society.[67]

Rawls maintains that his political conception of justice is freestanding, not dependent on any specific metaphysical or epistemological doctrine: it is designed to gain the support of an overlapping consensus among citizens whose religious, philosophical, and moral doctrines not only diverge but are "opposing and irreconcilable."[68] This explains why he insists that valid political conceptions must be conceived as reasonable rather than true—because citizens hold conflicting and irreconcilable positions as regards the truth of political values, truth is not an appropriate standard for measuring their validity: "[h]olding a political conception as true . . . is exclusive, even sectarian, and so likely to foster political division."[69] Rawls's methodological starting point is the historicity, plurality, and irreconcilability of human conceptions of epistemic validity, that is, of the good and the true. From his political constructivist viewpoint, not only is there nothing to be gained from deliberation on the truth of the specified political principles, to do so would encourage social divisiveness and would prevent the achievement of "a just and stable society of free and equal citizens, who remain profoundly divided by reasonable religious, philosophical, and moral doctrines."[70]

Rawls's constructivist strategy has certain advantages in the context of political theory—even if one does not share his premise that intractable ethical conflicts are irreconcilable,[71] or agree with his view that public deliberation on the truth of political values would foster sectarianism.[72] One advantage is that it releases the political theorist from the burden of unproductive discussion of fundamental ontological and epistemological questions and allows her to concentrate instead on constructing the political principles and constitutional framework most congruent with the deeper self-understandings and aspirations of those who inhabit a given historical, sociocultural context.

However, even from the perspective of political theory, the limitations of Rawls's constructivist strategy are evident. Since his approach disallows questions concerning the truth of the deep-seated, normative intuitions and expectations with which his political principles are deemed congruent, it is unable to argue for the superiority of these principles over those governing the lives of inhabitants of rival sociocultural contexts. Its combination of constructivism with a nonepistemic interpretation of political and legal validity means that it can gain no purchase in sociocultural contexts in which the value of "reasonableness" does not already prevail. Not surprisingly, therefore, political constructivism runs into problems when extended to international law and practice.[73]

Habermas strongly rejects what he sees as Rawls's reduction of normative concepts of political and legal validity to the ideas of reasonableness prevailing in particular sociocultural orders.[74] As we have seen, however, his own theory of legal-political validity is open to the same kind of objection. Unless it is supplemented by an account of the context-transcending validity of the deep-seated, normative intuitions and expectations that form the basis for his recon-structive strategy, it, too, stands accused of purchasing its critical power at the cost of its cognitive validity claim.

Axel Honneth's critical social theory can be seen as a direct response to Habermas's efforts to reactivate a dialectics of immanence and transcen-dence.[75] As we have seen, Honneth endorses Habermas's replacement of a subject-object model of cognition and action by an intersubjective one. However, he discerns both a cognitivist and a functionalist bias in Habermas's theory of communicative action. By "cognitivist bias" I take him to mean a tendency to construe human flourishing primarily in terms of the interests of human subjects: interests of which the subject is self-consciously aware, or can be made aware by therapeutic or other means.[76] Honneth argues that Habermas shares this tendency with the majority of Left-Hegelian theorists. He contends that Habermas, like his predecessors in the tradition, identifies only those obstacles to human flourishing whose effects can be described as violations of (rational) "interests."[77] Honneth sees this cognitivist bias at work not only in Horkheimer and Adorno's critique of instrumental rationality, but also in Habermas's critique of the colonization of communicative rationality by functionalist rationality. Just as Horkheimer and Adorno criticize the expan-sion of instrumental rationality on grounds that it prevents human beings from realizing their interest in reconciliation with all living beings, Habermas criti-cizes the expansion of functionalist rationality on grounds that it prevents human beings from realizing their interest in achieving mutual understanding (*Verständigung*). For Honneth, this leads to a regrettable narrowing of the scope of social criticism. It permits only normative deficits of certain kinds to come into view. Social disorders such as those Émile Durkheim describes, for example, which take the form of the dissolution of social bonds and impact only indirectly on the cognitive dimensions of subjectivity, are ignored by Habermas's critical gaze.[78]

Thus, Honneth maintains that Habermas's theory fails to exploit the full potentials of an intersubjective framework, leading to a form of critical social theory that is too thin and weak to provide a basis for critique of the principal pathologies of contemporary capitalism. He proposes, instead, an intersubjec-tive model that does not prioritize the cognitive dimension of human flourish-ing but takes account of its bodily-affective and creative-productive aspects as well. Rather than securing the social conditions for the realization of (rational) interests, Honneth's good society secures the social conditions necessary for the full social recognition of individual needs, rights, and contributions to society as a whole.

In addition to criticizing the cognitive bias of his theory, Honneth attributes to Habermas a tendency to give a functionalist interpretation of social pathologies.[79] By "functionalist" I take Honneth to mean an interpretation that disregards subjective—bodily, emotional, and cognitive—responses to the normative deficits of a given social order, considering only their lack of rationality as measured against some abstract conception of human interests. Habermas's theory of communicative action stands accused of neglecting the individual human being's subjective experiences of social injustices or pathologies, for it tends to treat impairment of the social conditions necessary for individual human flourishing from a purely functionalist point of view. Consequently, damage to the presuppositions of communicative action is not experienced by human subjects as an ethical *violation*. Habermas, we might say, tends to conceive of ethical violations as errors to be corrected rather than as painful experiences or traumas. Honneth does find some evidence in *The Theory of Communicative Action* that Habermas acknowledges the importance of subjective experiences of suffering as a motivation for critical social thinking and action.[80] However, these passages are counterbalanced by Habermas's tendency to give a functionalist interpretation of the idea of a social pathology.[81] Rejecting this kind of functionalist approach, Honneth emphasizes, instead, the intellectual, emotional, and bodily resistance of human subjects to pathologies in the social order.[82] Against Habermas, he argues that the subjects involved in communicative action "experience an impairment of what we can call their moral experiences, that is, their 'moral point of view,' not as a restriction of intuitively mastered rules of language, but as a violation of identity claims acquired in socialization."[83]

Honneth's deviation from Habermas in these two respects is reflected in a deviation in his justificatory strategy, which also diverges from Habermas's in two main ways. The first difference has to do with the kind of theory each draws on for support for their emancipatory, critical perspectives. Honneth shares with Habermas a concern to find empirically based, theoretical support for his normative conception of human flourishing; indeed, he even agrees that his strategy, too, could be described as "reconstructive."[84] In contrast to Habermas, however, who draws on reconstructive studies of pretheoretical, intuitive, linguistic knowledge, Honneth—particularly in his most recent work—draws on contemporary psychoanalytical findings relating to the early development of the human subject.[85] Whereas Habermas claims that formal pragmatics reveals idealizing presuppositions of communicative action that are sufficiently substantial to ground his critical perspective, Honneth seeks to anchor his perspective in the normative expectations relating to recognition that can be uncovered by psychoanalytic theory. Thus, the difference between Habermas's linguistic interpretation of individual human flourishing and Honneth's more holistic one is reflected in their respective appeals to formal pragmatics and psychoanalytic theory.

However, the two approaches diverge not only with regard to the kind of empirically based theory to which they look for support for their emancipatory, critical perspectives, they also differ as regards the scope of the empirically based, theoretical reflections on which their theories rest. As we have seen, Habermas maintains that the idealizing presuppositions uncovered by formal pragmatics that ground his critical perspective are features of communicative action in all societies;[86] by contrast, Honneth—at least in his most recent work—accepts that, on their own, the normative expectations uncovered by psychoanalytic theory are insufficient to ground his critical perspective.[87] He now acknowledges that such normative expectations amount to no more than minimal conditions for human flourishing—in his terms, "intact identity formation" or "ethical personality"—that take on different shapes in different sociocultural contexts.[88]

The three types of recognition that form the basis for Honneth's critical perspective build on these minimal conditions of intact identity formation; he accepts, however, that they have emerged as normatively substantial conditions for individual human flourishing only under the conditions of bourgeois capitalism. In other words, Honneth's position now is that recognition from others in a number of dimensions is a universal condition of intact identity formation, but the object and form of recognition vary from historical context to historical context. Moreover, normative expectations relating to social recognition are internalized and institutionalized in different societies in different ways; since the standards of justice are determined by the manner in which the "order of recognition" is normatively anchored in a given society, such standards, too, vary from historical context to historical context. Thus, even if there are good anthropological arguments for assuming the universality of the general, recognition-related, conditions under which human beings can form an intact identity, for the purposes of critical social theory these general conditions are insufficient. The standards to which the critical social theorist must, in the first instance, appeal, are the normative expectations relating to recognition that have been internalized and institutionalized in concrete ways in a given social-cultural context.

Honneth is concerned in particular with the specific expectations of recognition that have been institutionalized socially since the emergence of bourgeois capitalism. He identifies three mutually irreducible spheres of social recognition that have been differentiated historically in the transition process from the feudal to the bourgeois-capitalist social order.[89] First, love is identified as the normative idea guiding intimate relationships; it refers to the loving concern for the well-being of the other in the light of his particular needs; the positive self-relation corresponding to it is "self-confidence." Second, the principle of legal equality is identified as the norm for relationships of legal right; it refers to the equal status of each citizen before the law, based on an equality of respect for his dignity or autonomy; the positive self-relation corresponding to it is "self-respect." Third, the principle of individual accomplishment (*Leistungsprinzip*) is identified as the standard according to which social hierarchies are established; it refers to the individual human being's distinctive contribution to the industrially organized, social division of labor; the positive self-relation corresponding to it is "self-esteem."[90] These three normative expectations of recognition project an idea of the good society in which the social conditions for the full recognition of ethical personality would be secured.

Just as Habermas seeks to anchor his emancipatory perspective immanently, in the idealizing presuppositions of everyday communicative practices, Honneth seeks to anchor his emancipatory perspective immanently, in the expectations of recognition that exist in modern capitalist social orders. Moreover, just as Habermas seeks to use these idealizing presuppositions to expose discrepancies between an idealized procedure of argumentation and what happens in specific contexts of communicative action, Honneth seeks to use these expectations of recognition to expose discrepancies between the normative ideas contained in these expectations and the possibilities for recognition that are available in specific contexts. Thus, both theorists agree that a potential for criticism is built into the existing social order. Despite these points of convergence, however, there are at least two significant differences between Habermas's and Honneth's understanding of what immanent criticism involves. One difference concerns its form: Habermas envisages the exchange of reasons in processes of intersubjective deliberation;[91] Honneth envisages social struggles that have a bodily-affective as well as a rational aspect. A second difference is Honneth's reliance on the idea of a "validity surplus" (*Geltungsüberhang*). Despite superficial similarities between Habermas and

Honneth in this regard, closer consideration reveals some interesting points of divergence.

Honneth's critical perspective relies on the idea that each of the three spheres of social recognition possess a validity surplus vis-à-vis the existing social order, both separately and as they interact to constitute a complex socio-moral order.[92] This surplus of validity refers to the normative potential inherent in the idea of love and in the principles of legal equality and individual accomplishment. Insofar as the existing bourgeois-capitalist social order institutionalizes social relations of recognition that are one-sided or restrictive, inhabitants of this social order can rationally object on the grounds that these social relations lack justification. Love and the principles of legal equality and individual accomplishment thus represent normative ideas in relation to which subjects can rationally make claims to the effect that prevailing interpretations and modes of institutionalization of norms of recognition are not appropriate or not sufficient and need to be expanded and developed.[93] Thus, for example, the ways in which the principle of individual accomplishment have been interpreted and institutionalized under conditions of bourgeois capitalism can be—and have been—criticized on the grounds that they privilege the activities of one social group (economically independent male citizens) and discriminate against, and exclude, those of others.[94]

Honneth's idea of a validity surplus does not merely refer to the discrepancy between deep-seated intuitions and expectations, on the one hand, and actual modes of interpretation and institutionalization, on the other. If that were all, it would be hard to distinguish it from the version of immanent criticism to be found in Habermas's writings. It has some additional connotations that make it different from Habermas's conception. One is that no actualization of a particular normative expectation can ever satisfy its own inherent normativity: "even where there is no apparent gap between *de facto* practices and implicit norms, the ideals associated with the distinct forms of recognition always call for greater degrees of morally appropriate behavior than is ever practiced in that particular reality."[95] Thus, for example, Honneth attributes a semantic surplus (*Überschuss*) to the idea of social equality, which may gradually be opened up by way of innovative interpretations without ever being completely or finally determinate.[96]

As we shall see, this motif of an ineliminable gap between the inherent normativity of a norm or practice and its realization in concrete historical instances links Honneth with poststructuralist critical social thinking (and, indeed, with Adorno).[97] In both cases, it expresses a dynamic yet nonteleological conception of the historical process: Honneth sees history as a never-ending series of struggles for recognition; poststructuralists tend to see it as a never-ending series of practices aimed at the rearticulation, restaging, and reenactment of key concepts. However, Honneth's interpretation of the significance of the gap is different from the usual poststructuralist interpretation. Whereas poststructuralists typically leave open the question of whether new actualizations of the norm can be seen as more adequate in some context-transcending sense, Honneth regards the historical endeavor to overcome the discrepancy between ideal and practice as a learning process—as part of a permanent pressure to learn that is part of the historical process itself. As he puts it: "... norms of recognition ... continually demand, from within themselves, the further perfection of our moral action, such that the historical process is characterized by a permanent pressure to learn."[98] This constitutes a further respect in which Honneth's idea of a validity surplus diverges from Habermas's conception of immanent criticism. For Honneth, the idea of a validity surplus does not merely imply an ineliminable gap between normativity and actuality; it has the additional connotation that norms and practices have an inherent rationality: the potential for transcendence contained within them is a potential for rational transcendence.[99] Accordingly, his theory of recognition is also a theory of ethical (and, more generally, social) progress.

In his recent work Honneth makes clear that the critical force of his idea of a validity surplus depends on such a theory of progress.[100] For, evidently, the idea of a validity surplus vis-à-vis the existing social order provides a basis only for context-immanent critique. Although it allows the theorist to expose the gap between the normative ideas guiding his critical diagnoses and emancipatory projections, and the normative ideas prevailing in a given social order, it does not provide the conceptual resources necessary for cross-cultural and transhistorical social criticism. In order to acquire a critical force that extends beyond the given social order, it must be supplemented by an account of collective moral learning in a context-transcending sense.[101] As part of such an account Honneth relates the three normative expectations at the center of his theory to moral ideas of social inclusiveness and individuality; these are presented, in turn, as indisputable achievements of modernity; from this premise, love and the principles of legal equality and individual accomplishment are to be justified by extension.

However, like Habermas's account of collective moral learning, Honneth's account is underdeveloped. By presenting social inclusiveness and individuality as indisputable achievements of modernity he raises more questions than he answers. The point is not to show that love and the principles of legal equality and individual accomplishment can be justified through reference to the ideas of social inclusiveness and individuality. The point is to show that the latter ideas are valid in a context-transcending sense—that they constitute historical achievements. So far Honneth has given no indication as to how he would go about showing this in a manner congruent with the antiauthoritarian impulses that I have expressed by the idea of situated rationality.

An additional justificatory task arises from the fact that the ideas of social inclusiveness and individuality are compatible with a number of conceptions of human flourishing and corresponding ideas of the good society. There is no necessary or exclusive link between these ideas and the idea of the good society projected by Honneth's three normative expectations of recognition. The ideas of social inclusiveness and individuality are compatible, for example, not only with Honneth's idea of love and his principles of legal equality and individual accomplishment but also with Habermas's idea of a communicatively rationalized social order and (as will become apparent in the next chapter) Ernesto Laclau's idea of hegemonic democracy. Thus, in addition to showing that the ideas of inclusiveness and individuality constitute ethical progress in a context-transcending sense, Honneth has to make his case that the three normative expectations of recognition he identifies in modern capitalist social orders point to an idea of the good society that is ethically superior to the ideas evoked by Habermas or other contemporary critical social theorists. With regard to Habermas's conception of what constitutes successful identity formation, for example, he has to justify his claim that this conception is seriously curtailed by showing why the concept of ethical personality cannot be confined to the capacity for reason giving but extends also to the singularity of the embodied subject and her distinctive contributions to the reproduction of the social order. To be sure, Honneth's use of empirically based psychoanalytic, historical, and sociological studies to support his theory of recognition indicates his concern to do precisely this. However, what is missing from his justificatory efforts on the context-immanent level is an attempt to show that the identified attributes of ethical personality are ethical in a context-transcending sense. As things stand, the idea of ethical validity at work in his conception is quite unclear; Honneth has not addressed these issues explicitly.[102] Nor can any theory of ethical validity easily be extracted from his writings.[103]

In sum, Honneth's justificatory strategy requires further development on both the context-immanent and on the context-transcendent levels. On the context-immanent level, he must elucidate what it means for the inhabitants of modern capitalist orders to be able to regard the conception of personality projected by his theory as *ethically valid*. On the context-transcending level, he must elucidate what it means for the inhabitants of modern capitalist orders to regard this idea of ethical personality as a *historical achievement* that could be recognized as such by everyone, everywhere.

Although Honneth's justificatory strategy is in need of development along these lines, we find no attempt in his writings to elucidate the idea of context-transcending validity in a manner congruent with the idea of situated rationality; moreover there is an empiricist strain in his writings that hints at residual foundationalist tendencies and is at odds with the antiauthoritarian impulses of his own theory and contemporary critical social thinking more generally.

An empiricist tendency has been apparent in Honneth's writings from the outset. In his earlier writings, he called for historical and sociological studies to establish evidence of moral experiences of suffering and resistance to suffering. There, he advocates studies concentrating on the experiences of suffering among the lower social classes on grounds that the members of such classes are not culturally specialized in articulating moral experiences.[104] He held the view that, due to their theoretical innocence, the critical social theorist would be able to perceive in their utterances—"prior to all philosophical or academic influence, as it were"—their normative expectations relating to recognition; these results could then be generalized beyond their immediate research context to arrive at the conclusion that the normative presupposition of all communicative action is the expectation of social recognition. In this way, the responses of the lower social classes to the moral experience of lack of recognition[105] would constitute a pretheoretical resource for critical social theory, replacing the classical Left-Hegelian appeal to the negative work-related experiences of the proletariat.[106]

It is clear, however, that, on their own, historical and sociological studies can carry the burden neither of justifying the theory of recognition nor of explaining its motivating power. The critical social theorist inevitably uses such studies selectively, picking out trends and patterns that seem to support her already existing theoretical framework. Moreover, Honneth's earlier appeal to the philosophically uninformed—that is, pretheoretical—reactions to the suffering of the lower classes seems naive today, following a decade in which "recognition" has become the catchword of new social movements in the United States and elsewhere.[107] As Honneth now acknowledges, it is implausible to suppose that simply any feelings of a lack of recognition, together with a readiness to engage in social struggle, is evidence of the truth of his emancipatory perspective.[108] One reason for this, pointed out by Honneth himself, has to do with the dependence of publicity on social power. Under conditions of unequal power relations, certain kinds of experiences tend to be suppressed, with the result that certain forms of socially induced suffering and injustice never achieve the level of political thematization and organization in the first place.[109] A further difficulty, not explicitly mentioned by Honneth, has to do with the recent popularization of the vocabulary of recognition. Over the past decade, claims to social recognition have become part of the standard political discourse in the United States and other contemporary capitalist social orders.[110] This has led to a situation in which most forms of resistance to perceived socially induced suffering are articulated in terms of recognition, making it difficult to distinguish between pretheoretical responses and theoretically informed ones.

Difficulties such as these may account for the fact that Honneth no longer focuses on the need for sociological and historical studies of the moral experiences of the lower social classes. (This is not to say that his theory no longer draws on studies of these kinds. In fact, it continues to make productive use of a range of historical and sociological reflections.)[111] In his most recent work, he concentrates instead on the theoretical results of psychoanalytical investigations into early childhood development to substantiate his theory of recognition. Drawing on work by Daniel Stern, for example, he seeks support for his anthropological thesis that human identity formation is guided by a core set of—verbal and nonverbal—expectations relating to social recognition.[112] Elsewhere, he draws on other recent developments in object-relations theory to find support for his antiteleological thesis that relations of recognition are constantly marked by the possibility of conflict, making the struggle for recognition a permanent feature of human social behavior.[113]

However, for the purposes of answering the questions of justification and motivation, psychoanalytical theories are no more adequate than historical and sociological studies. Certainly, such theories lend support to the social critic's diagnoses of social evils, and to the idea of the good society that guides them. However, they cannot substitute for the philosophy of history that, in classical Left-Hegelian theory, guaranteed the truth of the theorist's critical perspective. Indeed, for any contemporary critical social theory that seeks to take account of the ethical and epistemological demands of situated rationality, no simple substitute is possible. For such a theory, *no* authority—be it history or sociology or psychoanalysis—can underwrite the validity of the theorist's critical diagnoses and emancipatory projections. Rather, as I will show in chapters 5 and

6, the validity of the theorist's diagnoses and projections is a matter for argumentation, guided by a concern for an answer that is right in a context-transcending sense and that proceeds in a historicist, comparative, open-ended, and concrete way. This lends an ineluctable contextual dimension to the justificatory process.[114]

At times, in Honneth's justificatory enterprise, the contextual dimension threatens to disappear from view. On the one hand, he is clearly aware of the limited support his theory can gain from psychoanalytic and other empirically based studies. As we have seen, he now acknowledges explicitly that the normative expectations uncovered by object-relations theory are, on their own, insufficient to anchor his emancipatory, critical perspective; moreover, that the normative expectations (love and the principles of legal equality and individual accomplishment) that anchor this perspective must be seen as the result of specific historical and cultural developments. In addition, he underscores the provisional nature of his theoretical framework, characterizing his moral-psychological categories as hypotheses that are open to empirical contestation.[115] On the other hand, the language he uses when dealing with the immanent component of critical social theory has, on occasion, a foundationalist undertone. Thus, for example, he speaks of the need to identify social discontent "independently of *all* public recognition" or even "*completely* independently" of such recognition.[116] His recent approving references to the idea of a latent subjective rational interest in emancipation call on him to clarify how this idea can be made fruitful without violating the demands of situated rationality; his use of the term *vorwissenschaftliche Instanz* (translated as "pretheoretical resource") is symptomatic in this regard. Whereas the English word "resource" captures the pragmatic, contextual aspect of justification, the German word "Instanz" has an unequivocal connotation of "authority." Moreover, it is striking that the bulk of his theoretical efforts in recent years has been directed toward strengthening the anthropological core of his theory with the help of psychoanalytic studies; he has paid less attention to the question of the kind of model of practical rationality—and guiding idea of context-transcending validity—that might be used to justify the normative validity of love and the principles of legal equality and individual accomplishment.

This chapter has considered two contemporary attempts to sustain a dialectics of immanence and transcendence without falling prey to epistemological and ethical authoritarianism. In the discussion of Habermas's theory of communicative action, I showed that, in its universalist form, formal pragmatics provides inadequate (or unsuitable) support for his critical perspective and emancipatory projections. Rather than abandoning it, however, I suggested that he historicize it, self-consciously acknowledging its sociocultural specificity. A historicist interpretation of formal pragmatics would not only enable Habermas to maintain his critical perspective on certain forms of social exclusion and inequality; it would fit well with the justificatory strategies he has employed in other writings, for example, with the critical-hermeneutic approach employed in *The Philosophical Discourse of Modernity* and the reconstructive approach he adopts in *Between Facts and Norms*. However, the proposed historicist interpretation of formal pragmatics as well as the other justificatory strategies remain on a context-immanent level; accordingly, they are open to the problems of radical contextualism. In order to avoid these problems, I advocated a second justificatory step. With this step, the theorist moves, so to speak, to a second, context-transcending level; justification on this level amounts to a willingness to engage with the question of the context-transcending validity of the deep-seated, normative intuitions and expectations to which she appeals in her critical diagnoses and emancipatory projections. As we have seen, Honneth seems prepared to embrace this kind of two-step strategy. However, like Habermas, his account of the second step is underdeveloped. Furthermore, on occasion, Honneth slips into a foundationalist use of language that is at odds with the kind of historicist, comparative, open-ended, and concrete model of justification that, I will argue, is best suited to the anti-authoritarian self-understanding of contemporary critical social theory. Before moving to a closer consideration of this model of justification, and of the idea of context-transcending validity that guides it, I wish to consider the dialectics of immanence and transcendence as it relates to critical social thinking outside the Left-Hegelian tradition. In the next chapter, accordingly, I discuss the poststructuralist theories of radical democracy proposed by Judith Butler and by Ernesto Laclau.

4

Restaging and Re-Presenting Universality

Among contemporary theories we find a diversity of views with regard to the emancipatory goals of critical social thinking, the forms it should take, the conception of agency appropriate to its aims, and the universality of the ideas of validity to which it appeals in its critical diagnoses and emancipatory projections. So far, our main concern has been with the last of these issues, presented in terms of a dispute between radically contextualist and context-transcending approaches. On one side of the divide, I place critics such as Rorty, who contest the usefulness of ideas of context-transcending validity and restrict the scope of critical interrogation to the inhabitants of a particular sociocultural context. On the other side, I place critics such as Habermas and Honneth, who defend the importance of ideas of context-transcending validity and conceive of critical interrogation as universal in reach, extending across historical and cultural contexts. However, the very terms in which I have conducted the dispute are open to objection. It could be argued that, by setting up a debate between radically contextualist and context-transcending approaches, I display a bias in favor of a particular mode of critical social thinking, prejudicing the discussion from the outset; the mode of social criticism allegedly favored is one for which questions of justification are of central concern.

It is certainly true that some contemporary approaches to critical social theory do not engage with justificatory issues. In some cases, this is due to a blanket rejection of normative political thinking. Thus, for example, in their book, *Empire*, Michael Hardt and Antonio Negri dismiss normative political thinking as anachronistic, on the grounds that its transcendent dimension is deeply incongruent with the defining features of the new imperial form of sovereignty that they attribute to contemporary processes of globalization.[1] In the new imperial order described in *Empire*, the principle of immanence has been fully realized, in the sense that there is no longer any "outside"; this renders normative political concepts such as justice, democratic legitimacy, and political autonomy obsolete. Hardt and Negri argue that such concepts rest on a distinction between inside and outside, for they presuppose some external, transcendent standpoint from which criticism of actual modes of social and political organization and regulation is possible. Since there is no longer any boundary between inside and outside, "[t]he transcendental fiction of politics can no longer stand up and has no argumentative utility. . . ."[2] In the same vein, the authors argue that ideas of context-transcending validity have become unthinkable, since "all the transcendental determinations of value and measure . . . have lost their coherence";[3] instead, "[p]olitics is given immediately; it is a field of pure immanence . . . it articulates being in its global extension."[4] A principal aim of the present book is to show, against critics such as Hardt and Negri, that ideas of context-transcending validity have not become unthinkable—that the idea of transcendence and the idea of immanence are not deeply incongruent but must be set in dialectical motion.

In other cases, however, the reluctance to engage with justificatory issues is not due to an outright rejection of normative political thinking but to a perceived connection between an emphasis on justification and conceptions of agency, democratic politics, and the good society that are rationalist and reconciliatory. In the work of Judith Butler and Ernesto Laclau, for example, a noticeable unwillingness to address questions of justification is coupled with a hostility toward the rationalist and reconciliatory modes of thinking that they associate with Habermas and his followers.[5] Although neither Butler nor Laclau rules out a context-transcending approach to social criticism, each is likely to reject the very terms of the debate as I have constructed it, regarding it as biased in favor of a mode of critical social thinking they find deeply uncongenial.

It is true that our discussion so far has considered only approaches to critical social theory that confront questions of justification, specifically those relating to the universality of the normative ideas guiding processes of critical interrogation. Rorty, Habermas, and Honneth accept the basic terms of the debate between radically contextualist and context-transcending approaches to critical social thinking, and position themselves at various points within it. It is also true that justification involves an appeal to an idea of rational agency. Rorty and Habermas may disagree as to the transcendent aspect of the kind of reasoning required for social criticism and democratic politics, but both are committed to an idea of agency in which argumentative reasoning is a core component.[6] Not surprisingly, therefore, they advocate models of social criticism and democratic politics in which argumentative reasoning plays a central role. Moreover, it is hard to deny that this kind of reasoning is linked with the ideas of harmony and reconciliation: the purpose of the exchange of reasons in argumentation is to reach an agreement of some sort, be it with all other natural persons (Habermas) or merely with others who inhabit the same sociocultural context as "us" (Rorty).

Thus, critics such as Butler and Laclau are correct to perceive a connection between an emphasis on justification and the commitment to an idea of rational agency; they are also right to discern further connections with argumentation-based models of social criticism and democratic politics, and with the ideas of harmony and reconciliation built into such models. However, they are wrong if they see these connections as grounds for ignoring questions of justification and for dismissing the debate between radically contextualist and context-transcending versions of critical social theory as irrelevant or inimical to their own concerns. Questions relating to the universality of ideas such as truth or justice arise even for approaches to critical social theory that question the ideal of rational agency, advocate models of criticism and democratic politics that are not argumentation based, and reject harmonistic and reconciliatory ideas of the good society.

As I shall show, the limitations of Rorty's radically contextualist approach are equally limitations for approaches that do not subscribe to his deliberative model of democratic politics; the dilemmas encountered by Habermas and Honneth in their efforts to maintain a context-transcending perspective are also dilemmas for approaches that reject their normative conceptions of agency. From this I draw the conclusion that Butler and Laclau, too, must confront the question of context-transcending validity and develop accounts of context-transcending validity that permit cross-cultural and transhistorical interrogation. They cannot simply ignore questions of justification; rather, they must join Habermas and Honneth in the endeavor to develop justificatory strategies that negotiate the tensions between immanence and transcendence without falling prey to epistemological and ethical authoritarianism.[7]

Both Butler and Laclau acknowledge poststructuralism as a significant influence on their thinking.[8] It seems permissible, therefore, to affiliate them with poststructuralist modes of social criticism.[9] It is not easy to pinpoint the reasons for the deep lack of sympathy between poststructuralism and the kinds of social criticism it associates with Habermasians.[10] The explicitly formulated objections seem clear enough. Poststructuralist social critics such as Butler and Laclau reject the foundationalism of Habermas's critical theory, his prioritization of a capacity for rational agency, and the reconciliatory aspects of his model of deliberative politics. However, the first objection is by no means unique to poststructuralism: it is not just poststructuralist critics who accuse Habermas of foundationalism; thinkers who associate themselves with his basic concerns and endorse key elements of his communicative paradigm are equally critical of this aspect of his theory. In fact, the foundationalist residues in Habermas's thinking do not appear to be the main focus of poststructuralist hostility.[11] In his recent writings, Laclau himself proposes a conception of the subject that is, in a sense, foundationalist: the subject is conceived as having been structured by an originary incompleteness that it attempts to fill by way of representations of an "impossible object" that cannot be grasped conceptually.[12] Interestingly, Butler's response to Laclau's critical social thinking is cordial, even though she vehemently rejects the idea of constituting exclusions that are foundational and structurally static. This suggests that Laclau's and Butler's hostility toward Habermasians would most likely persist even if Habermas succeeded in eliminating foundationalist residues from his thinking, for example, by self-consciously acknowledging the historicity of his conception of communicative rationality. It appears that it is less foundationalism than the appeal to a capacity for rational agency, together with the reconciliatory aspect of the idea of communicative rationality, which evokes the ire of poststructuralist critics—but even here it is not easy to see what they find so enraging. In subsequent chapters I look briefly at Butler's objections to Habermasian accounts of rational agency (chapter 6) and at Laclau's objections to the harmonistic and reconciliatory content of Habermas's idea of the good society (chapter 7). In the present chapter I concentrate on Butler's and Laclau's non-Habermasian proposals for radical democracy.

I have argued that, in contemporary critical social theory, radically contextualist and context-transcending approaches are united in an antiauthoritarian impulse that I expressed by the concept of situated rationality. This notion, as we have seen, has two main features. First, it acknowledges the inescapable conditioning effects of history and context on human thought and action, accepting that they are never neutral; moreover, it rejects the view that there can be any privileged access to truth or knowledge. Second, it pays tribute to the ethical idea of autonomous agency by making human subjects responsible—rationally accountable—for their assignments of ethical meaning and value. This commitment to the idea of situated rationality and, in particular, to its ethical aspect leads contemporary critical social theorists to ascribe a rationality or truth value to the deep-seated, normative intuitions and expectations embedded in a given sociocultural context; as we have seen, this rationality or truth value can be interpreted either purely contextually, as valid only for the inhabitants of a particular local context, or it can be given a context-transcending interpretation, whereby it is deemed valid across historical and sociocultural contexts. I have suggested that the concept of situated rationality calls for an approach to critical social theory that avoids epistemological and ethical authoritarianism. Butler's theory is certainly guided by this antiauthoritarian impulse, although she is likely to find the term "situated rationality" unacceptable and to distance herself from the ethical idea of autonomous agency as I have formulated it.[13] Her critical social thinking seeks to avoid epistemological authoritarianism by acknowledging that truth never appears outside a particular presentation, in the sense that we are fundamentally dependent on historically and culturally specific forms of language to say and understand what is true.[14] It can be said to avoid (what I refer to as) ethical authoritarianism by self-consciously operating within the evaluative horizon of Western modernity and by appealing to the democratic possibilities inherent in the key terms of liberalism, thereby allowing in principle for the rational acceptability of its emancipatory, critical perspective to those it addresses.

Butler advocates the innovative reuse of the *main terms of modernity*.[15] For her, the normative and optimistic aspect of critical social thinking consists "in the possibilities for expanding the key terms of liberalism, rendering them more inclusive, more dynamic and more concrete."[16] She describes her work as "motivated by a desire for a more radically restructured world, one which would have economic equality and political enfranchisement imagined in much more radical ways than they currently are."[17] In positioning itself within the evaluative horizon of Western modernity, therefore, her thinking can be said to practice a form of immanent critique and be formulated in terms that are supposed to resonate intellectually and affectively with the subjectivities of its addressees.

At the center of Butler's critical social thinking is a notion of the subject as incomplete. In her view, the identity of the subject is constituted through exclusions. We might also say that identity, for Butler, is always posited in a field of differential relations. The crucial point, however, is that she construes this incompletion of identity[18] in a radically historical way: what is excluded in every positing of identity depends on specific political and social factors that are subject to alteration by way of disruptive enactment, innovative restaging, and other kinds of verbal and nonverbal performances. She insists that the negativity at the heart of identity can—indeed, must—be operationalized in order to revise and transform the political field. If negativity is to be politically salient, however, it may not be posited as foundational or structural. Thus Butler strongly criticizes what she sees as Slavoj Žižek's and Laclau's ahistorical recourse to an originary lack within the subject that, as a quasi-transcendental limitation on all possible subject formation, is indifferent to politics.[19] Against any attempt to exclude in advance certain kinds of negativity from democratic contestation, rearticulation, and restaging, Butler insists on the radical performativity of identity, whereby subjects constitute their identities entirely by way of multiple acts within a field of political and social signifiers.

It is not just the identity of the subject that is incomplete, however. For Butler, *all* identity is characterized by negativity—a negativity that is politically salient. In consequence, although any particular articulation of a concept posits an identity that is exclusionary, its exclusions can be revealed by way of practices of critical interrogation that may spark off a creative rearticulation and restaging of the concept. For this reason, Butler does not reject universal concepts such as democracy, freedom, truth or, indeed, the concept of universality itself. What she rejects is the closure of such concepts: static conceptions that refuse to acknowledge their own dependency on particular cultural values, fail to respond to their own constitutive exclusions, and block attempts to rearticulate them in more inclusive and emancipatory ways.[20] Against such static conceptions, she advocates ideas of universality, democracy, freedom, and so on, that are "futural," "unconstrained by teleology," and not "commensurate with any of [their] 'realizations.'"[21] Her concern is to preserve the ideality of such ideals by highlighting the distance between their ideality and the givenness of any of their modes of instantiation.[22] In her view, this calls for practices of criticism that seek to unsettle and disrupt prevailing norms, exposing the contingency of what is presented as necessary and the incompleteness of what is presented as complete.[23] Since a tendency to subsume, exclude, and order is endemic to reason, argumentative modes of criticism are not well suited to the task. This is certainly one reason why she finds the deliberative models of social criticism and democratic politics proposed by Habermas deeply uncongenial.[24] Instead, Butler advocates practices of criticism that suspend judgment. In her view, rather than setting up standards for assessing the goodness or badness of particular elements of a given social order, criticism should seek to uncover the system of evaluation at work in these elements, at the same time pointing toward new possibilities for social order.[25]

Furthermore, in keeping with her suspicion of approaches to social criticism that attach importance to the public exchange of reasons, Butler draws attention to the somatic dimension of practices of criticism.[26] She reminds us that political claims do not have to be articulated in language, for "lives make claims in all sorts of ways that are not necessarily verbal."[27] Thus, bodily interventions in the public sphere can fulfill important critical functions. Subversive or anomalous public performances that are not primarily linguistic may open up new conceptual horizons and provoke innovative ways of rearticulating and restaging social norms and social relations.[28] She sees the figure of Sophocles' Antigone as exemplary in this regard: by her (linguistically mediated) actions Antigone challenges apparently immutable foundational social norms, in particular, norms relating to kinship relations, and opens new dimensions to what it means to be human.[29]

Butler's praise for Antigone is indicative of the context-transcending orientation of her social criticism, although this is never thematized explicitly. This orientation is implicit in her emphasis on the radical interrogation of concepts and norms, even foundational ones such as kinship rules. (Foundational rules are what Claude Lévi-Strauss calls "threshold rules": the rules that make culture possible and intelligible. They may thus be described as transcendental rules.)[30] Butter emphasizes that no premises should be beyond interrogation, removed from the possibility of creative reenactment and innovative rearticulation. Accordingly, even the frame of intelligibility within which criticism operates must be acknowledged as historically variable and revisable.[31]

She insists, furthermore, that the transformation of norms and concepts is an inherently open-ended process. This follows from her view that all instantiations of norms or concepts are partial and exclusive, creating their own "outside" that can never be fully internalized. Thus, no conception of universality eliminates particularity, no conception of democracy gives equal power to all citizens, and no conception of freedom puts an end to oppression. It is this gap in principle between the ideality of the ideal and its historical actualization that provides a space for the critical transcendence of the given. For Butler, we might say, norms and concepts carry the possibilities for their own transcendence within themselves. From the point of view of our present discussion, however, the question is not just whether there are possibilities for transcendence inherent within the norm or concept; it is whether these possibilities are the basis for the kinds of cognitive and social transformation for which validity in a context-transcending sense can be claimed.

Butler does not confront this issue. However, certain elements in her critical social thinking suggest that she cannot regard it as a matter of indifference. One such element is her reference to the revisablility of the frame of intelligibility within which the creative rearticulation and restaging of norms and concepts take place. In order to speak of progressive, emancipatory revisions (such as those she attributes potentially to Antigone's actions), Butler has to allow for a critical perspective that is not confined to any specific frame of intelligibility, but extends across historical epochs and sociocultural contexts. Otherwise, she would be obliged to regard changes in foundational rules as normatively arbitrary. We will recall that Rorty encounters a similar problem. Just as Butler has to answer the question of whether revisions to the frame of intelligibility can be regarded as progress in some context-transcending sense, Rorty has to clarify the normative status of the transformations in ethical and intellectual vocabulary that accompany paradigm shifts. As we have seen, this presents him with a dilemma, for, on the one hand, his radically contextualist stance forbids him from seeing such shifts as anything other than arbitrary; on the other hand, he has been obliged to admit that such changes are rationally motivated, since they result from the need for new ways of thinking for the purpose of making sense of anomalies. In consequence, he ends up in the unstable position of at once describing paradigm shifts as learning experiences and denying the coherence of adopting the transhistorical perspective necessary to characterize them as such.

To be sure, unlike Butler's model of social criticism as performativity, Rorty's model is argumentation based. Accordingly, the implication to be drawn from his radically contextualist stance is that it is incoherent to speak of rational deliberation with regard to fundamental changes in ethical and intellectual vocabularies. However, similar implications follow from nonargumentative versions of radical contextualism. For, it is not just rational deliberation that is denied a coherent role in this regard—it is the critical attitude in general. The radically contextualist position rules out the possibility of a critical interrogation of ethical and intellectual vocabularies, foundational rules, frames of intelligibility, and so on, *whether or not* this criticism is argumentatively—or even verbally—articulated. Nor can it coherently allow for responses to new conceptions relating to the good for human beings—in particular, conceptions emerging from changes in frames of intelligibility—that are not just a matter of strategic interest or subjective preference; here, it makes no difference whether such responses are formulated argumentatively or enacted nonverbally. The evaluative language employed by Butler in relation to revisions to frames of intelligibility suggests that she could not happily accept this implication of radical contextualism.

There is a further element in Butler's thinking that makes the debate between radical contextualism and context transcendence relevant to her concerns: her notion of concrete universality. For Butler, universality is tied to particularity—it emerges in concrete contexts of interaction by way of disruptions to particular ideas of universality. Moreover, it is inherently temporal—it is deemed to have no content beyond its stagings at multifarious scenes of embattlement and no location apart from the interstice in which it momentarily occurs.[32]

Butler proposes restaging the notion of universality in terms of cultural translation.[33] As we have seen, she does not reject universal concepts but only their closure by way of immobilizing interpretations that refuse to acknowledge their own partiality. She sees closure at work in proceduralist as well as substantive accounts of universality. The latter seek to base their normative views of what a political order ought to be on a description of human beings that is universally applicable: for example, a description in terms of desire, speech, deliberation, or dependency. Butler objects to all attempts to identify universal features of human beings, since they fix contingent features as invariant, removing them from the field of political action. However, she also rejects proceduralist approaches such as those proposed by Rawls and Habermas on the grounds that, in different ways, both of these writers seek to establish universalizability as a criterion for justifying the normative claims of any social and political program. Her objection here seems twofold. She finds the proceduralist approach guilty of prioritizing the rational capacities of human beings, looking suspiciously on ostensibly nonrational modes of human conduct in the domain of politics.[34] She objects also to what she sees as proceduralism's too-ready assumption that a "we" exists that deliberates on the validity of a given norm or proposition and that is able to act on the outcome of its deliberations.[35] Against all attempts to ground universality in aspects of human nature, and against all attempts to identify specific social practices as paradigms of universality, Butler insists on its inherent temporality. For her, universality is a "not yet"; it is essentially constituted by that which remains unrealized by it.[36] Thus, universality must be restaged as an open-ended practice of postcolonial cultural translation.

Such translation practices are of various kinds. Butler's model, to begin with, is the kind of postcolonial translation proposed by Gayatri Chakravorty Spivak as a theory and practice of political responsibility.[37] The postcolonial translator works with the texts of subordinated cultures, seeking to make us aware of the "founding violence" of the culturally dominant discourse ("episteme") by bringing into relief its exclusions. Her aim thereby is not to extend a violent regime to include the subordinated other, for it is precisely the ways in which she is already included in the regime that efface her subjectivity and make her agency illegible. Her aim, rather, is to bring into relief the nonconvergence of discourses, in order to facilitate perception of the founding violence of the dominant episteme amid the ruptures of narrative.

Where the texts to be translated are themselves part of the dominant episteme, the translator can expose the limits of what the dominant language can handle. Here, Butler's model is the innovative "misuse" of dominant terms along the lines of the "mimetic doubling" made famous by Homi Bhabha in his writings on colonialism.[38] Translations do not simply repeat the original text; they displace it, appropriating it in a way that robs it of some of its putative authority. The repetition can have an emancipatory dimension, for it may offer the possibility of disrupting the established discourse that controls and defines the parameters of the universal within politics.[39] Translation practices such as these expose the failure of norms of universality to effect the universality for which they stand. For Butler, the normative aim guiding such practices is to extend and render more substantive the notion of universality itself; to push the limits of our language, thereby opening up new possibilities in our endeavors to achieve our deepest hopes and aspirations.[40]

She sees another kind of translation practice as necessary in order to compose an overlapping set of aims from the heterogeneous visions of universality that motivate particular political formations of resistance and movements of enfranchisement.[41] Even on the Left, there is no single idea of universality shared by groupings such as those struggling against racism, against homophobia, or against the international monetary fund. For this reason, the universal claims intrinsic to such groupings have to be articulated in the context of a project of translation in which the terms in question are not simply redescribed by a dominant discourse. Instead, the dominant discourse itself has to alter by virtue of admitting vocabularies alien to it into its lexicon, a process that involves rearticulating the idea of universality itself. In this restaging, particular competing claims to universality are threaded together "into an unwieldy movement whose 'unity' will be measured by its capacity to sustain, without domesticating, internal differences that keep its own definition in flux."[42] Translation of this kind is also required by the politics of multiculturalism.[43] Here, too, emancipatory politics should not be understood as the formation of strategic alliances among particular groupings but as the composition of a set of competing overlapping universalisms through which the universal "announces . . . its 'non-place.'"[44]

Butler implies that forms of cultural translation that fail to restage universality are open to criticism, thus suggesting that cultural translations of the kinds she advocates are normatively valuable. It seems that the value of the activity of translation is bound up with its outcomes: translation is valued precisely because it restages the universal, resulting in new articulations and enactments of the idea of universality. It appears, moreover, that Butler regards these new articulations and enactments not just as new but as better: cultural translation appears to be part of a broader critical enterprise that seeks to reuse the key terms of modernity in ways that constitute an improvement over existing conceptions. "Improvement," as we have been told, is a matter of expanding democratic possibilities, making the key terms of modernity more inclusive, more dynamic, and more concrete. Her references to cultural translation as "the project of extending and rendering substantive the notion of universality itself" are unambiguous in this regard.[45] Thus, the normative language in which Butler presents her idea of cultural translation raises questions concerning the idea of validity guiding her conception. Clearly, the practices of restaging and rearticulation she advocates do not leave the normative horizon of Western modernity intact; instead, more or less systematically and gradually, they bring about profound transformations in its ethical and intellectual vocabularies. If Butler wants to claim that it is good that they should do so—and that the changes brought about are themselves good—she has to appeal to an idea of validity that transcends the values established by the frame of intelligibility of any particular sociocultural context. Otherwise, she once again runs up against Rorty's problem. If she accepts his radically contextualist position, she will be unable to advocate cultural translation on normative grounds, since the only kinds of reasons available to her are decisionistic or strategic ones; this will require her to reformulate her argument in nonnormative terms. On the other hand, if she does accept the need for a context-transcending perspective, she runs up against the difficulties encountered by Habermas and Honneth in their attempts to negotiate the tensions between immanence and transcendence.

Like the other thinkers whose work we have examined, Laclau's critical social thinking is guided by an antiauthoritarian impulse that has an epistemological as well as an ethical dimension. His epistemological antiauthoritarianism is evident in his antiessentialism, which denies the existence of an essence of things independent of the influences of history and context and maintains that "the idea of a truth outside all context is simply nonsensical."[46] This antiessentialism has consequences for the ethical domain, for it leads him to reject the idea that social agents have "objective interests" of which they are not conscious;[47] this could be seen as indicative of a commitment to the value of (what I refer to as) ethical autonomy for it seems to indicate the need for critical theory to be rationally acceptable to those it addresses. A commitment of this kind might also be discerned in the fact that, like Butler, he takes the deep-seated intuitions and expectations of the inhabitants of Western modernity as the normative reference point for his radical democratic project. Describing his aim as that of expanding and deepening liberal-democratic ideology in the direction of a radical and plural democracy, he unequivocally endorses the constitutive values crystallized in this ideology. Rather than rejecting the principles of liberal democracy, he calls for a deepening of what Tocqueville referred to as the "democratic revolution" whereby democratic struggles for equality and liberty would be extended to a wider range of social relations.[48]

Like Butler, Laclau appeals to a notion of the incomplete subject, regarding the negativity at the heart of identity as of crucial importance for his project of radical democracy. For Laclau, as for Butler, identity is differential, constituted in relation to an "other" that "prevents me from being totally myself."[49] The theoretical category he uses to conceptualize this negativity is "antagonism." Antagonisms establish the limits of identity: the boundaries of the discursive formation of the subject and of society.[50] However, although Laclau agrees with Butler that "what is produced as the 'constitutive outside' of the subject [or society] can never become fully inside or immanent,"[51] he disagrees with her on two important points.

The first point of disagreement concerns their explanations for the incompleteness ("incompletion") of the subject. In *Hegemony and Socialist Strategy*, his earlier work with Chantal Mouffe, Laclau drew on an Althusserian idea of identity as being overdetermined, which affirmed the incomplete, open, and politically negotiable character of every totality or identity.[52] On this view, all identity is constituted discursively and no discursive totality exists in the form of a simply given and delimited positivity: it has a discursive exterior that deforms it and prevents it from achieving intactness.[53] Laclau and Mouffe account for the nonfixity—overdetermination—of identity through reference to Jacques Derrida's deconstruction of the concept of structure as a self-contained space unified by a fixed center.[54] In Derrida's well-known account of the history of "structure," the center comes to be thought of as a function rather than as a natural site or fixed locus: as "a sort of nonlocus in which an infinite number of sign substitutions came into play. . . . The absence of the transcendental signified extends the domain and the play of signification infinitely."[55]

Laclau and Mouffe follow Derrida in attributing the incomplete character of all discursive fixation to the absence of a fixed center and the consequent infinite expansion of the play of meaning, concluding that it is "polysemy that disarticulates a discursive structure."[56] In his recent writings, however, Laclau has moved from an Althusserian-Derridean account of the negativity of identity to one that draws on Jacques Lacan's idea of the Real.[57] Now, it is the Lacanian Real that constitutes an inherent limit to the symbolic, maintaining a gap between reality and its symbolization and setting in motion the process of revision to particular formations of the subject and other positings of identity. Whereas Laclau's earlier account conceived of negativity as an infinite play of substitutions, his later view is that it is an originary void, an empty place to be filled by a succession of representations that are constitutively inadequate to it. Moreover, the subjective motivation guiding the process of filling this empty place by way of (failed) representations is a desire for a transcendent ethical object.[58] On this later view, therefore, the subject is construed as a constitutive lack, structured by a gap that it ceaselessly strives to fill by way of representations of totality. This conception of the subject has the advantage that it permits a conception of *intentional* agency, which is often difficult to accommodate within poststructuralist accounts: for, insofar as it reduces the subject to the effect of processes of signification that are essentially nonsubjective, poststructuralism runs the risk of eliminating the possibility of intentional action.[59]

An added advantage of Laclau's later view is its ability to allow for the possibility of *ethical* agency. On his later, psychoanalytic account, the subject's striving is not ethically indifferent since his acts of identification—his decisions about how to establish himself as a fully achieved identity—are oriented by a desire for a transcendent object that has an ethical connotation. Thus, by positing a notion of the subject as prior to the social processes whereby he develops his subjectivity, Laclau allows for the possibility of intentional agency;

by positing the subject as a constitutive lack that searches desperately (though in vain) for a signifier that can fully express his identity as an ethical being, he allows for the possibility of ethical agency.

A second significant point of divergence between Butler's and Laclau's notions of the incomplete subject concerns their views on representation. In contrast to Butler, who conceives of universality as a "non-place" that announces itself in the interstices between particularities, Laclau conceives of it as an "an empty place" that is filled by a succession of particular (failed) representations of universality.[60] Whereas, for Butler, universality manifests itself fleetingly in ephemeral spaces, for Laclau, universality exists only in its incarnations in some particularity that unsuccessfully endeavors to represent it. Thus, for Laclau, universality is always mediated by way of representations. Consequently, he sees representation as an indispensable component of the relations by which the democratic political field is constructed: "insofar as the universality of the community is achievable only through the mediation of a particularity, the relation of representation becomes constitutive."[61]

The idea of a complex dialectic between particularity and universality, mediated by representations, has remained at the center of Laclau's theory of hegemony since he formulated it initially in his collaborative work with Mouffe: "[w]ithout representation . . . there is no hegemony."[62] The concept of hegemony refers to practices of political articulation whereby a political field is constructed together with a political subject.[63] A political field is a contingent configuration of power relations, which is constructed antagon-istically from dissimilar elements; a political subject is a contingent *representation* of universal aims, which is constructed in opposition to an oppressive regime. The hegemonic relations established in these processes of construction are the product of a dialectics between universality and particularity.

In this conception, social groups occupy differential positions within the discourses that constitute the social fabric and are, in this sense, particularities. A plurality of particularities join together in opposition to oppressive forces by establishing "relations of equivalence." These alliances between particularities are based on opposition to a certain system of domination that is regarded as oppressive; an oppressive regime is one that comes to be seen as "the *notorious crime* of the whole of society"[64]—as the obstacle preventing society from coin-ciding with itself, from achieving the "fullness of society."[65] In the process of alliance, a political subject is constructed in opposition to a particular oppres-sive regime; this entails one particularity's assumption of the function of uni-versal representation; if it is to be able to assume this function, it must come to be seen as the one that can open the way to universal political emancipation, to achieving the "fullness of society." In other words, in hegemonic alliances a contingent plurality of particularistic demands are joined in a chain of equivalence by way of a process of identification; in this process the aims of a particular group are identified with the emancipatory aims of the whole community. However, despite claiming universality for its aims, the particularity remains particular—it is simultaneously above the chain of equivalences (as a representation of universality) and within it; the very condition of a hegemonic relation is that "a *particular* social force assumes the representation of a *totality* that is radically incommensurable with it."[66] Moreover, the chain itself is always exclusive—it includes some particularities, but not others.[67] Accordingly, all manifestations of universality are contaminated—they live in an irresolvable tension between universality and particularity and are, in addition, always reversible.[68] Laclau insists, however, that hegemonic universality is the only form of universality that a political community can reach.[69]

In his view, the universal, which is always mediated through particular representations, is a *necessary but impossible* object.[70] (As we shall see, it is also an *ethical* object.) On the one hand, objects such as the "fullness of society" and its correlate, the "notorious crime of the whole of society," are *necessary* if the coincidence between particular and general aims is to take place at all. On the other hand, they are *impossible* because universality cannot be represented in a direct way—no concept corresponds to the desired universal object (the "fullness of society"). Political representations are merely names for a universal object to which no concept corresponds.[71] For Laclau, therefore, terms such as universality, the ethical, truth, justice, and the like are "empty signifiers pointing to the absent fullness of the community."[72]

As in Butler's practices of cultural translation, establishing a chain of equivalence is not just a matter of establishing strategic alliances between competing interests.[73] In contrast to strategic alliances, in which the identity of the particular interest groups remains unaffected, in hegemonic relations the very identity of the groups is modified.[74] Unlike in Butler's conception, however, the cohesive force of the alliance is established by way of *representations* of universality. In Laclau's view, such representations may usefully be compared and contrasted to the revolutionary myths whose importance for revolutionary activity is emphasized in the work of Georges Sorel.[75]

Sorel insists that no socialist revolution—or more generally, heroic activity—is possible without what he calls "myths": imaginary constructions that inspire human beings to battle against the existing state of affairs. He maintains that a study of the great historical movements reveals a fundamental psycho-logical law: that "we do nothing great without the help of warmly-coloured and clearly-defined images, which absorb the whole of our attention."[76] Exam-ples he gives of such absorbing pictures and images are the myth of the general strike and Marx's myth of the proletarian revolution.[77] In contrast to the rational plans for social order that he associates with utopian thinking, such myths are not analyzable rationally and must be taken as a whole; nor can they be refuted for "they are not astrological almanacs."[78] For Sorel, their sig-nificance lies in their power to stimulate creative—heroic, socially transforma-tive—activity rather than in what they achieve in fact. A central thread running through his writings is that human beings are creators, fulfilled only when they are creative, and unfulfilled when they passively receive or drift unresistingly with the current. In his view, creative—revolutionary, heroic—activity is neces-sary for the realization of full humanity.[79] Thus, whether or not any of the social hopes and ideals expressed in these myths are realized is irrelevant. The point of myths is to motivate human beings to engage in revolutionary activity; this is valued not for its ability to achieve a better state of affairs but for its humanizing effects on the individuals who engage in it. This may explain why Sorel appears indifferent to the content of the myths that are deemed indis-pensable for revolutionary activity.

The most interesting point of connection between Sorel's and Laclau's conceptions is their common awareness of the affective pull of an imaginative construction. Sorel reminds us repeatedly that revolutionary myths are not blueprints for a good society; in contrast to utopian schemes, they cannot be subjected to rational analysis but must be taken as a whole; consequently, their motivating power does not reside in their power to convince but in their power to excite the passions. Moreover, their motivating force derives at least in part from their unattainability: in addition to arguing that it is unimportant whether the hopes and ideals expressed in revolutionary myths are ever realized, Sorel suggests that lack of realizability is part of their very attraction. These features of his conception recall Laclau's conception of political representations as constitutively inadequate attempts to incarnate the universal—the absent object of desire that is at once necessary and impossible. Political representa-tions, as we have seen, excite the political imagination and motivate social groups to form hegemonic alliances. Moreover, like Sorel in his description of myths, Laclau emphasizes that the object of desire resists symbolization and has an unfixed and tropological character.[80]

To be sure, the points of connection with Sorel to which Laclau himself draws attention are slightly different. He focuses not on the motivating power of the object of desire orienting social struggles, but on the emptiness of its content. He point out that, like the impossible objects incarnated in representations of universality, Sorelian myths are "empty places"; although they can be filled only by the particular, they utterly transcend any particular targets. In addition, at least on occasion, Laclau discerns similarities with respect to the ethical aspect of both conceptions.[81] Taking as his example Sorel's myth of the general proletarian strike, he argues that this "has all the characteristics of an ethical principle: in order to function as a proper myth, it has to be an object devoid of any particular determination—an empty signifier."[82] Here, however, Laclau seems to overlook an additional requirement that he himself attributes to ethical principles: a connection with a transcendent ethical object. Whereas, in his own work, the Lacanian Real provides a basis for establishing such a connection, Sorel's account of revolutionary myths does not evidently appeal to any comparable category. Although Laclau is correct to assert that Sorelian myths transcend any particular targets, it is not at all obvious that they are aimed at ethical targets. In fact, Sorel seems to leave this question open. His account of the motivating force of myths stresses their sensual, nonrational component, making no explicit connection between this and a transcendent ethical object. For this reason, Laclau's reading, which locates the motivating force of Sorelian myths in a desire for a transcendent ethical object, could be countered with a reading that locates it, for example, in an amoral will to power; indeed, the latter possibility seems especially congruent with the strong vitalist elements in Sorel's thinking. Moreover, Laclau's ethical interpretation of Sorel is at odds with his acknowledgement on other occasions that Sorel's emphasis on will rather than (ethical or nonethical) content opens up ambiguous possibilities, from bolshevism to fascism. He recognizes that, for Sorel, the relation between working-class demands and the "fullness of society" is purely contingent; what matters is not *what* the proletariat fights to obtain but *that* it engages in violent confrontations.[83]

Even leaving aside this particular point of dispute, there is a further reason why Laclau's ethical reading of Sorel's myth of the general strike should be treated with caution. It is not just that Sorel makes no clear reference to a transcendent ethical object; his notion of myth lacks a feature crucial to Laclau's own account of this object's ethical dimensions. Whereas, in Laclau's conception, the transcendent ethical object is mediated by way of particular representations, in Sorel's conception, myths such as the general strike are not *mediated* by "warmly-coloured and clearly-defined images": they are *themselves* such images. To be sure, here, too, there is room for dispute as to the correct reading. It could be argued that Sorel's reference to pictures and images makes sense only if these are taken to assume functions of representation, mediating between the "general strike" as a transcendent object and the subjects who seek to attain it. But the argument could be countered by pointing out that there is little evidence of any disjunction between object and image in Sorel's account. Although it seems sensible to leave such questions of textual interpretation to Sorelian scholarship, there is a point to my warning against overly hasty comparisons between Sorel's and Laclau's conceptions. As I see it, the two conceptions may usefully be compared with regard to the affective component of political-revolutionary motivation and with regard to the imaginative aspect of myths and political representations. However, these instructive comparisons should not be allowed to obscure significant differences in their accounts of the transcendent object that are relevant to our present discussion. As indicated, these differences concern the *ethical* character of the transcendent object and the need for it to be mediated by way of (constitutively inadequate) representations. This brings us back to our initial question concerning the notion of validity at work in Butler's and Laclau's critical social thinking.

As we have seen, Butler does not address the question of the scope of the normative perspective operative in cultural translation or in other contexts in which the "frame of intelligibility" itself is challenged by way of disruptive or innovative rearticulation, restaging, and renactment. Interestingly, Laclau reads Butler in a Rortyan vein, suspecting that, for her, "it is not possible to state any principle or rule whose tentative validity extends beyond a certain cultural context."[84] Whether or not his suspicions are justified—again, we can leave aside such questions of textual interpretation—it is clear that a radically contextualist position of this kind would raise problems for Butler's advocacy of cultural translation and similar practices of rearticulation, restaging, and reenactment.[85] This is why I suggest that it is not a matter toward which she should be indifferent. By contrast, Laclau himself unequivocally adopts a context-transcending position.[86] Against Foucault—and possibly Butler—he warns against confusing the contingency and context-dependency of the speaker's position of enunciation, on the one hand, and the range of applicability he attributes to his categories on the other. He points out that historicizing

the place of enunciation says nothing about the degree of universality attributed to the statements, positioning himself as historicist with respect to the
former and universalist with respect to the latter.[87] At the same time, he
acknowledges that, in his work so far, the universalist-ethical dimension of his
thinking—the dimension of normative argumentation—has advanced less
rapidly than the descriptive-normative dimension.[88] In other words, (what I
refer to as) the context-transcending dimension, although increasingly prominent in his more recent work, is in need of further development.

If the critical social theorist's normative categories are to be construed as
universal in reach, applicable across historical epochs and cultural contexts,
they must appeal to some idea of context-transcending validity. Presumably,
the idea of validity underpinning Laclau's universalist perspective corresponds
to the idea of the universal in his account of hegemonic politics. As we saw
in our discussion of his reading of Sorel, Laclau attributes an ethical dimension
to the necessary but impossible object of desire that motivates democratic
political activity; accordingly, the "empty places" that political representations
seek to fill with their imaginative constructions of universality are *ethical*
spaces.

According to Laclau, "the moment of the ethical is the moment of the
universality of the community, the moment in which, beyond any particular-
ism, the universal speaks by itself."[89] Since society consists only of particularities, universality has to be incarnated in something other than itself.
Universality—the ethical—becomes incarnated in the normative hopes and
ideals of a particular group. However, although there is an ethical *investment* in
particular normative orders, no normative order is, in and for itself, ethical.[90]
Instead, the relation between the ethical and the normative is inherently
unstable.[91] As he puts it, the ethical moment is the moment in which the "fullness of society" manifests itself as both impossible and necessary.[92]

It is clear from this that Laclau's account of hegemony is an account of an
ethically oriented struggle for political power. The transcendent objects of
desire motivating hegemonic politics are ethical objects. What remains unclear
is the precise nature of the relation between the transcendent ethical object
and its particular representations. So far, Laclau has not provided any satisfactory account of this relation.

As we know, hegemony describes a situation in which particular political
subjects assume the function of universality by virtue of their ability to symbol-
ize the promise of general emancipation. However, though these particular
political subjects are constitutively inadequate representations of the

transcendent ethical object (which is given names such as "universality" or "the fullness of society"), they must stand in *some* kind of relation to this object. If they did not do so, Laclau would not be able to attribute an "ethical investment" to particular representations. More significantly, his conception would be open to the objection that the particular representations of universality that emerge from hegemonic struggles are ethically arbitrary. This problem has accompanied his theory of hegemony from the outset. Already in *Hegemony and Socialist Strategy*, Laclau and Mouffe acknowledged that the "discursive compass of the democratic revolution opens the way for political logics as diverse as right-wing populism and totalitarianism on the one hand, and a radical democracy on the other."[93] To be sure, as already mentioned, Laclau at that stage favored an Althusserian-Derridean theory of the subject that made it difficult to accommodate a conception of ethical—or even intentional—agency. In the meantime, as we know, he has adopted a Lacanian perspective that is better able to accommodate an ethical conception.

However, notwithstanding the new theoretical resources he has at his disposal, Laclau's view of ethical agency, like his view of the ethical investment of particular representations, remains seriously underdeveloped. In particular, clarification is called for as to how the ethical exercise of agency may be distinguished from its nonethical exercise, and as to how ethical forms of investment in particular normative orders may be distinguished from nonethical forms. Pending satisfactory clarification of these issues, his theory is open to the objection—recently raised against it by Žižek[94]—that the "glue" binding together the social body in the theory of hegemony could just as well be fascist as liberal democratic; moreover, that Laclau offers no normative grounds for his own preferred option of radical democracy.

Laclau's dilemma is the following. On the one hand, since the transcendent ethical object is deemed to have no ethical content,[95] it can offer no guidance as to how the claims to universality raised by particular political representations can be ethically evaluated. On the other hand, the hegemonic construction of a political representation cannot be ethically arbitrary; otherwise his reference to "ethical investment" would make no sense; moreover, he could have no nonstrategic, nondecisionistic reasons for advocating (some version of) liberal democracy rather than a fascist democratic regime. Laclau is not prepared to grant any ethical content to the transcendent object, yet is equally unhappy with pure decisionism. He attempts to avoid decisionism by arguing that the horizon of options available to the plurality of particularities whose decision constructs a political subject is normatively limited.[96] These limits are set by "the ensemble of sedimented practices constituting the normative framework of a certain society."[97] Thus, the hegemonic decisions whereby particular political subjects are constituted are not normatively arbitrary but "must show their verisimilitude to people living inside these orders."[98]

However, the question is not whether hegemonic decisions are *normatively* arbitrary but whether they can be distinguished from one another on grounds that are ethical in a context-transcending sense. In appealing to the *Sittlichkeit* of particular communities Laclau avoids the accusation of decisionism, but at the price of opening himself to the charge of conventionalism. The weaknesses of a conventionalist approach are evident: the ensemble of sedimented practices constituting the normative framework of a certain society may be right-wing or totalitarian in tendency and therefore hostile to the liberal democratic ideas of freedom and equality.

The problem lies with Laclau's insistence on the emptiness of the transcendent ethical object. It is one thing to insist on a gap between the transcendent ethical object and its particular representations—this is the gap that allows for the idea of context-transcending validity, for a notion of validity that transcends any existing normative order: it is also the gap that prevents authoritarianism by keeping open the democratic process. Laclau rightly observes that if a community is to be a democratic one, "everything turns around the possibility of keeping always open and ultimately undecided the moment of articulation between the particularity of the normative order and the universality of the ethical moment."[99] However, the presupposition here—not mentioned by Laclau—is that the subjects engaged in democratic politics are motivated by concerns that are ethical in a context-transcending sense.

If it is one thing to insist on a gap between the transcendent ethical object and its particular representations, it is another to assert that this object is empty. In denying it any content at all, Laclau denies the possibility of an ethical relation between object and representation, with the result that the transcendent object loses its regulative functions. We could also say: by positing a relation between the transcendent object and its particular representations that is ethically invariable, Laclau makes all representations of the transcendent object ethically indifferent. If the danger connected with closing the gap between the transcendent ethical object and its particular representations is authoritarianism, the dangers connected with an invariable gap are decisionism and conventionalism. In order to avoid these dangers, Laclau has to allow for an ethically variable gap between particular representations of universality and the transcendent ethical object. Otherwise, the "ethical invest-ment" of which he speaks would be indistinguishable from investments based on mere subjective preference (decisionism) or the prevailing *Sittlichkeit* (conventionalism).

At a minimum, this requires Laclau to clarify the sense in which particular representations are presumptively ethical: the sense in which they are pre-sumed to be ethical until their ethical deficiencies are made apparent. Another way of putting this is to say that he must specify the relation between the transcendent ethical object and its particular representations in a way that allows for ethical progress—for improvement in the ethical quality of particu-lar normative orders vis-à-vis the ones they have replaced. If he is to succeed in doing so, however, he must indicate some means of evaluating ethical defi-ciencies and assessing the ethical quality of particular representations of the transcendent object. Since in company with most contemporary critical social theorists he rejects as nonsensical the idea of validity independent of all context, this requires him to identify modes of evaluation that are at once context dependent and context transcending. It is clear from this that the chal-lenge confronting Laclau is exactly the same as the one facing Habermas and Honneth in their attempts to maintain an idea of context-transcending validity while taking account of the demands of situated rationality.

I have argued that if particular political representations are to be open to ethical assessment, the transcendent ethical object cannot be as devoid of content as Laclau maintains. But what kind of content should we attribute to it? Laclau seems reluctant to allow any ethical content to the transcendent object for fear that singling out certain goals in advance as ethically valid ones would lead to a closure of the democratic process. In the next chapter I address the question of how we should think about the content of the transcendent ethical object. Here I want to note that Laclau himself has not yet tackled this difficult question; in consequence, he remains caught on the horns of a dilemma whereby authoritarianism is avoided only at the cost of conventionalism or decisionism. The question confronting him can also be formulated as a ques-tion of justification. Laclau owes us an answer to the question of how particu-lar representations of the transcendent ethical object can be regarded as ethically justified in a context-transcending sense. This question has to be answered not only with regard to the particular representations that gain hegemony as a result of democratic struggles, but also with regard to his own claims for the superiority of hegemonic politics over other—democratic and nondemocratic—forms.

In this chapter, I have sought to show that the debate between context-transcending and contextualist approaches to critical social thinking is relevant for contemporary social criticism in general, irrespective of whether the thinkers in question explicitly address questions of justification, endorse a normative model of public reasoning, or emphasize the importance of rational agency. I argued that Butler, who does none of these things, cannot ignore the questions of context-transcending validity and the scope of the critical interrogation of social institutions and arrangements that she advocates. She, too, must elaborate a justificatory strategy that negotiates the tensions between immanence and transcendence while avoiding the pitfalls of epistemological and ethical authoritarianism. To do so, she must be prepared to accept some notion of subjectivity as prior to its formation in multiple social and political discourses. Otherwise, she will not be able to account for the ethically oriented, context-transcending motivation she attributes to subjectivities engaged in processes of cultural translation or other ways of restaging cultural norms. By positing the subject as an originary lack, Laclau is able to avoid this problem. However, Butler worries that Laclau's (and Žižek's) Lacanian view of the incompletion of the subject immunizes the negativity at the heart of identity against alteration by way of democratic challenges: it seems to remove certain contents from the realm of political contestation. In the next chapter, I refer to this as the problem of ideological closure in the pernicious sense. It is in order to avoid such closure that she underscores the political salience of even constituting exclusions. Laclau's insistence on the *emptiness* of the transcendent dimension that he attributes to subjectivity could be seen as a response to this kind of worry; since the transcendent ethical object is empty, no contents are removed from the realm of critical interrogation. The difficulty, here, however, is that its emptiness threatens to render it ethically vacuous. If the transcendent object (the ethical, the universal, truth, justice, and so on) motivating hegemonic politics is utterly devoid of content, then it cannot help us ethically to assess the particular representations of it that, at any given time, assume a position of hegemony. Consequently, normative democratic politics succumbs to either decisionism or conventionalism. The key question that has emerged from this chapter, therefore, is how to conceive the relation between the transcendent ethical object and particular representations of it. In the next chapter I address this question more directly.

5

Re-Presenting the Good Society

Context-transcending social criticism requires a concept of context-transcending validity. If the critical power of critical social theory is to extend across historical epochs and sociocultural contexts, it must make use of concepts of validity (truth, justice, the ethical, the universal, and the like) that are similarly context transcending in scope. Rorty sees correctly that the question of context-transcending validity is at the core of his dispute with Habermas. Against Habermas, who regards ideas of universal validity as indispensable for the project of a critical social theory, Rorty maintains that the utility of such ideas is extremely limited. He contends, furthermore, that they have undesirable effects: they encourage the mistaken belief that access to things as they are "in themselves" is possible. Indeed, in his view, this belief is not just mistaken, it is arrogant, unhealthy, and immature. In chapter 2 I queried Rorty's advocacy of a radically contextualist position. I agreed with his view that no external standpoint is available that would permit authoritative judgments in matters of truth or justice. However, I suggested that he goes too far by rejecting the need for reference to validity in a context-transcending sense, pointing out that by doing so, he robs social criticism of the power to respond to the challenges posed by cross-cultural encounters, engagements with the historical past, technological innovations, ecological developments, new life situations, and so on; moreover, that he himself is unable to maintain this position consistently.

It is one thing to argue that ideas of context-transcending validity play an indispensable role in critical social thinking; it is another to find ways of understanding context-transcending validity that permits it to retain its traditional functions of evaluation, regulation, and motivation without falling prey to epistemological and ethical authoritarianism. In this regard, a key question that has emerged from the last chapter concerns the relation between context-transcending validity and historically specific representations of it. The question can be formulated in various ways. In Laclau's writings, it is formulated in terms of the relation between the transcendent ethical object and particular representations of that object. In Rorty's and Habermas's writings, it is formulated in terms of the relation between truth and justification. From the point of view of my concerns in this book, the question can be formulated in terms of the relation between the good society and the particular representations of it that are offered in particular critical social theories.

The first issue here is the need for a gap between the transcendent ethical object (for example, the good society) and its particular representations, between truth and justification. The second issue is the way in which the gap should be construed, if it is needed. As the discussion of Rorty made clear, the challenge facing advocates of a radically contextualist approach is to show that *no* gap is needed for the purposes of democratic politics and critical social thinking. As the discussions of Habermas, Honneth, and Laclau demonstrated, the challenge facing advocates of a context-transcending approach is to find a way of maintaining the gap that enables a context-transcending, critical perspective without violating the demands of situated rationality.[1]

If the gap is closed, the result is radical contextualism and the limitations it imposes on the scope of social criticism. This is the difficulty with Rorty's position. But the gap that is posited in Laclau's account has similarly unwelcome consequences. By construing "the ethical" as an empty signifier, Laclau posits a gap between the transcendent ethical object and its particular representations that is ethically invariable. In his account, every particular representation of universality is equally distant from—or close to—the transcendent ethical object. This opens the door for conventionalism or authoritarianism: the only available bases for preferring one representation to another are either conformity with socially institutionalized ideas of ethical rightness or conformity with the dictates of some transcendent authority. From the point of view of democratic politics and critical social thinking, therefore, the negative implications that follow from Rorty's closure of the gap between truth and justification also follow from Laclau's positing of a gap that is ethically invariable.[2]

In other words, by insisting on the emptiness of the transcendent object, Laclau runs the risk of losing the dimension of context transcendence that he regards as essential for democratic politics. However, attributing ethical content to the transcendent object is also risky. Laclau is right to be wary in this regard. Butler, as we have seen, draws attention to one serious risk that arises. In her view, any attempt to give normative content to transcendent ideas runs the risk of denying the political salience of these normative contents—of concealing their inherent contestability by removing them from the realm of critical inter- rogation and immunizing them against the possibility of creative rearticulation and reenactment. She attempts to avoid this danger by insisting on the *negativity* of the universal. In the terms of our discussion up to now, the danger of denying the political salience of normative contents is that it leads to episte- mological and ethical authoritarianism—removing normative contents from the realm of critical interrogation grants them a normative status that is ahis- torical, absolute, and independent of their rational (and affective) acceptability to those for whom they have binding force. However, the term "ideological closure" better captures the dimension of concealment implied in Butler's view of the dangers arising from the postulate of a substantive transcendent object.[3]

In our attempt to answer the question of how to construe the gap between the transcendent object and particular representations of such objects, it is helpful to look more closely at the idea of ideological closure as it is used in the work of Laclau. Closer inspection of Laclau's interpretation of this idea is helpful for a number of reasons. To begin with, examination reveals that Laclau tacitly employs the idea of ideological closure in two senses: a harmless sense, in which it refers to what I call "metaphysical closure," and a pernicious sense, in which it is the object of ideology critique. In both cases, ideological closure involves concealment (I come back to this point below). However, the concealment is regarded as dangerous only in the second case. The difficulties Laclau encounters in his attempts to allow for a robust conception of ideologi- cal closure—one that would allow for ideology critique—are instructive: they help us to see the limitations of his view of the transcendent ethical object as an empty place. However, Laclau's tacit distinction between harmless meta- physical closure and pernicious ideological closure is also suggestive. By allow- ing for the possibility of harmless forms of ideological closure, it enables us to see that the metaphysically closed aspect of representations of the good society is not a flaw to be eradicated but an indispensable feature of critical social thinking. This will prove particularly useful in our discussion of the utopian dimension of critical social theory in chapter 7. For our immediate purposes, highlighting the metaphysically closed aspect of representations of the good society has the advantage that it draws attention to their imaginary character, opening the way for the suggestion that such representations are imaginative constructions of a transcendent ethical object and may, accordingly, be understood as *fictions*.

Laclau explicitly addresses the question of ideological closure as part of a concern to rescue the idea of ideology as false consciousness, and to make it fruitful for radical politics and critical social thinking.[4] He acknowledges that the notion of ideology as distortion—as false representation or false consciousness—may seem dubious today in light of its apparent reliance on a privileged vantage point from which distortions can be perceived as such. As he points out, categories such as "false consciousness" or "distorted representation" make sense only so long as something "true" or "undistorted" is considered to be within human reach. But once a viewpoint beyond ideology becomes unreachable, such notions lose all meaning.[5] On the other hand, simply abandoning the concept of ideological distortion is not an option for theories that adopt a critical perspective on society. Giving up the practice of ideology critique, which relies on categories such as false consciousness, leads to new forms of positivism and objectivism. Whereas the idea of distortion seems to imply the accessibility of a reality that would speak without discursive mediations, relinquishing it means that the positivity and graspability attributed to that reality is transferred to the discourses organizing social practices, for these now appear as incommensurable and on an equal footing with all others. As he puts it: "[I]f we entirely do away with the notion of 'distortion' and assert that there are only incommensurable 'discourses,' we merely transfer the notion of a full positivity from an extra-discursive ground to the plurality of the social field."[6] Such a position is clearly unacceptable to any theory that sees itself as engaged in social criticism.

For this reason, Laclau makes a case for retaining the category of ideological distortion while simultaneously denying the accessibility of a privileged vantage point from which the distorted character of representations and consciousness would be visible. The crux of his argument is that the assumption of the availability of an extraideological viewpoint is the ideological misconception par excellence. At the same time, such an assumption is necessary. Consequently, "[i]deology is a dimension which belongs to the structure of all possible experience."[7]

In his account of the inevitability of ideological distortion, Laclau pursues a strategy that is reminiscent of his argument concerning the simultaneous necessity and impossibility of the universal. As we saw in the last chapter,

Laclau argues that the universal—the transcendent ethical object motivating hegemonic struggles—is at once necessary and impossible: it is necessary in order for the aims of particular social groups to come together as a *general* aim, incarnated in some representation of the universal, yet impossible since no actual representation of the universal corresponds to the transcendent object itself. His argument that ideological distortion belongs to the structure of all possible experience runs along similar lines. It starts from the premise that the idea of distortion makes sense only on the assumption of a primary meaning that is not distorted. Such a meaning would be complete in itself and fully transparent to itself. These attributes of self-sufficiency and self-transparency amount to an idea of closure—to the idea of a closed identity that does not need to go outside of itself in order to become and know what it is in itself.[8] I shall call closure of this kind "metaphysical closure," distinguishing it—*pace* Laclau—from ideological closure in the pernicious sense. Laclau argues that the projection of such an originary meaning is both impossible and necessary. It is impossible since meaning is in fact never final. It is necessary since without this kind of "fictitious fixing of meaning there would not be meaning at all."[9] Closure is thus the very condition of meaning.[10]

To be sure, the latter part of the argument, at least, is debatable: it could be objected that meaning does not presuppose the closure of identity but merely the assumption of some degree of coherence. However, we can leave aside such difficulties, since for our present purposes a weaker version of Laclau's thesis is sufficient. The question concerning us at the moment is whether attributing normative contents to the transcendent ethical object leads to ideological closure in the pernicious sense—to the removal of those contents from the realm of critical interrogation. From the point of view of this question, it is unimportant whether the idea of closure is a condition of meaning as such; it is enough to show that metaphysical closure is a condition of the representation of the transcendent ethical object motivating hegemonic struggles. In fact, this seems to be Laclau's main point in his discussion of ideological distortion. He appears less concerned with theories of meaning than with their implications for the representations of the transcendent ethical object (specifically, the universal) at work in hegemonic politics. His argument seems designed to show that the idea of the universal is the idea of a self-sufficient, self-transparent, primary meaning that, though posited as accessible, is not in fact within human reach. The ideological distortion built into political life is the illusion that a metaphysically closed identity (denoted by empty signifiers such as "the fullness of society," "truth," or "justice") is in fact accessible. This closure is projected onto some object—some political representation of the universal—that is constitutively incomplete. Accordingly, such representations can be described as the illusory presence of an absence—the illusion that the absent completeness is fully present in the representation in question.[11] This absence has to be concealed, however, for otherwise hegemonic struggles would lose their point.

From chapter 4 we will recall that the "glue" binding the particular groups that join together in chains of equivalence is the idea of the universal as incarnated in some representation of it. The glue's cohesive powers depend on the illusion that a particular representation of the universal is adequate to it; without this illusion the chain of equivalence would disintegrate. It seems, therefore, that when Laclau writes that the "illusion of closure is the main source of a distorted consciousness"[12] or endorses Žižek's view that "it is precisely the assumption . . . of a pure extra-discursive reality, which constitutes the ideological misconception *par excellence*,"[13] his main concern is to show that hegemonic politics is inherently ideological insofar as it depends on the double illusion that access to an entirely self-sufficient and self-transparent transcendent object is possible, and that this transcendent object is represented fully by a particular political representation. The important point here is that ideological distortion in the sense of metaphysical closure is regarded by Laclau as harmless. He maintains that the assertion of ideological distortion has no pejorative connotation, since it is "a dimension of society which cannot be suppressed."[14]

But Laclau is also concerned to rehabilitate the notion of ideology in the sense of false consciousness. As we have seen, he is alert to the danger that new kinds of positivism and objectivism may result from abandoning the notion of ideological distortion in a pernicious sense. This is why he attempts to rescue that notion from the epistemological authoritarianism implicit in the idea of an extradiscursive standpoint from which reality could speak without discursive mediations. However, though his rescue attempt is useful from the point of view of the theory of hegemony, it is inadequate as a contribution to the theory of ideology. This is because it leaves open the question of the basis on which ideology critique can be carried out once the thesis of the availability of an extradiscursive viewpoint becomes untenable. If, as Laclau maintains, ideological distortion is a dimension of society that cannot be suppressed, it is unclear how a critique of ideology is supposed to be possible. On the one hand, Laclau assures us that his interpretation of ideological closure as (what I call) metaphysical closure does not mean that ideological critique is impossible: it merely implies that all such critique has to be thought of as *intra*ideological.[15] On the other hand, he gives no hints as to the evaluative basis for intraideological critique.

Presumably, intraideological critique would start from the premise that the inherent inadequacy of representations of the universal must be denied; from this starting point it would move on to attack unacceptable forms of this denial of inadequacy. But Laclau gives no clues as to the evaluative basis from which such an attack could be undertaken. For this reason, although his idea of ideological closure as metaphysical closure casts light on what is involved in political representation and in the formation of chains of equivalence, it does not help us to analyze the kinds of ideological distortion that are the proper object of ideology critique. To make the idea of ideological distortion fruitful for critical social thinking, therefore, Laclau must establish some basis for criticizing claims to universality as unacceptably distorted. In other words, he must establish some basis for distinguishing constitutive ideological closure from ideological closure in a critically robust sense. A first step in this direction could be taken by defining ideological closure, along the lines indicated by Butler, as the denial that certain normative contents are politically salient. However, a second step is also necessary. In addition to providing an account of what he means by (pernicious) ideological closure, Laclau has to clarify why ideological closure in this sense is *ethically* unacceptable. For this, however, he requires a suitable conception of ethical validity.

The problem with Laclau's account of ideological distortion is similar to the problem with his account of the transcendent (ethical) object as an empty place. In this account, as indicated, the relationship between the transcendent object and the political representations that gain hegemony as a result of democratic struggles is ethically invariable; although these representations are allegedly ethically invested, by completely emptying the transcendent object of ethical content he denies us any ethical means of assessing their claims to validity. From an ethical point of view, each claim is equally deserving—or undeserving—of merit, for the gap between the transcendent ethical object and its particular representations never varies. Similarly, his account of ideological distortion fails to provide any means of criticizing the distortedness of particular representations of the transcendent ethical object over and above their constitutive inadequacy. What is lacking in both cases is an idea of validity that would permit ethical criticism of validity claims, even where these are acceptable from the point of view of the prevailing *Sittlichkeit*.[16] So long as he lacks a conception of ethical validity of this kind, Laclau's endeavor to retain a transcendent moment in radical politics and critical social thinking, and to rehabilitate the idea of ideology as false consciousness, will remain unsuccessful.

Despite this serious shortcoming, however, Laclau's discussion of ideological distortion does help us to move forward in our consideration of the question of the relation between the transcendent ethical object and historically specific representations of it. Laclau's discussion is useful in that it casts light on what is involved in representation: it shows that representations of the universal grant a transcendent status to particular normative contents and by doing so involve *metaphysical* closure. It is also useful in its suggestion that this kind of closure is harmless: although described by Laclau as ideological closure, it is deemed to have no pejorative connotations and to be no cause for concern. Admittedly, as an attempt to resurrect the notion of ideological distortion it is inadequate, since its conception of ideological closure lacks critical bite; nonetheless, its implicit suggestion that metaphysical closure is not in itself a problem is fruitful, for it permits a more differentiated view of the relation between the transcendent object and its representations. If political representations inevitably involve metaphysical projections—projections of an object that is self-sufficient and self-transparent—then it remains an open question whether such projections lead to ideological closure in the pernicious sense of removing normative contents from the political field of open-ended interrogation. Later in this chapter I suggest that ideological closure in the pernicious sense can be avoided by a self-conscious acknowledgment of the metaphysically closed, fictive status of representations of the transcendent object. First, however, I want to show that Laclau's idea of metaphysical closure suggests an interpretation of Habermas's idea of the ideal speech situation that helps to make sense of the relation between truth and justification in Habermas's critical social theory.

Like Laclau, Habermas must find a way of maintaining a gap between the transcendent object and its historically specific articulations that can be operationalized for the purposes of context-transcending social criticism, while avoiding the danger of ideological closure in the pernicious sense. Whereas in Laclau's work, this gap is formulated as one between the transcendent ethical object and particular representations of it, in Habermas's thinking it is formulated as a gap between truth and justice, on the one hand, and the agreements reached in real processes of discursive justification, on the other.

Unlike Laclau, who denies the transcendent object any ethical content, Habermas, at least in his earlier writings, defines truth and justice in terms of an ideal speech situation (we shall see that he has now revised his position regarding truth). The idea of the ideal speech situation is the idea of ideal justificatory conditions: it projects the image of a condition in which participants in argumentation would be motivated only by the search for the single right answer, in which only the force of the better argument would prevail, in which the exchange of arguments would be completely unconstrained, and in which all relevant arguments would be considered on their merits (in the case of truth), or all parties affected would be included in discussion and be accorded an equal opportunity to exchange reasons within it (in the case of justice). Recalling Laclau's remarks on originary meaning, we can see that the projected condition is one of self-sufficiency and self-transparency: it has no need to go outside of itself to become and to know what it is in itself. For, the idea of the ideal speech situation projects a condition in which participants in argumentation would have acquired complete and final knowledge, of the world, of themselves, and of other persons, and also perfect mutual understanding. This suggests an interesting analogy with Laclau's idea of political representation: with its attributes of self-sufficiency and self-transparency, the ideal speech situation might be understood as a representation of truth (or justice), in the sense of a constitutively inadequate, particular articulation of a transcendent object.

To be sure, this does not appear to be Habermas's own understanding of the ideal speech situation. Although over the years he has revised his account of its status within his theory, it is unlikely that he would accept this way of construing it. For, if construed as a representation of a transcendent object, the ideal speech situation appears to undermine Habermas's professed commitment to postmetaphysical conceptions of truth and justice (I come back to this below); if construed as a constitutively inadequate representation of a transcendent object, it appears to lose the regulative powers with which Habermas equips it. Nonetheless, I want to argue that the analogy with Laclau's idea of political representation is instructive: it can help us to resolve certain problems connected with Habermas's account of truth, in particular, and with his account of context-transcending validity more generally; it also helps to clarify the challenges facing Habermas in his attempt to defend the idea of context-transcending validity without falling prey to epistemological and ethical authoritarianism. To see the usefulness of the analogy, we must first look briefly at the role played by the ideal speech situation within Habermas's theory.

Habermas's idea of the ideal speech situation is central to his attempt to elaborate postmetaphysical conceptions of truth and justice in a context-transcending sense.[17] Since the early 1970s, the endeavor to elaborate post-metaphysical conceptions of truth and justice has been a central part of his critical social theory.[18] For our present purposes, postmetaphysical thinking—regarded by Habermas as one of the most significant impulses of twentieth-century philosophy[19]—can be taken as roughly equivalent to the idea of situated rationality. As in other parts of his critical theory, formal-pragmatic reflections play a key role in his attempt to steer a course between immanence and transcendence, between the situatedness of reason and the context-transcending scope of claims to truth and justice.

As we saw in chapter 3, Habermas uses formal-pragmatic studies of every-day language to show that communicative action is the primary mode of language use. Even in its everyday forms, communicative action amounts to a rudimentary practice of argumentation, for it is action centered on the activity of raising and responding to validity claims. This validity-centered action is guided by a host of idealizing presuppositions concerning both the conduct of discussion and its outcome. As regards its conduct Habermas maintains, for example, that participants in argumentation are guided by the assumption that all relevant arguments will be considered and that the only permissible force is that of the better argument. As regards its outcome he maintains, for example, that participants are guided by the assumption that a valid outcome—a true proposition or a just norm—will command universal agreement as to its validity.

Habermas's thesis is that the idealizing presuppositions guiding everyday communication serve to establish an internal connection between context-transcending validity and concrete practices of argumentation. The thesis of such a connection is a crucial aspect of his postmetaphysical project, for it is supposed to enable him to assert the context-transcending power of truth and justice while acknowledging that we can arrive at truth and justice only by way of communicative processes that are subject to the influences of history and context.

Initially, Habermas defined truth and justice as argumentatively reached, universal agreement. He asserted not only that valid propositions and norms would command universal agreement; he made the stronger claim that the truth of propositions, and justice of norms and principles, *is* the outcome of argumentation conducted under ideal justificatory conditions. In other words, he used the normative model of argumentation extracted from formal-pragmatic investigations of everyday communicative practices as a basis for *definitions* of truth and justice. In both cases, he argued that an intersubjectively achieved, rational agreement provides a criterion of valid knowledge, on the condition that the agreement is reached through a process of argumentation that satisfies certain demanding procedural requirements (approximating to the requirements of the ideal speech situation). Clearly, therefore, in this conception, procedure and outcome are intimately connected. The validity of propositions or norms cannot be established purely on the basis of the openness, fairness, and inclusivity of the argumentation procedure; argumentatively achieved agreement is also necessary. Conversely, agreement—even universal agreement—is not a sufficient basis for establishing the validity of propositions or norms; the agreement has to be reached in open, fair, and inclusive procedures of public argumentation.

Thus, in the original version of the thesis, truth and justice were defined as a rational consensus achieved under ideal justificatory conditions. We could also say: context-transcending validity was deemed to be *constructed* by way of the argumentative exchange of reasons under the conditions of the ideal speech situation.[20] In the meantime, however, Habermas has modified his position with regard to truth. Although he continues to defend a constructivist view of justice,[21] he has now abandoned the claim that truth is the outcome of an idealized rational consensus—that it is constructed argumentatively under ideal justificatory conditions.

Habermas appears to have abandoned his constructivist view of truth in response to criticisms of his use of the idea of an ideal speech situation. Generally speaking, these criticisms fall into two broad categories. One set of criticisms focuses on difficulties connected with operationalizing the idea of the ideal speech situation—on difficulties arising once we try to use it as a criterion of truth or justice. A second set of criticisms focuses on difficulties connected with the metaphysical character of the social condition it projects—on difficulties arising from its projection of a condition that is self-sufficient and self-transparent.

The first line of criticism focuses on the gap between idealized rational consensus and any consensus reached in actual processes of justification. As critics such as Cristina Lafont have shown, Habermas's constructivist model is inherently unstable.[22] For it either implies an unbridgeable gap between an idealized rational consensus and de facto agreements—in this case, the idea of an idealized rational consensus is so far removed from human practices of justification as to undermine the authoritative power ascribed to it—or it closes the gap between the ideal and the actual; in this case, truth and justice lose their cognitively construed, context-transcending force.

A second line of criticism is directed against the very notion of an ideal speech situation. Here, objections are of two main kinds. The first kind of objection focuses on the problem of motivation, drawing attention to the paradoxical aspect of regulative ideas. This kind of objection has been raised most forcefully by Albrecht Wellmer.[23] Regulative ideas are ideas of perfection that prompt human beings to endeavor to attain them but transcend their powers to do so.[24] For Wellmer, the idea of the ideal speech situation is an idea of this kind; he argues that to strive to attain any ideal condition is paradoxical and that the paradoxical nature of the endeavor undermines the projected condition's motivating power. For this reason, he rejects approaches to the question of context-transcending validity that rely on regulative ideas. The paradoxical character of ideas such as the ideal speech situation consists in their imputing to human beings the motivation to realize an aim whose realization would mean the end of human history. This is because the ideal speech situation, as noted, evokes the idea of a condition in which participants in communicative action would have acquired complete and final knowledge of the world, of themselves and of other persons, and also perfect mutual understanding; in achieving such a state of perfection, however, they would be no longer human.

We are reminded here of Kant's point that human imperfection is the positive condition of freedom: if God had not limited our cognitive capacities and had granted us direct access to "things in themselves," we would be blind automata rather than free, responsible agents.[25] The difficulty, as Žižek points out, is that this seems to undermine Kant's notion of a regulative idea. Such an idea is supposed to regulate human activity, in the sense of motivating human beings to think and act in accordance with its idea of perfection. But in order to do so, the unattainability of the goal must be forgotten or overlooked; otherwise, it will provoke only cynicism or naivety. As Žižek puts it: "either we must blind ourselves to the necessary ultimate failure of our endeavour—regress to naivety, and let ourselves be caught up in the enthusiasm [for the impossible goal]—or we must adopt a stance of cynical distance, participating in the game while being fully aware that the result will be disappointing."[26] Like a Kantian regulative idea, Habermas's idea of an ideal speech situation raises a question about its capacity for motivating moral or political thinking and action.

The second kind of objection concerns the problem that arises if ethical contents are attributed to the transcendent object (the universal, truth, the good society, and the like). The danger here, as we have seen, is pernicious ideological closure: denial of the political salience of the ethical contents in question. This is the worry that Butler expresses with regard to substantive transcendent ideas. It is shared by Laclau, who criticizes Habermas's idea of the ideal speech situation on the grounds that it specifies the normative content of the transcendent ethical object prior to all democratic struggles and decisions;[27] as we know Laclau attempts to avoid the danger of pernicious ideological closure by construing the transcendent object as an empty place. By defining truth and justice as the outcome of an agreement reached under ideal justificatory conditions, Habermas stands accused of making something essentially unrepresentable representable, and of denying the constitutive inadequacy of all representations. By doing so, he can be charged with immunizing a particular representation of truth or justice against critical interrogation, rearticulation, and reenactment in processes of political contestation.

In response to these and related criticisms, Habermas has replaced his constructivist model of truth with a weaker, nonconstructivist one.[28] In the modified conception, truth is not *defined* as the outcome of an idealized intersubjective process of deliberation. Rather it is described as a "Janus-faced" concept.[29] It has two aspects: a discursive one, which connects it to the argumentative exchange of reasons, and a pragmatic one, which ties it to everyday contexts of action. On the one side, truth is the concern of participants in argumentation who are guided by the idea that a proposition, if true, would withstand any attempt to refute it under ideal justificatory conditions.[30] On the other side, truth is a pragmatic presupposition of participants in everyday communicative practices who are guided by the need for behavioral certainty.[31] Truth's "Janus face" refers to the dynamic interplay between everyday behavioral certainties and the process of rational discussion of these certainties once they fail to prove reliable as a basis for everyday action; the fallible results of these processes of rational discussion ("discourses") are fed back as truths into everyday contexts of action. They then provide a reliable basis for action until, for contingent empirical reasons, they no longer work—that is, they fail to prove their truth (*sich bewähren*) by preventing disappointment—and have to be reassessed discursively in light of new evidence and experiences.[32]

Three features of this modified conception merit particular attention: the first is that it acknowledges the constitutive inadequacy of all actual representations of truth. By giving up the idea that truth is a rational consensus reached under ideal justificatory conditions, it makes room for the notion of an object that always in some way transcends our descriptions and interpretations of it. Habermas now refers to a "recalcitrant reality," that has the power to surprise us, to disappoint our expectations, and to resist our interpretations.[33] This idea of a recalcitrant reality can be compared to Laclau's notion of the universal as a transcendent object that is always in excess of our representations of it. In both cases, a gap is postulated between the transcendent ethical object and our attempts to capture it by way of descriptions, interpretations, and other kinds of representations. To be sure, Habermas's main emphasis is on the power of a transcendent object to compel us to revise our descriptions and interpretations; Laclau, by contrast, emphasizes the way in which it conceals itself from us, encouraging the illusion that our representations of it are adequate. Despite this difference in emphasis, however, both Habermas and Laclau appear to rely on a conception of a transcendent object that is always in excess of our representations of it. This postulate of an ineradicable gap between the transcendent object and its articulations has several advantages: it accommodates the sense that truth, unlike justification, is unconditional, it captures the intuition that truth is a property that can never be lost, and it allows for the feeling, common even in everyday situations, that certain perceptual shifts are demanded of us. From the point of view of radical democratic politics (and, more generally, critical social thinking) it has the additional advantage of sensitizing us to the dangers of ideological closure, calling for an attitude of permanent suspicion with regard to the validity of even those representations of truth that appear indubitable.

The second noteworthy feature of Habermas's revised conception of truth is the changed status of argumentation. In the earlier version, truth was constructed by way of the exchange of reasons in idealized forms of argumentation. Now, it is deemed to transcend the results of any argumentative process, no matter how ideal the justificatory conditions under which it is conducted. I have already drawn attention to some advantages of the revised view: its ability to make room for intuitions concerning truth's unconditionality, permanence over time, and imperative force; in addition, its encouragement of a climate of suspicion with regard to all particular political representations. A further advantage is that it avoids overburdening the concept of argumentation. Habermas's modified conception allows him to avoid a position whereby argumentation becomes the privileged site of cognitive transformation. This was a serious difficulty with his earlier view of truth.

With his earlier assertion that reality is constructed through processes of argumentation, Habermas committed himself to the view that significant shifts in perception—changes in how we see the world or some part of it—come about primarily by way of the intersubjective exchange of reasons. Although Habermas himself did not explicitly endorse this consequence of his constructivist position, it is a corollary of such a position and his implicit commitment to it is evident today in his account of moral validity (justice). (I discuss the constructivist aspect of Habermas's account of moral validity in chapter 7.) However, such a view of reality is quite implausible. Shifts in perception do not come about solely—or, indeed, even primarily—as a result of the exchange of reasons through argumentation; typically they are prompted by experiences in other, nonargumentative contexts. Tying cognitive transformation to the exchange of reasons through argumentation is deeply counterintuitive. Nonetheless, Habermas's constructivist account of validity commits him to precisely that position. This provides an additional reason to support his move away from a constructivist view of truth.[34]

However, by relinquishing a constructivist account of truth, Habermas encounters a new set of problems. These have to do with the relation between truth and justification. They confront not just Habermas but any theorist who conceives of truth in terms of idealized rational acceptability.[35] For, if an idealized rational consensus fails to guarantee the truth of a proposition, it is unclear why it bears any relation at all to the concept of truth. The problem is compounded in the case of Habermas's conception. This is because he asserts a close relation not just between truth and the idea of a consensus reached under ideal justificatory conditions but also between truth and the argumentative exchange of reasons. As we know, the connection is important from the point of view of his project as a whole, specifically, from the point of view of his concern to anchor a context-transcending moment within everyday practices of intersubjective communication. For this reason, Habermas cannot lightly abandon his thesis of a close connection between truth and argumentation.

The earlier version of the theory of truth asserted a conceptual connection between truth and argumentation, both from the side of truth, where argumentation was held to be a necessary component of the attempt to establish it, and from the side of argumentation, where an orientation toward truth was held to be an unavoidable guiding presupposition of participation in it. Habermas is now faced with two difficulties. In giving up the idea that truth is constructed by way of the argumentative exchange of reasons, he has to deal with the problem of how to account for the necessity of argumentation.

In giving up the idea that a rational consensus reached under ideal justificatory conditions is a definition of truth, he runs up against the problem of how to explain why the idea of the ideal speech situation continues to play any role at all in argumentation.

I shall return to the problem of the need for argumentation in the next chapter. In the present chapter I want to concentrate on the problem of accounting for the continued importance of the idea of a consensus reached under ideal justificatory conditions. With this we come to the third noteworthy feature of Habermas's revised conception: the changed status of the idea of the ideal speech situation. In the earlier conception, this idea was supposed to provide a standard for assessing the validity of agreements reached in processes of argumentation. However, as indicated, this standard proved impossible to apply: critics such as Lafont pointed out that the idea of idealized rational consensus is unworkable as a standard for measuring agreements since we have no way of knowing the extent to which the justificatory conditions under which they were reached conform to or deviate from the conditions of the ideal speech situation. This is one reason why Habermas now accepts, at least in the case of truth, that the idea of agreement reached under ideal justificatory conditions cannot function as a standard for assessing consensus. However, we have also seen that the idea of the ideal speech situation continues to play a role in his account of truth. How should we understand its new role?

Habermas himself throws little light on this question. In his most recent writings he tells us that the idea of agreement reached under conditions of the ideal speech situation is not a *criterion* of truth. In other words, its purpose is not to provide a yardstick for measuring the difference between actual agreements as to the truth of propositions, on the one hand, and agreements that would be reached under idealized conditions, on the other. However, since he continues to describe the idea of the ideal speech situation as a presupposition guiding participants in argumentation, he evidently attributes to it some important function. But what exactly is this new function? The most obvious answer to this question is that it now functions as a regulative idea.[36] However, this answer, though plausible, raises further questions.[37]

The first question raised concerns the possibility of rational motivation. As we have seen, regulative ideas are ideas of perfection that prompt human beings to endeavor to attain them but transcend their powers to do so. In projecting an unattainable condition of self-sufficiency and self-transparency, they appear to give rise to a problem of motivation that, as Žižek puts it, leaves us with only the options of cynical detachment or regressive naivety. From the point of view of critical social theory, neither of these options is acceptable. Since critical social theory seeks to motivate autonomous agents to engage in transformative social thinking and action with a view to bringing about social change for the better, cynical detachment is clearly not an option; since it seeks to motivate autonomous agents, for whom rationally backed conviction is a requirement of autonomous thinking and action, regressive naivety is not an option either. If we are to understand the idea of the ideal speech situation as a regulative idea, therefore, then we will have to show that regulative ideas are able to exert a *rationally motivating* power. Showing this is one of the principal aims of my discussions over the course of this chapter and the following two.

The second question concerns the danger of ideological closure in the pernicious sense. Does the metaphysically closed character of regulative ideas—their projection of a condition of self-sufficiency and self-transparency—lead to pernicious ideological closure, understood as the removal of normative contents from the political field where they can be interrogated, rearticulated, and reenacted? This question will be addressed in the present chapter.

As a first step toward answering these questions, we need to gain clarity as to the main features of regulative ideas as they operate in critical social theories.[38] Since these features seem to me implicit in Laclau's account of political representation,[39] I suggest that his conception of political representation can fruitfully be applied to the ideas of the good society guiding critical social theories; this allows us to characterize these ideas as regulative ideas that are representations of the good society. It also enables us to see that they are imaginative constructions—fictions—and allows us to formulate the question of motivation as the question of how fictions can exert a rationally motivating power. It is helpful, therefore, to recall the key features of Laclau's account, highlighting the important points of comparison between his idea of political representation and Habermas's idea of the ideal speech situation. This has the added advantage of helping to clarify the role played by that idea in Habermas's revised theory of truth.

As we have seen, Laclau and Habermas now seem united in the view that there is an ineradicable gap between the transcendent object and its historically specific articulations (to be sure, Habermas allows for a gap only in the case of truth, not in the case of justice). By making the presupposition of a "recalcitrant reality" an integral part of his revised conception of truth, Habermas acknowledges the constitutive inadequacy of even apparently justified propositions and beliefs. In Laclau's terminology we might say that he now accepts that any particular representation of truth is incommensurable with its object. To be sure, using Laclau's term "representation" as synonymous with "propositions and beliefs" may cause confusion. Although many claims to truth are, in a sense, representations of truth,[40] Laclau's concern is not with truth claims in general. Although his account of the gap between the transcendent ethical object and its representations could conceivably be elaborated to produce a general theory of truth, his focus to date has been on *political* representations. These may be distinguished from other kinds of representations of the transcendent object by their material aspect and by their affectively imbued power to motivate action on the part of those who accept their validity. For Laclau, ideas such as "liberal democracy," "human rights," and "national socialism" are not purely abstract representations of an absent ethical object, they are incarnations: they take on flesh and blood, so to speak, assuming the attributes of a bodily presence. For this reason, Laclau's account of representation has the most relevance for representations of the transcendent object that have a certain materiality and, with this, an affectively imbued motivating power. I want to suggest that Habermas's idea of the ideal speech situation falls into this category.

The ideal speech situation is not an empty idea—indeed, it is precisely its lack of emptiness to which Laclau objects—but has material substance. It imaginatively evokes the idea of a social condition in which the coordination of social action and the reproduction of social order would take place according to the norms of communicative rationality. Specifically, it projects the utopian idea of a society in which linguistic interaction in all domains of the "lifeworld"[41] would be guided by the aim of reaching rational agreement in matters of validity; moreover, linguistic interaction would be conducted in a manner fully inclusive of all points of view, dealing fairly and openly with all claims to validity, free of strategic interests, motivated by a concern for the right answer, and regulated by no force except that of the better argument. In the projected society, cultural traditions would be passed on by way of this kind of linguistic interaction. In addition, it would constitute the basis for generating, and critically interrogating, the laws, norms, and principles regulating society. Finally, the internalization of the norms governing this kind of linguistic interaction would be central to the socialization of individuals, who would conduct their individual and collective lives in harmony with its governing principles.[42]

I want to suggest that it is the material, pictorial aspect of the idea of the ideal speech situation—its imaginative projection of a particular form of social cohesion and order—that enables it to exercise an affectively imbued, rationally motivating power. This power derives from what Laclau calls its "ethical investment": the relation it bears to the transcendent ethical object. Since this object, qua vacated space,[43] cannot exert a motivating force directly, it requires mediation by way of imaginative constructions. Without mediation by way of "warmly-coloured and clearly-defined images" (Sorel), the transcendent object would be unable to stimulate human agents to engage in transformative social thinking and action.

In analogy with Laclau's conception of political representations as incarnations of an absent object, therefore, we can understand the idea of the ideal speech situation as occupying the "empty place" of truth—the space vacated by Truth and its equivalents such as God, Progress, Reason, or History. As a representation of the unrepresentable, it is not an arbiter of truth (as Habermas's earlier interpretation maintained) but a stand-in for it. As a stand-in for truth, it operates in a metonymic fashion, signaling in a partly symbolic, partly substantive, and partly imaginative way something that cannot be fully represented in language or rendered fully transparent to our knowledge and practices.[44] We might also say that regulative ideas such as the idea of the ideal speech situation are fictions: fabricated myths (in the Sorelian sense) that allow us imaginary access to a mode of social life that is complete in itself—self-sufficient and self-transparent.

In sum, like Laclau's political representations, and, indeed, his own idea of hegemonic democracy,[45] the idea of the ideal speech situation is a fiction. It projects the idea of a social condition of self-sufficiency and self-transparency that can never be achieved by human beings. The question we must now consider is whether it is a *pernicious* fiction: whether it encourages cynicism and naivety or leads to the removal of normative contents from the realm of critical interrogation. In the first case, the problem would be one of motivation; as indicated, Wellmer and Žižek see this as a danger inherent in *regulative* ideas. In the second case, the problem would be one of pernicious ideological closure; Butler sees this as a danger inherent in *substantive transcendent* ideas.

The question of whether the ideal speech situation is a pernicious fiction can also be formulated in terms of concealment. Is the fictive character of the ideal speech situation—and of representations of the good society more generally—something that can openly be acknowledged or is it something that must remain hidden? We can approach this question by way of Laclau's contention that ideological closure always involves concealment. However, we must bear in mind his failure to distinguish clearly between metaphysical and ideological closure, for there is a corresponding ambiguity in his account of concealment.

At first glance, Laclau's contention that ideological distortion always involves concealment seems to make a straightforward conceptual point about ideology in the pernicious sense: ideology in this sense does not simply remove normative contents from the realm of critical scrutiny, it hides the fact that it does so. On closer examination, however, his position seems to be that all forms of metaphysical closure involve concealment, even those that cannot be criticized as perniciously ideological. He maintains that metaphysical closure conceals the absence of an extradiscursive reality—of a reality beyond the influences of history and context. We might say that metaphysical closure conceals the impossibility of closure: it masks its own impossibility. The important question for our present purposes is why it needs to do so. Laclau himself offers no clear answer to this. In fact, two different answers could be extrapolated from his writings; each would send his theory of hegemony in a different direction and give rise to different kinds of problems.

The first answer to the question of why closure must mask its own impossibility is that only projections of completeness—of self-sufficiency and self-transparency—can excite the ethical imagination and lead to politically engaged thought and action. In this case, making visible the operation of closure seems to lead to the kind of problem of motivation we have already mentioned. For, if we become aware that our ideas of context-transcending validity (the universal, the ethical, the fullness of society, and so on) are imaginative projections of a condition of self-sufficiency and self-transparency that is not attainable by human beings, it may be difficult to sustain a commitment to the idea in question as a meaningful object of human thought and action. We may react with cynical detachment or regressive naivety; in either case, its power to motivate thought and action is jeopardized.

The second answer to the question is that projections of completeness are necessary in order to protect human subjects from an originary trauma that is concealed within the symbolic order itself. This is the answer that Žižek favors: drawing on Lacan, he posits an originary trauma—a "kernel beyond redemption" or "spectral cut"—inhabiting the symbolic order as a primal wound that can never be healed.[46] In this case, making visible the operation of concealment seems to lead to ideological closure in the pernicious sense: for, if we become aware that we rely on the illusion of self-sufficiency and self-transparency for protection against an originary trauma, we may react by insisting on the need for such protection, on the grounds that blocking access to the trauma is less painful than confronting it. In that case, we would acknowledge that the painfulness of the wound necessitates the removal of certain contents from the realm of critical interrogation. Such an acceptance of ideology as a protection against the pain of an originary trauma may even be pleasurable: ideological closure may be accompanied by the narcissistic self-indulgence involved in enjoying one's own pathological condition.

In each case, however, an alternative reaction is also possible. Becoming aware that the illusion of completeness is necessary in order to excite the ethical imagination may lead not to cynical detachment or regressive naivety but to a self-conscious acknowledgment that fictions are an inevitable part of ethically invested thinking and do not negatively affect its motivating power. Becoming aware that the illusion of completeness is necessary to protect against an originary trauma may lead not to ideological closure (and the enjoyment of it) but to the attempt to come to grips with the originary trauma by way of a therapeutic process of (collective or individual) self-investigation. Of course, the very idea of an originary trauma seems to preclude the possibility of ever finally coming to terms with it, since it suggests that any reconciliation achieved by way of the therapeutic process can never be complete; nonetheless, it does not rule out the possibility of greater and lesser degrees of success in working through the trauma and does not, in consequence, imply the futility of efforts to deal with a traumatic past.

Although in both cases making visible what is concealed need have no negative effects, this is not true of affirming the need for concealment. Here there is an asymmetry between the two cases. In the first case, where concealment serves to promote the fiction of completeness, affirming its necessity may not be a problem—that is, it may be possible to acknowledge the necessarily fictive character of representations, without succumbing to cynical detachment or regressive naivety. In the second case, by contrast, where concealment serves to protect against the pain of an originary trauma, affirming its necessity can only be cause for concern—that is, if we acknowledge the necessarily fictive character of representations, we collude in the removal of normative contents from the realm of critical interrogation and, hence, in the perpetuation of ideological closure in the pernicious sense.

Laclau, as we know, maintains that ideological closure (by which he means metaphysical closure) has no pejorative connotations. It follows that he must take an equally benign view of the concealment necessarily involved in such closure. This enables us to see that only the first answer to the question of why closure must mask its own impossibility is available to him. His answer, *pace* Žižek, cannot be the need to conceal some originary trauma; rather he must see concealment as necessary to excite the ethical imagination and to motivate thought and action.[47] If this is so, the particular challenge facing his argument for the need for the illusion of closure is to show that this illusion does not encourage either cynical detachment or regressive naivety.

Applied to our discussion of Habermas, the task is to show that we can interpret his idea of an ideal speech situation as a fiction, understood as a representation of a transcendent object that conceals its own impossibility, without compromising its motivating power. Our task will be made easier if we can show that an allegiance to regulative ideas—and above all, an allegiance to representations of the good society—is not necessarily compromised by an awareness of their fictive character.

For this purpose, Hans Vaihinger's theory of fictions is a useful point of departure. In his seminal study, *The Philosophy of "As If,"* Vaihinger makes a number of observations of particular relevance to our present discussion.[48] The first observation is that fictions are structured by the "as if" principle: they require us temporarily to suspend disbelief in their illusory character. Accordingly, acknowledging that something is a fiction does not prevent us from (temporarily) attributing to it a certain reality. This is evidently true in the case of literary fictions. In entering the imaginary realm of literary fiction, we are required not only to suspend judgment on the reality of what we encounter there, but to behave as though its events and characters were real ones.[49]

The second observation is that fictions are practically useful.[50] Vaihinger draws attention to their expediency in science, mathematics, philosophy, and many other contexts of intellectual life: "[a]n idea whose theoretical untruth or incorrectness, and therewith its falsity, is admitted, is not for that reason practically valueless and useless; for such an idea, in spite of its theoretical nullity may have great practical importance."[51]

The third observation is that a self-consciousness awareness of their fictive character does not detract from the practical usefulness of fictions. Vaihinger underscores this self-conscious aspect and the absence of any claim to actuality.[52] In contrast to a hypothesis, which seeks to be an adequate expression of some still unknown reality and to mirror this objective reality correctly, a fiction "is advanced with the consciousness that it is an inadequate, subjective and pictorial manner of conception, whose coincidence with reality is, from the start, excluded and which cannot, therefore, be afterwards verified, as we hope to be able to verify a hypothesis."[53] He hints at a historical dimension to this awareness, however, acknowledging that many fictions are first described as hypotheses, an awareness of their fictive character developing only "in the course of time."[54] This resonates with theories of reflexive or "second" modernity, for which this historical dimension is central. For example, in their recent work, Ulrich Beck and associates describe the contemporary modern world as one of reflexive modernity—as a stage within the development of modernity that is characterized by an explicit awareness of the fictive nature of the mental constructions by which we make sense of and regulate our daily lives. They draw attention, in particular, to the way in which boundaries—for example, legal or political ones—are created whose artificial, fictive character is freely recognized, but which are accepted as legitimate boundaries all the same.[55] Similarly, they show how, under reflexive modern conditions, the idea of an acting and deciding subject has an "as if" character and is recognized as a necessary fiction.[56]

Contemporary theorists of reflexive modernity lend support to Vaihinger's contention that a self-conscious awareness of our use of fictions does not detract from their practical utility in many areas of life. If such theorists are correct, a consciousness of the fictive character of representations of the good society is at least compatible with an ability temporarily to suspend this consciousness and find the idealized social condition they project both affectively and rationally motivating.

These reflections suggest that it may be possible for representations of the good society to command our allegiance, even though we are aware of their fictive character. We may be able to find them affectively and rationally motivating, even though we know that the social condition they project is not realizable. They also suggest that it is not a belief in the realizability of the projected condition that makes representations of the good society motivating, but other beliefs concerning the projected condition. This raises the question of what it is it about representations of the good society that enables them to command the allegiance of autonomous agents, even though we are aware that they are imaginative constructions. My thesis is that the motivating power of such representations depends more on their persuasive capacity than on their ontological status: the ability of representations of the good society to command the allegiance of autonomous agents depends on the agents' belief that the validity claims raised by the political representation in question are indeed valid. By "ontological status" I mean the realizability of the social conditions projected by representations of the good society. By "persuasive capacity" I mean the power of these projections to arouse feelings of attraction and convince us rationally of their merits—their ability to make us feel that they are a better stand-in for the transcendent ethical object than any other available ones, and to give us good reasons for perceiving them as such. In other words, if a particular representation of the good society (such as liberal democracy or anarchic communism or the ideal speech situation or hegemonic democracy) is to motivate us to engage in ethically oriented, political action, then we must experience it as the best available representation of the transcendent object and be able to support it argumentatively as such. My contention, in sum, is that the fictive status of regulative ideas and, in particular, of representations of the good society, has little or no bearing on their power to motivate us; what is important is the success of their claim to verisimilitude—their ability to persuade us of their appearance of truth.[57]

My suggestion, therefore, is that the question of the motivating power of ideas of the good society is tied to questions of justification. As indicated in chapter 3, the presupposition here is that contemporary critical social theories address their critical diagnoses and emancipatory projections to autonomous agents—to human beings who are regarded as free to form and pursue their own conceptions of the good on the basis of reasons that they can call their own. I have more to say about the idea of autonomy in the next chapter. In the remainder of the present chapter I continue to pursue the question of whether the fictive character of ideas of the good society compromises their (affectively imbued) rationally motivating power.

So far we have established that the claims to validity raised by particular ideas of the good society are claims to be the best available stand-ins for the transcendent object—to represent something that can never fully be represented in language or rendered fully transparent to our knowledge and practices. Understood in this way, representations of the good society do not claim *authority* in matters of validity; rather, they claim to disclose the transcendent object more powerfully, and to articulate it in ways that provide better ethical orientation, than other, rival representations. If autonomous agents are to be able to accept such claims, they must be able to have reasons for doing so. Our task, therefore, is twofold: we must clarify the kinds of validity claims raised by particular representations of the good society and we must show how these claims can be rationally assessed.

The first part of the task requires us to consider more closely the functions fulfilled by particular representations of the good society in their capacity as stand-ins for the transcendent object. Here, we can distinguish between two kinds of functions: functions of disclosure and functions of orientation. These functions are intimately entwined. They correspond to the two analytically distinguishable yet practically inseparable components of the kind of validity claim raised by representations of the good society: the claim (1) to disclose the transcendent object more powerfully than rival ideas of the good society and (2) to project an idea of the good society that provides better ethical orientation than competing ideas. From the point of view of context-transcending critical social thinking that seeks to be in tune with the antiauthoritarian impulses of modernity, both components are indispensable.[58] For, a painting or a piece of music might disclose the transcendent object (the universal, justice, the good society) powerfully, but in a way that cannot be captured in words and, hence, can neither be shared nor assessed discursively. This would mean, in turn, that the ethical orientation it provides could not be subjected to intersubjective forms of criticism, opening it to charges of authoritarianism (I have more to say about this in the next chapter). Conversely, a particular view of the good society—for example, the view currently offered by some traditional forms of religion—might offer guidance in ethical matters that could be accepted as valid for purely conventional reasons ("this is the way our family has always behaved"). In that case, the disclosing component of ideas of the good society would disappear and with it their context-transcending dimension—the view in question would be accepted as valid, but it would not be equipped with a context-transcending force. Not only are the two components indispensable, they are dependent on one another. This interdependence must be borne in mind in contexts of critical evaluation. A particular claim to disclose the transcendent object powerfully cannot be assessed rationally in isolation from the corresponding claim to provide ethical orientation, and a particular claim to provide ethical orientation cannot be assessed rationally in isolation from the corresponding claim to disclose the transcendent object powerfully.

(1) In claiming to disclose the transcendent ethical object powerfully, particular representations of the good society claim to be vehicles that enable us to experience the power of that object. Bereft of their capacity to mediate experiences of the transcendent object, we would not be able to account for what Laclau calls the "ethical investment" of political representations—our supposition that they bear a relation to a transcendent ethical object—and we would have no nonauthoritarian ethical grounds for finding them convincing. Clearly, therefore, their disclosing function is crucial from the point of view

of context-transcending social criticism. At a minimum, the term "disclosure" implies that *something* is disclosed. For this reason, *pace* Laclau, the universal cannot be a space that is entirely empty (an "empty place") but at most a space that has been vacated. If we are to speak of disclosure, we must assume that something—some trace or residual power—has remained behind. On the other hand, Laclau is correct in his view that, for us, as inhabitants of a secularized modernity, access to the transcendent object is always mediated through historically specific descriptions and interpretations that are constitutively inadequate to it. For us, the space of the universal (justice, the good society) is not directly accessible and our representations of it are always partial and incomplete. If something is disclosed by way of representations of the good society, therefore, it cannot be the content of the transcendent object in its fullness and finality but, at most, some ghostly apparition of it. Derrida speaks of the "ghostliness" of the transcendent object and the vertigo that threatens to seize us when we attempt to peer beyond its many representations.[59] In a similar vein, Adorno draws attention to the essential opaqueness of what is glimpsed in moments of disclosure, referring to the absolute as always "veiled in black."[60]

Thus, representations of the good society allow us no more than glimpses of the specter of truth. We might say: what we gain from the disclosure of the transcendent object is less a revelation of its content than the sense that there is such an object. In other words, representations are a vehicle not for transmission of the determinate content of a transcendent idea, but for fleeting experiences in which the possibility of completeness is present for a moment. Charles Taylor reminds us that the Romantic and post-Romantic word for such momentary experiences is "epiphany." In striking contrast to the "blackness" of Adorno's description of the absolute, Taylor describes an epiphany as an experience of illumination—as a "manifestation which brings us into the presence of something that is otherwise inaccessible, and which is of the highest moral or spiritual significance; a manifestation, moreover, which also defines and completes something, even as it reveals."[61] We might say: in moments of epiphany, the possibility of truth, justice, or happiness becomes concrete for an instant. Or, as a character in a short story by Alice Munro puts it, such moments seem to mean "that we have a life of happiness with which we only occasionally, knowingly, intersect."[62]

It should be noted, however, that representations of the good society are not the primary vehicles for the disclosure of the transcendent object—even in this weak sense of disclosure as a momentary glimpse of the possibility of completeness. To be sure, such disclosure is intrinsic to all forms of language use in which validity in a context-transcending sense is at stake: as such it is part of scientific modes of language use as much as political, legal, or moral modes. It could be argued, indeed, that it is intrinsic to almost all forms of human communication—nonverbal as well as verbal, the everyday as well as the specialized. Nonetheless, under conditions of modernity, art, music, literature, and religion have become privileged sites for experiences of disclosure. Although it would be gravely mistaken to restrict the disclosing function to aesthetic and religious modes of communication,[63] it is correct to say that such modes of communication are designed to facilitate disclosure and do so by means of linguistic, visual, aural, and other kinds of techniques (using, for example, shock effects, unexpected juxtapositions, and innovative metaphors), and by means of exercises such as prayer and meditation. In sum, although the disclosure of the transcendent object is an indispensable function of representations of the good society, these are not as a rule constructed with a view to enabling such disclosure.

It should also be noted that the disclosing function of representations of the good society gives rise to problems of critical evaluation. As we have seen, the assumption of an ineradicable gap between the transcendent object and its particular representations implies the constitutive inadequacy of these representations. Using the language of disclosure we could say that what is disclosed is always partly resistant to linguistic (and nonlinguistic) articulation. Since the content of the transcendent object is always "veiled in black" and disclosed more as a sense that it exists than as a sense of what it consists in, the experience of disclosure cannot be captured fully by representations; moreover, at certain times and in certain sociocultural contexts, it cannot be articulated in the form of propositional contents that could be subjected to critical evaluation (I return to this point in the next chapter).

In this regard, too, we can learn from Adorno's reflections on metaphysical disclosure. As a number of commentators have observed, the ineffable dimension of disclosure—the disjunction between the experience of disclosure and its linguistic articulation, between intuition and concept—is central to Adorno's concept of, in particular, aesthetic disclosure.[64] In his account, it is the work of art that serves as the primary medium for experiences of the absolute; at the same time, however, what is experienced in the work of art remains beyond the complete and final grasp of conceptual language, forever partly resistant to interpretation and evaluation: "Discursive language wishes to express the absolute in a mediated way, but the absolute eludes its grasp at every turn, leaving each attempt behind in its finiteness. Music expresses the absolute directly, but the very moment it does so, the absolute is obscured, just as excessively strong light dazzles the eye so that it can no longer register what is clearly visible."[65]

Thus, although philosophy must endeavor to capture in thought what has been disclosed in aesthetic experience, its efforts are inherently inadequate. Just as aesthetic experience, for Adorno, escapes capture by discursive language, I want to say that the experience of the disclosure of the transcendent object is an experience that can never fully be captured by representations. And, just as philosophy, for Adorno, must nonetheless struggle to capture in words what is experienced in the work of art, critical social thinking must endeavor to *re-present* its guiding ideas of the good society. Moreover—and at this point I move beyond Adorno—it must do so in the form of validity claims that are open to intersubjective assessment. This brings me to the second main function fulfilled by representations of the good society: their function of orientation.

(2) I have described the ideas evoked by representations of the good society as fictions insofar as they project an idea of completeness—of self-sufficiency and self-transparency—that abstracts from the finitude of human knowledge and the contingency of human life and history. Their fictive character renders them unsuitable for the purpose of settling disputes in matters of validity. However, although they cannot be used as a means for adjudicating matters of validity, they do provide navigation points from which we can take our bearings.[66] Thus, the ideas of the good society evoked by particular representations are supposed to provide orientation to us in our ethical actions and reflections—to point us in the right direction in our endeavors to find the best ways of organizing and regulating our social lives. But evidently, the orientation provided by Habermas's idea of the ideal speech situation will be different to that provided by Laclau's idea of hegemonic democracy, which will be different in turn from the orientation provided by certain ideas of liberal democracy, national socialism, state socialism, anarchic freedom, and so on. If it is to avoid making the choice between representations of the good society a matter of arbitrary decision, an appeal to the prevailing *Sittlichkeit*, or a surrender to superior might, critical social theory has to find some nonauthoritarian, normative basis for assessing their relative merits.

In this regard, the material, pictorial aspect of representations of the good society—their ability to evoke more or less determinate *images* of the good society—is crucial. If the transcendent object—the universal, justice, the good society, and the like—were not mediated by way of *re-presentations*, its orienting powers would remain entirely abstract and the attempt to establish the merits of competing normative approaches would be futile. Interestingly, Habermas himself uses the word "picture" (*Bild*) to describe ideas such as the ideal speech situation.[67] Charles Taylor acknowledges the material aspect of representation indirectly in his discussion of epiphanies, when he stresses that what is manifested is inseparable from its embodiment.[68] Our reflections thus far shed light on why the pictorial aspect is so important. It is important, first, from the point of view of motivation: without mediation by way of more or less determinate pictures of the good society, the transcendent object would lack affective power and fail to stimulate ethical thought and action. But it is also important from the point of view of justification: if particular ideas of the good society did not take the form of more or less determinate pictures of a social order whose claims to validity can be formulated as propositions, norms, or principles, they would not be open to argumentative forms of critical interrogation.

At this point, however, the objection could be raised that critical interrogation does not have to take the form of argumentation; indeed, echoing Butler, it could be objected that this form of criticism places unacceptable limits on the exercise of human agency and denies the openness of the historical process. In chapter 4, referring to Butler's work, I made the point that we should avoid an overly narrow view of critical interrogation that fails to appreciate the multiple forms it may assume—nondiscursive as well as discursive, nonlinguistic as well as linguistic. Certainly, we must beware of reducing the concept of critical interrogation to its argumentative modes. We must also be careful not to exaggerate the power of argumentation to *bring about* insight: earlier in this chapter, I warned against a tendency to make intersubjective deliberation the privileged site for cognitive transformation. Nonetheless, argumentation plays an indispensable role in critical social theory. In the next chapter I show why critical social theory must acknowledge the intimate connection between validity and argumentation. Since this connection is premised on the importance of the idea of autonomous agency, I also outline the conception of autonomy that I regard as the most appropriate for the critical enterprise today. Finally, I propose a model of practical argumentation that fits well with the antiauthoritarian impulses of contemporary critical social theory, while allowing for rationally backed choice between competing representations of the good society.

The challenge identified at the start of this chapter was to find a way of maintaining a gap between the transcendent object and its historical articulations that is held to be both ineliminable and variable. I suggested that Laclau's account of political representations can help to meet that challenge. In this account, particular political representations maintain the gap since they are constitutively inadequate incarnations of the transcendent object. Their relation to this object is manifested in their attribute of metaphysical closure: the social condition they project is an "impossible" condition of self-sufficiency and self-transparency. I drew attention to some interesting parallels between Laclau's account of the gap between the transcendent object and particular representations of it and Habermas's account of the disjunction between truth and justification. I suggested, furthermore, that Laclau's account of political representations can help to make sense of the continuing importance of the ideal speech situation in Habermas's account of truth, by allowing us to see it as a constitutively inadequate representation of the transcendent object. However, the main advantage of Laclau's account of political repre-sentation is that it highlights certain key features of ideas of the good society: in particular, their metaphysically closed character, which suggests that we should regard them as *fictions*, and their material, pictorial character, by means of which we construct *images* of the good society; the significance of this, in my view, is that these images have a propositional content that (normally) allows them to be formulated as claims to validity and, hence, to be open to rational evaluation. To be sure, the fictive character of ideas of the good society seems to give rise to problems of motivation and justification: it seems to undermine their capacity to motivate autonomous agents, for such agents need to be able to see their judgments and actions as backed by good reasons that they can call their own; at first glance, at least, it is hard to see how we can have good reasons for accepting the validity of fictions. These problems will continue to occupy us in the next two chapters. As we shall see, I do not consider them intractable.

If we can use Laclau to make sense of Habermas, Habermas equally can be used to make sense of Laclau. In this chapter and the last I have argued that there are ambiguities in Laclau's conception of political representation that create difficulties for his account of the context-transcending dimension of critical social thinking. In particular, his understanding of the relation between the transcendent ethical object and its historical articulations is in need of clarification. Whereas he maintains that political representations, as particular articulations of the transcendent object, are ethically invested in a context-transcending sense, his theory as it stands is unable to make sense of this ethical investment. On the one hand, he argues that political representations raise claims to verisimilitude, by which he means they claim the appearance of truth. On the other hand, when challenged by Žižek as to the normative basis for assessing such claims, he simply appeals to the prevailing *Sittlichkeit*. What is missing from his account is a conception of practical rationality that allows for the possibility of ethical learning processes—for epistemic gains in the domain of ethical action. By insisting on the connection between truth and argumentation, Habermas reminds us of the need for a conception of this kind. Moreover, as we shall see in the next chapter, his notion of communicative rationality, if historicized appropriately, provides a fruitful point of departure for a model of critical evaluation that would be in tune with the antiauthoritarian impulses of modernity, while permitting rationally backed choice between competing representations of the good society.

6

Re-Presentation and Argumentation

This chapter continues the discussion of the relation between the transcendent ethical object and its representations (in Laclau's terminology) or between truth and justification (in Habermas's terminology). It focuses on the question of how the claims to validity raised by ideas of the good society can be assessed rationally in a context-transcending sense. This question of justification can also be raised as a question of motivation: can ideas of the good society have an affectively imbued, rationally motivating power that is context transcending? These questions are complicated by my proposal to interpret ideas of the good society as regulative ideas that have an imaginary character and may be described as fictions. Notwithstanding their imaginary, fictive character, however, I have suggested that ideas of the good society raise claims to validity. Our question in this chapter is how these claims may be evaluated (in a context-transcending sense).

A further question addressed in this chapter concerns the nature of the link between validity and argumentation. While rejecting the position that validity (for example, truth or justice) is *constructed* in argumentation, I make the case for an intimate link between the two terms. The link between validity and argumentation, as I establish it, is a historically contingent one. It presupposes a commitment to the antiauthoritarian impulses expressed by the idea of situated rationality, a commitment that emerges historically only within the socio-cultural contexts of modernity. As we saw in chapter 1, one of the core components of the idea of situated rationality is the idea of autonomous agency, understood as the individual human being's freedom to form and pursue her conceptions of the good on the basis of reasons she can call her own. The centrality of the concept of autonomy to the concerns of contemporary critical social theory calls for a reflection on the kind of conception that would be congruent with its antiauthoritarian impulses, while avoiding the principal objections raised by the communitarian, poststructuralist, and feminist critiques of autonomy. As a contribution toward such reflection, this chapter includes a proposal for a suitable conception of autonomy.

In the last chapter I suggested that Laclau's term "political representation" may usefully be applied to ideas of the good society such as Habermas's idea of the ideal speech situation or, indeed, Laclau's idea of hegemonic democracy. Political representations are ethically invested articulations of the transcendent object (the universal, the ethical, justice, and the like). They may also be described as regulative ideas. Their ontological status is fictive: they are imaginative projections of an unattainable transcendent object. As fictions, ideas of the good society do not claim to *be* the transcendent object but rather to be the best available *re-presentation* of it. In claiming to be valid, they claim what Laclau calls verisimilitude—the appearance of truth—or what Habermas calls justification—the ability to command the agreement of everyone on the basis of the best available reasons.[1] In other words, the claims to validity raised by particular representations of the good society are claims to be the best available stand-ins for the transcendent object—to represent something that can never be fully represented in language nor rendered fully transparent to our knowledge and practices. Understood in this way, political representations do not claim *authority* in matters of validity; rather, they claim to disclose the transcendent object more powerfully, and to articulate it in ways that provide better ethical orientation than other, rival representations. Contemporary critical social theories address their critical diagnoses and emancipatory projections to autonomous agents. If autonomous agents are to be able to accept such claims, they must be able to have reasons for doing so. Our task, therefore, is to provide an account of what it means for the validity claims raised by particular ideas of the good society to be open to rational assessment by autonomous agents. My suggestion is that, for such agents, validity is tied to public processes of argumentation.

There are a number of reasons for this: to begin with, critical social thinking has to take seriously the idea of a validity claim, understood as an assertion that calls for a rationally backed "yes" or "no" response from its addressees; in making a validity claim, the speaker relativizes her utterance against the possibility that it will be contested by others on the basis of good reasons.[2] If a critical social theory is to be in tune with the antiauthoritarian impulses expressed by the idea of situated reason, it cannot understand its own guiding emancipatory vision as a declaration of power or as an assertion of authority, but must conceive it instead as a contestable set of claims to validity.[3] Of course, it may seek to unmask the utterances of other theories—or, more generally, any other employments of the language of validity—as declarations of power or assertions of authority. However, it cannot regard its own claims to validity as expressions of power or authority without falling foul of epistemological and ethical authoritarianism. From this starting point, the case that argumentative assessment is an indispensable ingredient of critical social thinking can be established fairly easily. To do so, we must appeal once again to the idea of situated reason, and to the normative context of modernity from which it emerges.

For the inhabitants of modernity, the validity of claims cannot be assessed independently of public argumentation. In the wake of processes such as the desacralization of knowledge, secularization of authority, and democratization of political power, which are widely acknowledged as key features of modernity, the only acceptable basis for weighing up the strengths and weaknesses of claims to validity is individual and collective human reasoning. If we add to this the cluster of ideas constituting the idea of situated rationality, we can see why deliberation has to take the form of open-ended, inclusive, and fair practices of evaluating reasons in public spaces.

Social criticism that proceeds in accordance with the idea of situated rationality is obliged to acknowledge its limited viewpoint. Since there is no ahistorical or decontextualized access to the transcendent object, no final assessment of validity claims is possible; a judgment in favor of a particular claim is always open to challenge on the basis of new evidence, new experience, new social, technological, and ecological developments, and new insight; thus the idea of situated rationality requires us to understand the process of critical evaluation as open-ended. Furthermore, it requires us to construe it as maximally inclusive. Since there is no privileged access to the transcendent object, evaluation of the validity claim has to take into consideration all viewpoints. The idea of autonomous agency means that these viewpoints must be articulated by real human subjects; this follows, as we shall see, from the connection between autonomy and rational accountability for, if the subjects addressed by the claim are to be held to account for their judgments and actions, they themselves must be admitted to the discussion. The principle of equal respect requires, in addition, that all viewpoints be weighed up fairly; accordingly, the process of critical evaluation must be conducted evenhandedly. Finally, the norm of rational accountability, which I will posit as one of the four constitutive elements of the idea of autonomy, makes publicity an essential ingredient of the concept of a good reason: a speaker who claims validity for a particular utterance assumes an obligation to defend its validity publicly, if necessary.

Indeed, the idea of situated rationality, with autonomous agency as a core component, does not only imply the need for public processes of intersubjective deliberation that are open-ended, inclusive, and fair; it points toward a model of critical evaluation that bears a strong resemblance to the model of argumentation at the center of Habermas's theory of communicative action. Unlike Habermas's model, however, it is not based on universal presuppositions of linguistic interaction; instead it articulates a notion of rationality that has emerged with the development of modernity and has, as such, a specific historical and sociocultural index. Situated rationality is a conception of rationality that is itself situated. The connection between validity and open-ended, inclusive, fair, and public argumentation is not a feature of communication in general but has come about in certain sociocultural contexts as a result of historically contingent factors.

We are now in a better position to answer our earlier question concerning the relation between argumentation and context-transcending validity: as we saw in chapter 5, Habermas faces the problem of how to account for the necessity of argumentation once he gives up the idea that validity is *constructed* by way of the argumentative exchange of reasons. We can now see that the relation between validity and argumentation, though historically contingent, has a stable foundation. It is based on a constellation of ideas relating to the absence of absolute, ahistorical, and decontextualized standards for adjudicating validity, and to the equal moral worth of human beings, that is constitutive of the evaluative horizon of modernity. To be congruent with this constellation of ideas, truth and other instances of context-transcending validity have to be conceived as tied to open-ended, inclusive, and fair practices of evaluating reasons in public spaces. Since the ideas in question are formative of the individual and collective identities of the inhabitants of modernity, they cannot set these ideas aside at will. To be sure, the foundation they provide, though stable, is not immovable. Like the riverbed in Wittgenstein's famous metaphor in *On Certainty*, the constellation of values that comprises the modern worldview may shift over time; moreover, some of its interrelated elements may disappear or be displaced. In Wittgenstein's words, the riverbed of thoughts, like the bank of a river, ". . . consists partly of hard rock, subject to no alteration or only to an imperceptible one, partly of sand, which now in one place now in another gets washed away, or deposited."[4] However, Wittgenstein leaves open the question of whether shifts in the riverbed of thoughts are ethically arbitrary or open to ethical assessment. By contrast, a critical social theory that seeks to retain a context-transcending dimension is committed to the position that shifts of these types constitute changes that can be evaluated ethically as changes for the better or for the worse (or as a mixture of both).

The concept of autonomy plays a central part in the case I make for the intimate link between validity and argumentation,[5] and more generally, in my attempt to elaborate a concept of validity that is congruent with the antiauthoritarian impulses of contemporary critical social thinking. However, the concept of autonomy has itself come under attack on grounds of its reliance on normative pictures of identity that are alleged to be fundamentally misconceived.

Just as Nietzsche's critique of philosophical objectivity impels critical social theory to confront the question of the possibility and desirability of securing normative foundations for its critical diagnoses and emancipatory projections, his critique of the subject forces it to confront the question of the possibility and desirability of autonomous agency. For Nietzsche, the concept of the autonomous agent is part of a broader picture of a reason-driven, unitary subject that disregards the nonrational dimensions of human subjectivity and denies its fragmented character; he condemns this picture as a regressive illusion.[6] His critique of the notion of the reason-driven, unitary subject gains support in the early twentieth century from the discipline of psychoanalysis (Freud), resonates with sociological observations on the effects of modern urbanization (Simmel), and finds expression in the literature and poetry of modernist authors (Kafka, Beckett, the dadaists). More recently, the concept of autonomous agency has come under fire from a number of directions. In the last decades of the twentieth century, two broad lines of criticism have emerged: the poststructuralist line, which develops the Nietzschean critique of the reason-driven, unitary subject, and the communitarian line, which is suspicious of the modern emphasis on individual as opposed to collective values. These two lines of criticism came together in the feminist critique of autonomy which, by highlighting the caring and communal values that, historically, have been central to many women's sense of agency, provides additional reasons for mistrusting the idea.

The intuition I see at the heart of the concept of autonomous agency is the importance of the individual's freedom to form and pursue her conceptions of the good on the basis of reasons that she can call her own.[7] Thus, I interpret autonomy as *ethical* autonomy, as a form of freedom that involves an orientation toward the good. The task facing contemporary critical social theory is to elaborate a conception of autonomous agency that does justice to this intuition while avoiding the objections raised by poststructuralist, communitarian, and feminist critics; the elaborated conception would also, of course, have to be congruent with critical social theory's antiauthoritarian aims. The extended discussion such a task requires is the subject for another book; my reflections here are, of necessity, cursory and provisional. Moreover, I assume that most contemporary objections to the concept of autonomy can be understood as objections to the ways in which it has traditionally been interpreted.[8] Certain poststructuralist objections appear to challenge the very idea of autonomy; however, taking my lead from Judith Butler I shall suggest that they should be read as objections to static ideals of autonomy rather than to the central intuition on which the ideal is based. The conception of autonomy that I present here in outline develops that central intuition. It has four core elements: strong evaluation, rational accountability, independence, and purposive rationality. I shall comment on each element briefly, explaining in each case why I see it as a requirement of autonomy.

The first core element in the conception I propose is *strong evaluation*. This refers to the human agent's ability to construct her identity in reflective engagement with a range of important questions about the good. By attaching central importance to this capacity, the proposed conception of autonomy fits well with the antiauthoritarian impulse of contemporary critical social thinking, for it displaces responsibility for the validity of ethical judgments and actions from some absolute or conventional authority to the judging and acting human subjects themselves. Strong evaluation presupposes the ability and willingness to form second-order desires and volitions. Charles Taylor, drawing on an influential essay by Harry Frankfurt,[9] emphasizes the importance of the formation of second-order desires and volitions and uses it as a core element in his account of the modern self.[10] Indeed, Taylor presents the modern self as a "strong evaluator," as a person who can raise the question: do I really want to be what I now am? Such persons are able and willing to evaluate what they now are, and to shape themselves on the basis of that evaluation; in doing so, they make use of a language of evaluative distinctions (in which, for example, motivations are described as noble or base, courageous or cowardly, clairvoyant or blind, and so on) that is richer and deeper than the language required by a simple weighing of alternatives.[11] However, Taylor's account of strong evaluation goes beyond Frankfurt's account of second-order desires and volitions in its attention to the question of what it means to position oneself reflectively in relation to the good.[12] In Taylor's account, the good is that which is picked out as incomparably higher in a qualitative distinction. Some such higher goods are what he calls "constitutive goods": our actions and aspirations are constituted as good through their relation to these goods (examples are history, nature, art, God, or freedom). As such, constitutive goods are moral sources—objects, the love of which empowers us to do and be good.[13]

Taylor's position has the following significant implication. If autonomy involves strong evaluation, and if strong evaluation involves a relation to moral sources, autonomous agency calls for a *receptivity* to the power of these sources (I come back to this point toward the end of this chapter). Accordingly, the conception of autonomy advocated here attaches importance to openness to experiences of disclosure in which the power of the good makes itself felt. To be sure, strong evaluation presupposes several other capacities such as flexibility, open-mindedness, sensitivity to others, and imaginativeness. Evidently, too, it has a material aspect: if human subjects are to be able to engage reflectively with questions of the good, they must have at their disposal certain material goods such as food, clothing, and accommodation and must receive the upbringing and education that will facilitate the development of the required capacities. Furthermore, the capacity for strong evaluation presupposes a sociocultural context in which there is a plurality of conceptions of goods: if the semantic resources available in a given sociocultural context means that subjects can define themselves through reference to only one conception of the good, then strong evaluation is not possible.[14]

It is important to avoid the misconception that strong evaluation entails a split between the reason-giving dimensions of subjectivity, on the one hand, and the bodily and affective-emotional dimensions, on the other. As I shall show later on in this chapter, the kind of nonauthoritarian model of practical reasoning appropriate for the aims of contemporary critical social thinking rejects any kind of simple opposition between reason and feelings, intuitions and passions. Nor should this view of autonomy be taken to imply that the reason-giving dimensions of subjectivity are more important than its other aspects. The view that autonomy involves strong evaluation is readily compatible with views of the human subject in which the capacity for strong evaluation is only one among a number of important attributes. It is compatible, for example, with Butler's view of the subject as being in a constant process of restaging and rearticulating his identity (on the assumption that she does not rule out rational deliberation as one possible means of rearticulation) or with Honneth's view of the subject as seeking recognition not just of his capacity for autonomous agency but also of the bodily-affective and creative-productive aspects of his personality.

Strong evaluation is posited as a core component of the concept of autonomy in order to make sense of the perception that autonomy is valuable only when directed toward the good. Conceptions of autonomy that detach it from ethical motivation—from the subjective orientation toward the good—face the difficulty that they are unable to account adequately for the value of autonomy. In *Liberation from Self: A Theory of Personal Autonomy*, Bernard Berfosky runs up against this difficulty. Berofsky argues forcefully against interpretations of autonomy that connect it with the rational evaluation of desires and strong preferences from the point of view of their worth.[15] By "worth" Berofsky means what I call *ethical* worth: an ascription of value to certain strong preferences and desires through reference to some idea of ethical validity.[16] He criticizes approaches to autonomy that conceive of the autonomous agent as a rational evaluator of her assignments of ethical meaning and value, claiming that they "elaborate second-order acts to a metaphysical or ethical status far beyond what many of them deserve."[17] Closer consideration suggests, however, that his principal objection is to the tendency to define autonomy in terms of the subject's orientation toward the good; this objection is evident is his insistence that autonomy is possible without morality and without any reference to objective value or intrinsic worth.[18] By contrast, autonomy for Berofsky is a matter of objectivity: the autonomous person is open to the world as it is and is capable of adjusting his responses accordingly.[19] Autonomy as objectivity requires the subject to have a certain degree of openness, dispassion, stability, and flexibility, as well as an ability to respond appropriately to his environment; moreover, it presupposes that he is adequately informed about the world and is able to set goals and pursue them. However, it does not require the subject to be capable of moral emotions and attitudes. In short, it requires of the subject neither an orientation toward the good nor a critical evaluation of his assignments of ethical meaning and value.

By splitting off questions of autonomy from questions of ethical worth, Berofsky runs up against the problem of how to account for the perception that autonomy is valuable only if it is directed toward the good. This perception suggests a link between the value of autonomy and ethical motivation. As is often the case, the link is most evident in cases where it is absent: it is easier to see that the capacities comprising the concept of autonomous agency are commonly held *not* to be valuable if they are *not* directed toward the good. Thus, the capacities central to Berofsky's interpretation of autonomy such as dispassion, knowledgeability, and purposive rationality are commonly regarded as *not* valuable when they are used to achieve goals that could *not* be the proper object of ethical motivation. A cold-blooded murderer is not normally admired for the dispassionate and strategic thinking that enables her to carry out her crimes successfully; indeed, we tend to see this as making the deed more rather than less reprehensible and shudder at the perversion of the human capacities involved. In general, we do not value the exercise of the capacities connected with the idea of autonomous agency when they are disconnected from a concern for the good, indicating that the value of these capacities cannot be assessed independently of questions about the human subject's ethical motivation. The point can be extended to the concept of autonomy itself: generally it is *not* valued when it is *not* directed toward the good. This suggests that, at least on the commonly held view, the value of autonomy can be explained only through reference to its connection with the good. Of course, Berofsky could be read as attempting to challenge that commonly held view: as seeking to reorient our deep-seated intuitions and expectations by way of a series of provocative arguments. However, this reading is hard to fit with his repeated emphasis on the realistic character of his view of autonomy and on his extensive use of examples drawn from everyday life. Moreover, it is noteworthy that he makes no attempt to answer the question of why autonomy is—and should be—regarded as valuable; its value is simply presupposed.[20] Against Berofsky, therefore, I suggest that in order to provide an adequate account of the value of autonomy, we need to construe it as ethical autonomy—as involving a subjective orientation toward the good.

To be sure, it is one thing to assert that autonomy is valuable only if directed toward the good; it is another to maintain that it is valuable only if connected with an evaluative concern for the good. However, if we recall the normative intuitions and expectations comprising the idea of situated rationality, we can see that only a rationally evaluative concern is congruent with the antiauthoritarian impulses of contemporary critical social thinking. Since Berofsky denies a connection between the concept of autonomous agency and an evaluative concern for the good, he ends up with a foreshortened conception centered on the capacities for objective thought and action and instrumental reasoning.[21] This foreshortened conception of autonomous agency fails to do justice to the modern emphasis on taking responsibility for one's own assignments of

meaning and value and on respecting the distinct points of view of other subjects. Thus, although I share Berofsky's view that (some sort of) objectivity and
means-end rationality are core elements of the concept of autonomy, the
conception I propose posits strong evaluation as a further, core element.

The second core element of my proposed concept of autonomy is *rational
accountability*. This refers to the willingness and ability to take responsibility for
one's actions, judgments, and self-interpretations in the sense of being able to
explain and justify them to others, if need be. Again, the resulting conception
of autonomy fits well with the antiauthoritarian impulses of critical social
thinking for, by incorporating the obligation to account for one's ethical judgments and actions to others, it pays tribute to the principle of equal respect
for others as moral agents with a distinct point of view. It also fits well with
the receptivity to one's surroundings and to the power of the good, the willingness to learn from experience, and the openness to criticism that, as we shall
see, are presuppositions of practical reasoning on a nonauthoritarian conception. Here, too, however, we should beware of possible misconceptions. The
idea of rational accountability does not imply a commitment to the ideal of
the fully transparent self, which holds that all dimensions of subjectivity are
rationally retrievable.[22] In her willingness to account for her judgments and
actions to others, the human subject attests to the validity of these actions and
judgments, in Paul Ricoeur's sense of *attestation*. Attestation, as Ricoeur understands it, is "the assurance of being oneself acting and suffering":[23] a kind of
belief that the self has in its own ability to act and to suffer, to do and to
undergo things that it can impute to itself as its own actions and experiences.[24]
In attesting to the validity of her actions and judgments the human subject
makes public this kind of belief in her own capacities; she does not claim cer-
titude that these actions and judgments are her actions and judgments nor
does she claim that they can be rendered fully transparent, either to others or
to herself.

Rational accountability is an interpretation of what it means for the human
subject to be able to call her reasons her own. It shifts the emphasis from
ownership of reasons to responsibility for them. By doing so, it avoids the possessive-individualist pictures of human agency[25] that have been criticized
sharply by poststructuralists and communitarians, and by feminists influenced
by each of these movements. With their emphasis on self-ownership, such
conceptions stand accused of disregarding the ways in which human subjects
are formed in multiple contexts of meaning that are not of their making. They

also stand accused of denying the processual, fluid, and fragmented qualities of subjectivity. Similarly, by prioritizing capacities for detached choice and sovereign control, they disregard the importance of affective-emotional relationships, and of bodily and affective-emotional needs and desires. Possessive-individualist conceptions of self-identity give rise to models of politics that split off the bodily and affective-emotional aspects of human agency from deliberations on law, politics, and matters of justice, impoverishing these deliberations and encouraging the privatization of ethical concerns. They also point in the direction of the minimal state, a form of political arrangement regarded by many communitarians and feminists as destructive of community and the caring values that they wish to espouse.

Evidently, therefore, the unwelcome implications of conceptions of self-identity that are modeled on self-ownership, detached choice, and sovereign control make them unacceptable as a basis for the kind of conception of autonomy required by contemporary critical theory. For this reason, it is important to show that the human subject's freedom to act according to reasons that she can call her own does not entail allegiance to a possessive-individualist conception of self-identity. Two broad strategies are available here. The first strategy is to argue that the ownership of reasons does not commit us to a possessive-individualist model of self-identity. The second strategy is to argue that autonomy implies, not ownership of reasons, but a willingness to account for them to others.

The first line of argument is pursued by Jean Cohen in her defense of privacy rights.[26] Cohen endeavors to reconceptualize the idea of a right to privacy in a way that acknowledges feminist critiques of the possessive-individualist assumptions on which traditional liberal justifications of privacy have often relied.[27] To this end she proposes a conception of decisional autonomy as one of the core goods that privacy rights seek to protect, claiming that decisional autonomy does not presuppose a possessive-individualist conception of self-identity. Unlike Berofsky's conception of personal autonomy, decisional autonomy, as Cohen construes it, is given an ethical interpretation: it is understood as the human subject's ability to form and pursue her conceptions of the good. More precisely, decisional autonomy refers to the subject's freedom to decide for herself, without discussion or approval from others, certain matters constitutive of her personal identity. Cohen argues convincingly that autonomy in this sense is compatible with the situated and relational conceptions of individual identity advocated by communitarians; moreover, that it is able to take account of the identity-constituting role of deep commitments and convictions that communitarians—and others—emphasize. Unlike many communitarians, and in sympathy with poststructuralists, however, Cohen insists that individual identity is not simply the product of the community's values but a creative appropriation and interpretation of them. As she understands it, decisional autonomy refers to the self-creative synthesis that only the individual herself can fashion out of her various locations and commitments, in part through communicative association with others. It affords the individual a sense of control over the personal space in which she experiments with her self-definitions, granting her freedom from having to give reasons for choices that are the most crucial to her identity. Privacy is the "protective shield" for this personal space of exploration and experiment: "[it] protects the autonomy, judgment, creative imagination, and inviolability of the concrete (situated, socialized) individual in ways that society deems crucial."[28] Significantly, privacy is not a separate institutional sphere; individuals carry their shields with them, in public and in private, wherever they go. In short, privacy rights protect individuals' ethical self-determination by granting them control over their ethical deliberations (providing that principles of morality are not violated). They entitle individuals to choose with whom they justify or even discuss their ethical decisions, with whom they rethink conceptions of the good, and whose recognition matters.

A major strength of Cohen's argument is that it engages with some of the most serious concerns that have been voiced by poststructuralist, communitarian, and feminist critics of the concept of autonomy. Moreover, it expresses the valid intuition that autonomous agents require a personal space: a space of refuge from communicatively structured relationships, be these relationships with strangers or more intimate ones (I return to this point below). Its weakness, however, is that it retains residual traces of the possessive-individualist model of self-identity.[29]

In Cohen's account, individuals are not granted ownership of their bodies or property, but they are made owners of their decisions in areas of key personal concern. The use of the language of choice and control is a striking feature of this account, as can be seen in formulations such as: "a privacy right entitles one to choose with whom one will attempt to justify one's ethical decisions,"[30] and when we are told that privacy rights "secure control and power to the individual."[31] In view of this emphasis on control, her use of the language of defense in connection with privacy rights is hardly surprising: as we have seen, privacy rights are described as a protective shield, designed to protect the personal dimensions of one's life from undue scrutiny or interference.

Thus, Cohen grants individuals sovereign control over their reasons for their ethical choices and decisions (providing no moral principles are violated); she makes them owners of their interpretations of the good for human beings. This residual possessive individualism is accompanied by a residual voluntarism: ethical agents themselves choose whether or not to justify—or even discuss—their ethical choices with others.

The possessive-individualist, and accompanying voluntarist, elements in Cohen's account are directly connected with her rejection of the position that autonomy requires the subject's willingness to account publicly for her decisions. This position is currently associated most strongly with Habermas. In Habermas's writings, rational accountability is one of the central components of the idea of autonomy.[32] Here, we may distinguish between a stronger and weaker version of the Habermasian idea of rational accountability.[33] On the stronger version, in which rational accountability is part of what he calls moral autonomy, individuals are obliged to give reasons for their choices and decisions that everyone could accept as (universally) valid; on the weaker version, in which rational accountability is part of what he calls ethical autonomy, the obligation is to give reasons that members of a particular community or group could accept as valid. Cohen rejects the weaker as well as the stronger version: decisional autonomy is not just freedom from the obligation to justify one's actions by giving reasons that everyone could accept; it is freedom from the obligation to justify one's choices and decisions to anyone. To be sure, individual agents may choose to enter into discussion with others regarding their key personal choices and decisions, but this choice appears to be one among many dispensable preferences. Thus, in Cohen's conception, rational accountability is not a component of ethical identity but an option that the individual may or may not choose to exercise.

The residual possessive-individualist and voluntarist elements in Cohen's conception of decisional autonomy make it open to the same kinds of objections that poststructuralist, communitarian, and feminist critics raise against possessive-individualist models of self-identity more generally. Moreover, it is out of tune with attributes such as receptivity, openness to criticism, and willingness to learn from experience, which, as we shall see, are required for engagement in practical argumentation on a nonauthoritarian interpretation.[34] For these reasons, rather than pursuing Cohen's strategy of denying the connection between ownership of reasons and a possessive-individualist model of self-identity, the alternative strategy is more fruitful.

This alternative strategy offers a different account of what it means for the human subject to be able to call reasons her own. On this account, autonomy entails rational accountability: calling reasons one's own amounts to an acceptance of the responsibility to give reasons for one's judgments and actions to others, if necessary. On this account, reasons are not *owned* by the self but *owed* to others; moreover, they are not *protected from* the critical gaze of others but *opened up* to their critical judgments. Thus, not only does rational accountability constitute an interpretation of what it means to call reasons one's own that avoids even residual possessive individualism; it evokes a picture of the self as receptive to her environment and to the power of the good, willing to learn from experience and open to criticism, that is diametrically opposed to the picture of the self under siege evoked by Cohen's idea of decisional autonomy.

The third core element of my proposed conception of autonomy is *independence*. This refers to the human subject's capacity to engage with her surroundings, with other subjects, and with her own self-interpretations and life history in a receptive, flexible, open-minded, sensitive, and imaginative way, without undue reliance on the opinions of others. The capacity for independence should not be misconstrued as the view that human subjects are the origin of their will, desires, and behavior.[35] Nor does it imply that the autonomous agent can achieve complete freedom from the influences of natural environment, heredity, biology, social context, and so on.[36] Equally, it does not deny that autonomous agency is constituted in historically specific contexts of meaning, which involve various kinds of relationships with others.[37] Independence does not imply radical isolation, but the need for a certain kind of critical detachment—perhaps something akin to Berofsky's idea of objectivity. Independence in this sense not only warns against overreliance on the opinions of others in one's views of the world, relationships with others, self-definitions, and constructions of self-identity; it also calls for the attempt to free oneself from the pernicious influences of one's own earlier lives.[38]

The importance of making independence a core requirement of autonomous agency can be explained through reference to the requirements of rational accountability and strong evaluation. By making rational accountability the second core element of autonomous agency, we run the risk of undermining the very conditions that facilitate the flourishing of the first element, the capacity for strong evaluation. As we have seen, the capacity for strong evaluation presupposes a number of other capacities such as receptivity, flexibility, open-mindedness, sensitivity, and imaginativeness. In order for these capacities to flourish, the human subject may require a "space of her own," in the sense of a personal space of refuge from communicatively structured relationships, be these relationships with strangers or more intimate ones.[39] Without such a space, the requirement of rational accountability may lead to the subject's undue reliance on the opinions of others in his self-definitions and in his assignments of meaning and value. Such overreliance leads to the inauthentic form of self-love described by Rousseau as *amour propre*.[40] As Rousseau describes him, the inauthentic human subject lives "outside of himself," relying on the opinions of others for his picture of who he is. However, strong evaluation, which requires the subject to construct his identity in reflective engagement with a range of important questions about the good, presupposes a subject who "lives within himself" and, for this, a personal space of withdrawal from communicatively structured relationships may be necessary. A recognition of the importance of such a personal space seems to me the valid intuition guiding Cohen's conception of decisional autonomy. However, in order to avoid the residual voluntarism and possessive individualism of her conception, we must construe this space as a *permeable* enclosure, as a space for *temporary* withdrawal, which in the interests of rational accountability, may never be sealed off hermetically against the critical interventions of others.[41] Thus, the required "space of one's own" is a space of refuge from unwelcome intrusion; it is not a space over which the human subject may exercise sovereign control. The inclusion of independence in the proposed conception acknowledges the importance of such personal spaces for the development of autonomous agency.

The fourth and final element of the conception of autonomy I propose is *purposive rationality*. This refers to the ability to set and pursue short-term and long-term goals. Evidently, this ability is a prerequisite of strong evaluation, for without the capacity for goal-directed action, the human subject would be unable to *construct* her identity in reflective engagement with questions about the good. Purposive rationality should not be misconstrued as single-mindedness or rigidity: the autonomous agent may pursue multiple and heterogeneous goals and frequently change her tastes and opinions; the requirement of purposive rationality does not exclude some degree of fluidity, fragmentation, and heterogeneity of subjectivity. Nonetheless, a disintegrated self cannot be autonomous. In consequence, autonomy implies some degree of unity and coherence, and the ability to set goals and pursue them.[42]

Without minimal purposive rationality, autonomous agency of any kind would be inconceivable. Thus, conceptions of subjectivity that reject the attributes associated with purposive rationality do not merely call into question particular interpretations of autonomy; they threaten to undermine the concept of autonomy itself. Conceptions of subjectivity that reject attributes such as unity, coherence, and goal-directedness are closely associated with poststructuralism.[43] Thus, Judith Butler argues for a notion of the gendered body as radically performative, as a body that constantly invents and reinvents its identity and the unity of its life within multiple contexts of meaning.[44] Butler's gendered bodies are fluid and fragmented rather than fixed and coherent, and are constituted through multiple acts that are expressive of public and social discourse.[45] A difficulty with this kind of conception of subjectivity is that it seems unable to accommodate the kind of unified, integrated, goal-directed activity that is required for political struggles against suffering and oppression and, more generally, for transformative social action.[46] Butler's response to the problem is to allow for the political necessity of speaking and acting as a unified, coherent, goal-directed agent while insisting on the need simultaneously to interrogate the normative picture of subjectivity on which such speaking and acting are predicated.[47]

Thus, in line with my reading of her position regarding concepts such as democracy or universality,[48] Butler's objections to the idea of autonomous agency seem to be less objections to attributes such as unity, coherence, and goal-directedness than objections to the closure involved in static conceptions of identity. For Butler, such static conceptions effect a pernicious ideological closure, since they deny the political salience of normative contents, removing them from the political field. This is the most likely reason for Butler's antipathy to a Habermasian conception of rational agency, which I mentioned in chapter 4. Since Habermas's formal-pragmatic justificatory strategy grounds his conception of rational agency in supposedly universal communicative practices, it removes the attributes comprising it from the political field of contestation, rearticulation, and restaging. Otherwise, it is difficult to see why Habermasian conceptions of rational agency should be singled out for critical attention. One would expect Habermas's idea of rational agency (and autonomous agency in particular) to be more attractive to Butler, and to poststructuralist thinkers in general, than the disembedded and disembodied conceptions of agency commonplace within both the deontological tradition of moral theory and the contractarian tradition of political theory. By contrast with these traditions, Habermas's notion of agency is formulated in relational terms and has the potential to accommodate aspects of subjectivation emphasized by poststructuralist thinkers, for example, the subject's locatedness in multiple contexts of meaning, her bodily and affective-emotional constitution, and her qualities of fluidity, fragmentation, and innovation.[49] It looks, therefore, as though Butler objects less to the actual substance of Habermasian ideas of rational agency than to the attempt to give them an unshakeable foundation in the deep-seated, normative intuitions and expectations implicit in everyday linguistic behavior, thereby making them into static—ideological—conceptions.[50]

However, as we have also seen, static interpretations can be rendered dynamic by way of practices of critical interrogation that spark off creative rearticulations and restagings of the concept in question. Taking my lead from Butler, therefore, I suggest that its reliance on a degree of purposive rationality (or indeed, rational accountability, strong evaluation, or independence) is not in itself a reason to reject the very concept of autonomous agency. It is not autonomy's validation of attributes such as unity, coherence, and goal-directedness that is cause for concern but ideological conceptions of autonomy that remove such attributes from the political field, blocking attempts to rearticulate and restage them in more inclusive and emancipatory ways.

With these tentative and cursory reflections I have attempted to outline the kind of conception of autonomy that would make sense of the connection between validity and argumentation, while avoiding the most important objections raised by communitarian, poststructuralist, and feminist critics. We have now moved some way toward answering the question of what this conception of argumentation should look like.

So far we have established that, to fit with the core normative intuitions that shape modern identities, in particular, with the idea of autonomous agency, critical social theories must evoke a vision of the good society that is capable of being articulated in the form of validity claims; furthermore, that validity claims are subject to critical evaluation by way of public processes of argumentation that are open-ended, inclusive, and fair. We have ascertained, in addition, that the principal type of claim at issue in such public discussions is a claim that a particular idea of the good society discloses the transcendent object more powerfully, and provides better ethical orientation, than competing ideas. Our question, now, is how claims of this type may be evaluated critically.

Although the idea of situated rationality offers some assistance here, it is of limited usefulness. As we have seen, it points toward the need for public processes of open-ended, inclusive, and fair argumentation. However, it seems to have more to say about how we should conduct such argumentation than about how we should assess the propositions, norms, and principles that are the subject of argumentative dispute: although it offers clear normative guidelines as to how the public exchange of arguments should be institutionalized and carried out, it is less helpful with regard to evaluating the matters under consideration in argumentative exchanges. With regard to the conduct of argumentation, it stipulates open-endedness, maximal inclusiveness, and fairness. With regard to an assessment of the matters under discussion, however, it calls only for congruence with these stipulations.

In other words, the idea of situated rationality stipulates merely that the propositions, norms, and principles in question must be congruent with the antiauthoritarian ideas that are embodied in the argumentative procedures themselves. Although this places important normative constraints on the acceptability of the propositions, norms, and principles that are being argumentatively discussed, it does not help us to weigh up the merits of the multiple competing positions that would satisfy these constraints. We might say: it provides an insufficient basis for discriminating ethically among conflicting representations of the good society. To be sure, the constraints imposed by the idea of situated rationality do enable us to exclude some such representations; they rule out, for example, fascist forms of popular sovereignty or authoritarian forms of communism on the grounds that they contravene the principle of moral and political equality and fail to respect moral and political autonomy;[51] however, they allow us to include apparently competing representations such as Rorty's idea of a democratic society that would foster individual creativity, Habermas's idea of a democratic society that would be integrated and reproduced by way of communicative rationality, Honneth's idea of a democratic society that would make possible a full recognition of the three dimensions of personality, Butler's idea of a democratic society in which identities would be subject to permanent contestation, rearticulation, and restaging, and Laclau's idea of democracy in which competing political representations would struggle for hegemony. If the idea of situated rationality is unable to help us to decide between these and other representations of the good society, does this mean that they are simply incommensurable?

Representations of the good society are not incommensurable. They appear to be so only if we subscribe to a model of practical rationality that is ahistorical, absolutist, and abstract. By "ahistorical" I mean a model of practical rationality that fails to acknowledge its own historicity and the specific normative commitments that it assumes. By "absolutist" I mean a model of practical rationality in which judgments in matters of validity are finally and unquestionably valid. By "abstract" I mean a model of practical rationality that considers the validity of propositions, norms, and principles in isolation from their concrete articulation and realization in historical contexts. However, alternative models are available. Below I present the main elements of a model of practical rationality that fits well with the antiauthoritarian impulses of contemporary critical social thinking. Neither ahistorical nor absolutist nor abstract, this alternative model nonetheless allows for a rationally backed choice between competing representations of the good society; moreover, it does so not just from the point of view of their congruence with the idea of situated rationality (for, as we saw, many representations of the good society satisfy this requirement), but also from the point of view of their claim to disclose the transcendent object more powerfully, and to provide better ethical orientation, than rival representations.

In contrast to ahistorical models of practical rationality, the model that I propose acknowledges its own historicity, in this case, its indebtedness to core normative intuitions and expectations that shape modern identities. Accordingly, it is not merely committed to the idea of situated rationality, it also recognizes the historical situatedness of that idea. This means that critical social theory must acknowledge that its deep commitment to normative ideas such as autonomous agency, universality, and contestability—ideas that are constitutive for its own self-understanding—has a historical location: the social imaginary of Western modernity.

Here, it is crucial to note that this requirement of historicity does not necessarily lead to Rorty's radically contextualist position. To be sure, there is no escape from the contextualist circle:[52] this is especially clear in the case of key normative ideas such as autonomy, universality, and contestability. The advocated means for assessing the merits of the claims to validity raised by such ideas is a model of practical rationality that is based on the intuitions and expectations for which the claims are raised. However, this circle is cause for concern only to those who hold that knowledge of a reality independent of our descriptions, interpretations, and evaluations is possible. But, as we saw in chapter 1 above, contemporary critical social thinking is united in rejecting that possibility: thinkers such as Rorty who adopt a radically contextualist approach join with proponents of a context-transcending approach in acknowledging that our perceptions, interpretations, and evaluations of reality are always subject to the influences of history and context. From the premise that we are always bound to a context that determines our thinking and acting to some greater or lesser degree, the radically contextualist and context-transcending paths diverge. Proponents of a radical contextualist approach hold that the key normative ideas shaping modern identities are arational—outside the remit of reason. Proponents of a context-transcending approach hold that these normative ideas are connected with claims to validity that extend across sociocultural contexts and historical epochs. They maintain that it is possible and desirable to explore the validity of these ideas in engagement with the historical past and with the inhabitants of their own and other socio-cultural contexts, and to endeavor to rearticulate them creatively. For example, as we saw in our discussion of Butler in chapter 4, the concept of universality has been vigorously contested, resulting in creative new articulations of it. As mentioned in the present chapter, the idea of autonomous agency, too, has been the subject of contestation by communitarian, poststructuralist, and feminist critics, giving rise to attempts to rethink the concept in innovative ways. The same holds even for the idea of contestability: as is evident from the writings of Wellmer, for example, the question of which truths can be contested is itself a contested matter, suggesting the need to reconsider the concept of contestability itself.[53]

Critical social theories must also acknowledge the historicity of the other normative commitments that they assume. For, in addition to depending on a conception of situated reason, critical social thinking relies on at least two further assumptions that are necessary for the purposes of its context-transcending dimension. One of these is the assumption of an ineradicable gap between the transcendent object and its historical articulations. As we have seen, this assumption is necessary if critical social thinking is to have an inher-ently context-transcending dimension: if it is to be genuinely context tran-scending—context transcendent in a dynamic sense—it must assume that any particular representation of the good society is constitutively inadequate to its object. A further important assumption is the assumption that the gap, though ineliminable, is not invariable: it can be narrowed. If we did not presume that some representations of the transcendent object are able to bring us closer to it than other ones, we would have no nonauthoritarian, nonconventional, ethical grounds for finding the validity claims of some representations ethically more persuasive than others.

The second assumption could also be described as an assumption concern-ing the possibility of historical progress. As I argued in chapter 3, if critical social theory is to maintain a context-transcending dimension, it has to presuppose that learning processes on a sociocultural level are possible. A similar point can be extracted from Charles Taylor's reflections on Hegel's view of historical development. Taylor breaks down Hegel's view into a number of components.[54] Although he admits that, today, some of these are difficult to credit (for example, the idea that all human beings have the same potentiality, which unfolds in fixed stages), he maintains that one of the components remains indispensable in contemporary practical reasoning: the idea that each human being from the beginning has the potential within her to become what she later becomes.[55] This means neither that the realization of potentials is inevitable nor that the realization of potentials, when it occurs, follows some predetermined path. Equally, it does not imply that ethical progress is linear. What it does mean is that we need to presume that each human being and, more generally, each sociocultural form of life, contains within them the possibility of change for the better—and that such change is a kind of self-realization.

In sum, the context-transcending dimension of critical social thinking requires it to make at least two normative assumptions over and above the constellation of assumptions comprising the notion of situated rationality. To be sure, from the point of view of the question of historicity, it is less important which normative commitments are assumed by a particular model of practical rationality, than that the historically contingent character of these commitments is recognized.

In contrast to absolutist models of practical rationality, the model I propose regards judgments of validity as contestable rather than final and as comparative rather than absolute. In this regard, too, Taylor's reflections on practical rationality are useful, in particular his view that it is primarily a matter of reasoning in transitions.[56] As I understand it, the idea of reasoning in transitions comprises a number of elements. To begin with, the aim is not to establish that some position is correct absolutely but rather that some position is superior to other ones. Accordingly, practical rationality is concerned mainly with *comparative* propositions (recall my contention that a given representation of the good society seeks to disclose the transcendent object *more* powerfully, and to provide *better* ethical orientation, than competing representations).[57] Then, reasoning in transitions entails the idea of moving beyond a particular way of thinking or behaving. It is a matter of showing that the transition from one position to another constitutes an epistemic gain, for example, by resolving a contradiction or confusion in the first position, by taking account of an important factor that it had screened out, or by drawing attention to contexts in which the position is not sustainable. Once again, we are dealing with a thesis relating to ethical learning. This brings us to a further component of the idea of reasoning in transitions: the contestable character of claims to the effect that a given position constitutes an epistemic gain. As has been emphasized throughout our discussion, the claim that a certain position constitutes ethical learning is always open to dispute; moreover, such disputes can never be settled once and for all through appeal to fixed and given criteria. Whether or not something constitutes ethical learning is in principle a contested matter, the subject of open-ended discussions in which multiple kinds of empirical, theoretical, and normative arguments may be brought to bear. From this we can see that the comparative and contestable aspects of a nonabsolutist model of practical rationality go hand in hand.

In contrast to abstract models of practical rationality, the model I propose proceeds concretely. According to this model, the assessment of validity claims is not a matter of abstract evaluation of the ethical ideas expressed by the representation of the good society that is the subject of interrogation. Instead, it concentrates on the *materiality* of a given representation. Rather than abstractly deciding whether it is valid or invalid, assessment involves looking at the ways in which the ethical hopes and aspirations it expresses are actualized historically in social institutions and arrangements; more precisely, it entails considering the fit, or lack of fit, between these hopes and aspirations and what happens when they are translated into practice. Such consideration might show, for example, that in certain contexts the institutionalization of Habermas's idea of communicative rationality leads to a decrease rather than increase in personal and political autonomy; here, a connection might be made between the idea of a fully inclusive, final consensus and contemporary negative representations of political protest and the reemergence of the discourse of sedition.[58]

In the same vein, concrete examination might show that in certain contexts the institutionalization of Laclau's idea of hegemonic democracy leads to a less rather than more just society; here, a connection might be made between the idea of permanent conflict, contestation, and suspicion, and contemporary apathy in matters of economic redistribution and political participation. In exposing the gap between a particular representation's guiding ethical ideas and their historical actualization, criticism might be said to proceed *immanently*; this as we saw in earlier chapters is the method favored in the Left-Hegelian tradition of critical social thinking. Speaking generally, critical social thinking proceeds immanently when it investigates the discrepancy between a set of normative intuitions and expectations that are already implicit in a particular sociocultural context and their realization over time in social institutions and arrangements. As we know, the danger here is radical contextualism: a purely immanent method limits criticism to the exposure of the discrepancy between a particular set of hopes and aspirations and their historical realization; it abstains from judging the validity of the hopes and aspirations themselves. This is why it is important to underscore the context-transcending dimension of the proposed model of practical rationality.

We will recall that two normative commitments are crucial in this regard: first, the assumption of an ineliminable gap between the transcendent object and its historically specific articulations and, second, the assumption that ethical progress is possible. If the first assumption is made, immanent criticism does not merely point to the need for better—more adequate—actualizations of a posited set of normative ideas; it sets in train questioning processes that may call upon us to rethink their meaning or, indeed, eventually undermine their ethical validity. However, such processes of rethinking and undermining could be regarded as ethically arbitrary (this appears to be Rorty's position). For this reason, we need to make a second commitment and presume that collective ethical learning is possible. Otherwise, the questioning processes set in train by immanent criticism could not be viewed as rational (or irrational) in some context-transcending sense: they would have to be considered arational. Clearly, therefore, the second assumption is equally crucial if the critical interrogation of normative ideas is to lead to new or modified ideas that are not just different but ethically superior to the old ones. To be sure, as I have remarked repeatedly, particular claims regarding ethical learning are always open to processes of contestation that may lead to new articulations of our deepest ethical intuitions and expectations.

Finally, the model of practical reasoning outlined above rejects any kind of simple opposition between reason and feelings, intuitions and passions. On the one hand, if they are to be congruent with the antiauthoritarian ideas constitutive of modern identities, critical social theories are obliged to formulate their representations of the good society in terms of claims to validity—in terms of propositions, norms, and principles that seek to elicit from their addressees a rationally backed "yes" response. On the other hand, our discussion of such representations drew attention to their affective aspect: their ability to exert an affective pull that can be attributed to the transcendent ethical object they purport to represent. This is important, first, from the point of view of motivation. The success of representations of the good society in motivating thinking and acting depends on their ability to arouse the feeling that the social condition in question is attractive, to prompt the sense that it makes manifest the transcendent object, and to excite a desire to attain it. Thus, practical reasoning regarding the merits of particular representations of the good society is effective only when the images they project resonate with the feelings, intuitions, and passions of participants.

However, as we have seen, for autonomous agents motivation always has a rational component: such agents must be able to take responsibility for their judgments and actions by supplying reasons in support of them, if necessary. In this regard, too, the affective dimension is important. For, if others are to regard the reasons offered as good reasons, they must find them affectively as well as intellectually compelling. To be intellectually compelling, the reasons offered must be capable of being integrated into the frameworks of reasons that autonomous individuals construct for themselves in the course of their attempts to make sense of their own lives, of the lives of other people, and of the world around them. To be affectively compelling, the reasons offered must feel right, grant a sense of access to the transcendent object, and be capable of stimulating ethical thought and action. This does not mean that the reasons offered in support of a particular representation of the good society have to fit into existing frameworks of reasons and resonate with existing feelings, intuitions, and passions. Where the reasons offered are not in fact persuasive, a number of strategies are available. On the assumption that the antiauthoritarian orientation of critical social thinking rules out methods of persuasion that make use of violence, two kinds of strategy seem particularly useful. The first strategy is to work in conjunction with nonargumentative modes of bringing about (affectively imbued) cognitive transformation, such as the bodily practices of rearticulation and reenactment advocated by Butler.[59] The second strategy is to employ innovative modes of argumentation that set in train processes of (affectively imbued) cognitive transformation.[60]

I have said that the idea of situated rationality points toward a model of critical evaluation that bears a strong resemblance to the model of argumentation at the center of Habermas's theory of communicative action. However, since this model of argumentation does not help us to assess the merits of the many competing representations of the good society that satisfy its requirements, we need to develop it into an account of practical rationality that would allow for such an assessment. This account takes us beyond Habermas's account of practical rationality, at least in its existing formulations.[61] One of the most significant differences between the model of practical rationality outlined above and the one that can be found in Habermas's writings is its postulate of a transcendent ethical object that always exceeds its particular representations. This postulate, which I have formulated in the language favored by Laclau, has much in common with Charles Taylor's account of moral sources.[62] Taylor, as we have seen, presents the modern self as a strong evaluator, as someone who is motivated in a fundamental way to define herself from within a horizon of important questions about the good. Some of these questions refer to constitutive goods, or moral sources, which are neither fully independent of human perceptions and interpretations nor reducible to them. The relationship between the two sides is understood dynamically: on the one side, moral sources constitute good things as good and empower the realization of the good, in the sense of potentially motivating good thought and action; on the other side, articulation of the power of moral sources in the form of (linguistic or nonlinguistic) representations brings human beings into contact with the good.

In positing sources of ethical thinking and action that can never fully be captured by human representations,[63] Taylor's account of the modern self can be compared to Habermas's account of truth, which postulates a justification-transcendent, "recalcitrant" reality, and Laclau's account of hegemonic struggle, which postulates a transcendent ethical object. Like these it has several advantages: it accommodates the sense that truth, unlike justification, is unconditional, it captures the intuition that truth is a property that can never be lost, and it allows for the feeling, common even in everyday situations, that certain perceptual shifts are demanded of us.[64] Nonetheless, there are also important differences. Unlike Habermas, Taylor extends his postulate of a justification-transcendent reality to the moral-practical realm; accordingly, his approach fits better with the model of practical reasoning sketched above. Unlike Laclau, who, by positing an ethically invariable gap between the transcendent ethical object and its particular representations, fails to connect the two sides, Taylor shows how the transcendent object and its representations are connected; this places him in a better position to explain the purported "ethical investment" of representations of the good society: the claim that they articulate a transcendent ethical object.

The concept of articulation is central to Taylor's account of the modern self. Particularly interesting for our present purposes is his demonstration that articulation can be empowering. Although the sources of the good are granted some independence of our perceptions and interpretations, the activity of articulation is deemed to play an important role in recovering, reinvigorating, or releasing their power.[65] For Taylor, the power of moral sources depends largely on their proximity. Moral sources can be lost, can become remote, or can be as yet unknown or unfelt: articulation can bring them closer, grant us a clearer view of them, and enable us to grasp what they involve.[66] He acknowledges that not just any articulation enables proximity: some forms of articulation may be dead or have no power in a particular place or at a particular time or with particular people. Articulations are most empowering when the "speaker, the formulation, and the act of delivering the message all line up together to reveal the good."[67]

As passages such as these indicate, Taylor's focus is on *linguistic* articulation.[68] Moreover, the importance of the speech act as a whole is underscored: the power of articulation is greatest when a speaker delivers a message in a certain way, to a hearer, in a particular context. Habermas, too, emphasizes the way in which speech acts serve to establish a relationship between speaker and hearer based on the content of what they say. Drawing on Karl Bühler's schema of language functions, he presents language as a medium that simultaneously serves three different, but internally related, functions: expressions employed communicatively serve to express the intentions of a speaker, to represent states of affairs, and to enter into a relationship of obligation with an addressee.[69] The main difference between Taylor and Habermas in this regard is Taylor's emphasis on *the power of formulation*. Habermas shows little concern for the way in which the content of the utterance is articulated. A rare occasion on which he acknowledges the importance of the medium of communication is his discussion of Roman Jakobson's expansion of Bühler's three communicative functions by a fourth, "poetic" function.[70]

Jakobson defines the poetic function as the "focus on the message for its own sake."[71] An utterance is poetic to the extent that it relates reflexively to its own linguistic form, to the medium of language itself. His famous formulation of the poetic function is that it "projects the principle of equivalence from the axis of selection into the axis of combination."[72] Jakobson observes that in nonpoetic uses of language, words are *selected* on the basis of equivalence and combined on the basis of this selection. For example, "child" is selected as equivalent to "kid" or "youngster," and "naps" is selected as equivalent to "sleeps" or "dozes"; the words are then combined ("the child naps") on the basis of this selection. In the poetic use of language, by contrast, the words are *combined* on the basis of equivalence: equivalence is promoted to the constitutive device of the sequence.[73] His main examples here refer to the use of meter and sound: for instance, the equalization of one syllable with any other syllable of the same sequence ("Thirty days hath September") and rhymes, which are based on the regular recurrence of equivalent phonemes. Most important for our present purposes, however, is not his analysis of the use of equivalence in the poetic use of language but his insistence that any attempt to reduce the sphere of the poetic function to poetry, or to confine poetry to the poetic function, would be misguided.[74]

In the essay in question, Habermas follows Jakobson in claiming that the poetic function is operative not just in poetry but also in the ordinary language of everyday speech.[75] In general, however, Habermas's theory of communication tends to neglect the poetic use of language, paying little attention to the importance of the ways in which semantic contents are articulated.[76]

By contrast, Taylor's account of articulation opens the way for a consideration of the power of formulation. In the context of critical social thinking, this has the beneficial effect of drawing attention to the importance of modes of argumentation that make use of innovative linguistic strategies and devices. As we have seen, context-transcending social criticism challenges the validity of prevailing social institutions and arrangements through reference to some alternative idea of the good society. In doing so, it appeals to certain deep-seated, normative intuitions and expectations. Since these intuitions and expectations may have been lost or forgotten or may be grasped imperfectly, it cannot presume that its addressees will hear what it says: they may not be receptive to its critical diagnoses of the existing social reality and its projections of an alternative, better, social condition. Consequently, it may have to find ways of conveying its message that break through the various barriers to receptivity. Butler, as we know, highlights the possible effectiveness of non-linguistic interventions to induce the required awareness. Others pursue a linguistic path, attempting to develop new forms of philosophical expression. Thus, for example, Walter Benjamin's discussion of the concept of history takes the form of a series of theses whose connection is not logical in the strict sense; moreover, for the most part, the individual theses are explicated not discursively, but pictorially, in the form of images.[77] Similarly, Horkheimer and Adorno in *Dialectic of Enlightenment* practice a nontraditional mode of philosophical argumentation. They present their work as a series of fragments, and use aesthetic devices rather than philosophical arguments to make their point.[78] To be sure, philosophical experiments such as these, which rely heavily on the use of exaggeration, unexpected juxtapositions, and stories, run up against the problem of how their claims to validity may be rationally evaluated.[79]

Taylor does not confront this problem. He uses the concept of articulation in a very loose sense to include multiple forms of linguistic expression; in his account, articulations of moral sources do not have to take the form of generally intelligible propositions. However, if they do not take this form, they cannot be used as reasons and hence cannot be the subject of argumentative evaluation. Consequently, they cannot claim validity in a manner congruent with the idea of situated rationality, which, as we have seen, ties validity to public processes of argumentation that are open-ended, inclusive, and fair. The question of how articulations of moral sources can be evaluated rationally gains in urgency once we acknowledge that articulations are not always empowering. Taylor seems quite aware that they are not. He writes, for instance: "[t]rite formulae may combine with the historical sham to weave a cocoon of moral assurance around us which actually insulates us from the energy of true moral sources."[80] He seems prepared to admit that articulations may be "propaganda" rather than "words of power": they may insulate us from the power of moral sources rather than bring us closer to them, feed our self-conceit rather than empower us, and serve sinister purposes such as reinforcing a discreditable status quo.[81]

Here we encounter a limitation of Taylor's account of practical rationality. Its strengths include its postulate of transcendent objects (moral sources) whose power exceeds our representations of them, its commitment to the idea of ethical progress, its comparative and open-ended approach to reasoning, and its emphasis on articulation as the means whereby we gain access to the power of moral sources. Its weakness is that it stops short of confronting the problem of rational evaluation. At various points in the course of our discussion we have run up against this problem: the problem of how representations of the good society, whose validity depends on an experience of disclosure that may not be publicly intelligible, can be evaluated rationally in public processes of argumentation. Although Taylor is certainly aware of this difficulty, he does not pay it sufficient attention.[82]

But this objection could equally be raised against our discussion in the foregoing. I have argued that particular ideas of the good society claim to disclose the transcendent ethical object more powerfully than rival ideas and that this disclosing power is closely bound up with their claims to provide better ethical orientation (I stressed, in particular, that an assessment of the one involves an assessment of the other). The disclosing function of representations seems to threaten the possibility of critically evaluating their claims to validity: recalling our earlier discussion of Adorno, we may worry that discursive lan-

guage cannot succeed in fully capturing what is disclosed by way of representation, and that without a formulation in such language, there can be no critical
evaluation. Closer consideration shows that a number of issues here require
disentangling.

To begin with, we should be clear that the difficulties arising from the disclosing function of representations cannot simply be attributed to the ineliminable gap between the transcendent object and its particular representations.
The difficulties arise only if we posit the further thesis that ethical progress
entails narrowing this gap. If the gap were invariable, all representations of
the transcendent object would be equally adequate (or inadequate). In that
case, no ethical evaluation of the claims raised by particular representations
would be possible. This, I suggested, is the unwelcome position into which
Laclau is forced when he conceives of the transcendent object as an empty
place. Clearly, such a position is uncongenial to critical social theories concerned to maintain their context-transcending moment. This is one reason
why such theories must reject the view that the gap between the transcendent
object and its particular representations is invariable, and instead assume that
the gap can be narrowed: this, as we saw, amounts to the assumption that
ethical progress is possible. However, once we make this assumption, the disclosing function of ideas of the good society becomes a potential problem. We
must then presume that some representations of the good society disclose the
transcendent object more powerfully than others, providing better ethical orientation. If, in particular cases, we are to be able to defend their claims to do
so with reasons, we must be able to find words to express their disclosing and
orienting power that are intelligible to others. As Adorno knew, discursive
language may prove inadequate for this task; as Taylor reminds us, there is
often a need for powerful "poetic" formulations.

However, it would be equally wrong to attribute the problem of critical
evaluation to the poetic character of the formulations that may be required
for the purposes of expressing the power of the transcendent object (as disclosed by way of its particular representations). As Jakobson observed, the
poetic function is operative not just in verbal works of art but also in everyday
language and causes no particular problems of understanding. The frequent
use of metaphor in ordinary language and in ordinary philosophical discourse
bears this out: where metaphors draw on the existing reservoir of meanings
in a particular sociocultural context, they are readily intelligible and may be
used without difficulty as reasons in argumentations. If some articulations of
the transcendent object are not readily intelligible, this is due in the first

instance not to their poetic but to their novel character: to the fact that they fail to connect with the already existing sociocultural vocabulary—with the semantic contents contained in the existing sociocultural reservoir of meanings.

In order to see the difficulty here it is useful to bear in mind one general feature of the concept of a reason. To treat something as a reason is to treat it from the point of view of its general validity.[83] Valid reasons are reasons that could be accepted as such by everyone (who had the requisite information, expertise, experience, interpretative skills, empathy, and so on). Thus, if they are to be treated as reasons in argumentation, the claims to validity raised by ideas of the good society must claim general validity. In order to be capable of being accepted as valid (or invalid) by everyone, they first have to be intelligible to everyone. But, for the inhabitants of modernity, intelligibility, too, entails knowledge of validity conditions.

We have seen that the concept of evaluation most congruent with the cluster of normative intuitions and expectations shaping modern identities is argumentative: the assessment of claims to validity is tied to the exchange of reasons in public processes of argumentation that are inclusive, open-ended, and fair. For related reasons, a similar point can be made for the concept of intelligibility: for the inhabitants of modernity, the most appropriate interpretation stipulates a knowledge of the conditions under which an utterance could be accepted as valid. This idea is central to Habermas's pragmatic theory of meaning.[84] As he puts it: "We understand an utterance when we know what makes it acceptable."[85] This involves knowing "the *kinds of reasons* that a speaker could adduce to support the validity claim raised for what is said."[86] In other words, understanding a linguistic expression entails knowing how to use it in a discussion with other persons who may challenge its validity; this requires knowledge of the kinds of reasons that could be provided in support of the claims raised for the utterance in which it is used. However, as hearers we can only know the kinds of reasons that could be provided when we share a vocabulary with the speaker, or are able to establish a common vocabulary by means of translation. This is not possible in the case of novel articulations of the transcendent object. In such cases, the existing reservoir of reasons is insufficient; it is unable to supply the kinds of reasons necessary to support the claims to validity raised. This poses an at least temporary failure of intelligibility and also, of justification.

Although this may seem like a serious problem for critical social theory, I want to suggest that it is not. The difficulties involved in rationally assessing the validity claims raised by novel articulations of the transcendent object are evidence neither of a shortcoming of language in general nor of any specific sociocultural vocabulary. Rather, they are difficulties that may arise at any time and in any sociocultural context, indicating that the reservoir of reasons available to its inhabitants is in need of regeneration and renewal. From the point of view of critical social theory, this is surely a desirable state of affairs. A lack of such difficulties would indicate semantic stagnation—that the streams feeding into the sociocultural reservoir of reasons have dried up. Thus, it would be wrong to view the difficulties in question negatively, as a deficiency of language in general or of a particular sociocultural vocabulary; instead, we should view them positively, within the framework of a dynamic model that conceives of a sociocultural vocabulary as a reservoir of semantic contents that is ceaselessly in a process of enrichment and renewal.

It may be noted, furthermore, that the difficulties involved in rationally assessing the validity claims raised by novel articulations of the transcendent object point in the direction of a particular interpretation of autonomous agency. They suggest the need to interpret the idea of autonomy in ways that acknowledge the need for *receptivity* to the transcendent object. Nikolas Kompridis puts the point well: "Reconfiguring agency in terms of the demands of receptivity opens up a different perspective on transformative practice, making it possible to think of ourselves as facilitators, rather than heroic creators, of new disclosures and new beginnings."[87] As we have seen, the conception of autonomy outlined earlier in this chapter recognizes the importance of receptivity as well as activity by making strong evaluation—self-definition in reflective engagement with questions about the good for human beings— one of its core components.

Nonetheless, though the difficulties involved in rationally assessing the validity claims raised by articulations of the transcendent object can (and should) be given a positive interpretation, they also call for an attitude of suspicion. The disclosing function of representations of the good society means that we must, at times, treat their claims to validity with caution. In the case of novel articulations of the transcendent object, we must recognize that we have no means of distinguishing "words of power" from "propaganda" (Taylor) until the existing sociocultural vocabulary has been transformed in such a way that reasons in support of the claims they raise become available. How this happens depends on a host of contingent factors that, suddenly or gradually, in relatively complex or straightforward ways, on personal and on collective levels, produce the shifts in perception and cognition that render the articulations in question no longer novel, allowing hearers to know the "kinds of reasons" (Habermas) that could be adduced in support of the claims raised.

In this chapter and in the previous one I have attempted to find a way of thinking about context-transcending validity that would be in tune with the idea of situated rationality. The discussion has implications for the utopian dimension of critical social theory. To begin with, through showing that the transcendent object is always *re-presented* in particular imaginative projections, it calls into question modes of utopian thinking that claim to proceed purely formally or that advocate an abstract utopianism. Then, through showing that imaginative projections of the good society inevitably involve metaphysical closure, it raises a question concerning so-called *post*metaphysical approaches to critical social thinking. The discussion in the next chapter seeks to clarify these and related issues.

7

Re-Presenting Utopia

Utopian thinking projects vivid ethical pictures of a good society in which certain social conditions unfavorable to human flourishing would finally have been overcome.[1] Our discussion has suggested that the ideas of the good society guiding critical social thinking may be described as regulative ideas that have an imaginary, fictive character and re-present an idealized social condition. Evidently, therefore, they may also be described as utopian projections. However, critical social theory has an uneasy relationship with utopian thinking. Despite evident utopian elements in his own critical project, Karl Marx criticizes the "fantastic pictures of future society" painted by utopian socialists such as the Comte de Saint-Simon, Charles Fourier, and Robert Owen. Since their social criticism fails to take into account the economic conditions necessary for emancipation and does not adequately consider the actual state of the proletariat, it becomes a mere "fantastic scheme" in which personal inventiveness takes the place of historical action.[2] Here we find one common motif in the critique of utopian thinking: its distance from the actual historical process, leading to a lack of connection with the potentials for emancipation implicit within existing social reality. This motif recurs, for example, in the work of Herbert Marcuse, who rejects utopias as impossible projects, not realizable through the efforts of human beings.[3]

A critical social theory that fails to connect with the actual historical process stands accused of "bad utopianism." This problem arises when a particular critical social theory offers an emancipatory perspective that cannot be acted upon by those addressed by the theory—the theory is unable to stimulate the human subjects whose suffering or oppression it diagnoses to engage in action with a view to bringing about social change for the better. We can distinguish between two different types of bad utopianism; although in both cases the problem is one of motivation, the focus is different in each of the two cases. In the first case, the focus is on the poor quality of the theory's explanations: the theory stands accused of bad utopianism because it fails to identify the real causes of the social evils it describes. This is the kind of bad utopianism criticized by Marx. In the second case, the focus is on the inability of the theory's emancipatory projections to connect with the particular constellations of reasons shaping the identities of its addressees: the theory stands accused of bad utopianism because it fails to offer reasons that its addressees can find affectively and intellectually compelling. This is the kind of bad utopianism of which Horkheimer and Adorno stand accused as a result of their thesis, mentioned in chapter 3 above, that a repressive instrumental rationality has pervaded the consciousness of the inhabitants of the twentieth-century capitalist social order.[4]

In the next chapter I consider issues relating to the explanatory component of critical social theory. My discussion there proposes that an explanation of the causes of social evils is not a fruitful focus of enquiry for contemporary critical theories. If this is so, then the first type of bad utopianism, which points to the social critic's failure to explain the real causes of social evils, is not an issue for today's critical enterprise. In the present chapter I concentrate on the second type of bad utopianism, which arises when the theory fails to connect with the constellations of reasons shaping the subjectivities of those to whom it addresses its critical diagnoses and emancipatory projections.

Marx's ambivalence regarding utopian thinking is shared by Georges Sorel, though for different reasons. Again, despite the strong utopian impulse in his own social criticism, Sorel rejects utopian projections, unfavorably contrasting their "rationalist blueprints" for a good society with nonintellectual, imaginative constructions.[5] Here we find a second motif in the critique of utopian thinking: its denial of the finitude of human knowledge, the contingency of human life and history, and the creativity and freedom of human will. Critical social thinking that sees the good society as a condition attainable by human beings stands accused of "finalism," of an absolutist and ahistorical conception of human knowledge that gives rise to totalitarian models of social order. This motif can be found, for example, in the work of Isaiah Berlin, who denounces utopian schemes as morally repulsive visions of a closed world, praising Sorel for his "revolt against the rationalist ideal of frictionless contentment in a harmonious social system in which all ultimate questions are reduced to technical problems, soluble by appropriate techniques."[6]

Some contemporary critical social theorists attribute the problems of bad utopianism and finalism to forms of metaphysical thinking that are authoritarian and ahistorical and maintain that a postmetaphysical approach is necessary in order to avoid them. The theorists who hold this view seek to avoid bad utopianism by locating emancipatory potentials within existing historical reality that can be actualized by autonomously thinking and acting human beings. In contrast to the later Marx, for example, for whom emancipation is the result of the necessary dynamics of historical development, postmetaphysical approaches to critical social theory make the realization of these potentials contingent on the transformative social action of autonomous human agents. In addition, they seek to avoid finalism, and its accompanying risk of totalitarianism, by eschewing substantive ideas of the good society in favor of purely formal or purely abstract conceptions. By projecting their ideas of the good society formally, in terms of structural prerequisites rather than as fully fleshed-out pictures, they endeavor to keep open the process of history by taking account of the finitude of human knowledge, contingency of human life and history, and creativity and freedom of human will. Similar concerns motivate contemporary approaches that present their guiding ethical ideas in purely abstract terms. By conceiving of the universal (and related concepts such as the ethical, or justice) as a "non-place" (Butler) or an "empty place" (Laclau), they seek to maintain a utopian moment yet avoid the closure implicit in any representation of context-transcending validity.[7]

A concern to avoid problems of these kinds is evident in the conception of utopia that can be extracted from Habermas's theory of communicative action.[8] As we have seen in previous chapters, in his projected good society communicative rationality would flourish in the main domains of the "life-world." In the domain of sociocultural reproduction, cultural traditions would be passed on from generation to generation by way of public processes of rational deliberation. In the domains of moral, legal, and political validity, valid norms, principles, laws, and policies would be the outcome of public, open-ended, fair, and inclusive processes of intersubjective deliberation guided solely by the search for the single right answer. In the domain of personal identity formation, human beings would develop as autonomous agents for whom no aspect of their own subjectivity is in principle immune from rational criticism.[9] (Furthermore, the three domains governed by the norms of communicative rationality would maintain a harmonious relationship with the functionalist imperatives of the social system.)[10]

This conception of utopia is equipped with the features necessary in order to avoid bad utopianism and finalism. As we know Habermas claims that the idea of a communicatively rationalized social condition is already implicit within everyday linguistic practices.[11] Thus, it expresses an emancipatory potential that does not stand abstractly removed from history and the complexities of social reality but is already contained within existing social contexts. Furthermore, he emphasizes that communicative rationalization is not a process that can be taken for granted but is one that is contingent on the transformative action of autonomous human agents. Thus, his good society is seen not as the natural or inevitable result of the developmental dynamics of modern societies but as a possibility whose realization is dependent on the activity of autonomous agents in actual, historically specific, social orders. Finally, communicative rationality refers primarily to a procedure for dealing with validity claims and not to the content of these claims. Thus, his good society is defined formally; rather than describing the concrete shape of exemplary forms of life, it merely specifies the structural characteristics of possible ones.[12]

However, closer consideration shows that only the first and second features of Habermas's postmetaphysical idea of the good society are important if bad utopianism and finalism are to be avoided; the third feature, by contrast, is not essential for these purposes.

The first requirement, that the projected good society should express a potential already contained within existing social reality, recalls our discussion of the ethical component of the idea of situated rationality. In this respect, there is little difference between ethical authoritarianism and bad utopianism. Just as critical social theory must seek to avoid ethical authoritarianism by connecting with the particular constellations of affectively imbued reasons shaping the subjectivities of its addressees, it must seek to avoid bad utopianism by making the same kind of connection. Otherwise, it would be unable to motivate autonomous agents, in the sense of winning their affectively imbued, rational approval.

The second feature of Habermas's postmetaphysical conception of utopia, too, is clearly a key ingredient of any approach that seeks to avoid the accusation of finalism: this is its dependence on the activity of actual human agents. If utopian thinking is to avoid finalism, it must avoid teleological conceptions of the historical process. Instead, it must keep open the process of history by making emancipation a contingent matter, dependent on the perceptions, interpretations, and interventions of concrete, historically situated, autonomous agents who respond to specific experiences and exigencies.

The third feature is less straightforward, however: this is the formality of the proposed utopian conception. In emphasizing its formal character, Habermas is at one with several other contemporary critical social theorists. Formality is deemed a key requirement of the idea of the good life projected by Axel Honneth's theory of recognition, for example, and it is also a central feature of the theory of happiness proposed by Martin Seel.[13] For thinkers such as Habermas, Honneth, and Seel, critical social theories are supposed to identify only the formal characteristics of possible good societies, avoiding all substantive images.

Formal conceptions of the good society have at least two advantages. First, on the assumption that they are addressed to human agents with divergent life experiences and in different kinds of life situations, they are likely to appeal to a wider range of people than conceptions that specify the details of social organization and regulation. Second, by refusing to specify such details, they pay tribute to the openness of the historical process—to the need to revise social institutions, distributive mechanisms, and social practices in the light of new experiences, technological, ecological, and social developments, and insights that come about as the result of the exercise of human imagination. Consequently, formal conceptions of the good society seem more in tune with the idea of situated rationality.

At the same time, however, formality must be recognized as a matter of degree: there is no sharp dividing line between formal and substantive conceptions of the good society. Furthermore, even the most formal conceptions have to have some determinate content; otherwise, they would be unable to arouse the ethical imagination and would lack motivational and justificatory power. In fact, as we have seen, Habermas's utopian vision of a communicatively rationalized social condition is by no means indeterminate: it conjures a more or less concrete image of a society in which communication would be perfectly open, in which the outcomes of validity-oriented deliberation would be perfectly rational, in which there would be perfect mutual understanding, and in which subjects would have full access to their inner lives. Moreover, there does seem to be a connection between the determinacy of the image and the kind of metaphysical thinking that many contemporary critical social theorists find deeply uncongenial. As we saw in chapter 5, critics such as Albrecht Wellmer point out that ideas such as Habermas's idea of the ideal speech situation or, more generally, of a communicatively rationalized lifeworld, do not merely evoke a picture of a (more or less) specific social condition; they conjure a picture of a society that transcends the contingencies of human life and history and in which human finitude would have been overcome. In chapter 5 I described such idealizing projections as metaphysically closed: as projecting a condition of self-sufficiency and self-transparency that is impossible—not attainable by finite human beings. Wellmer, too, describes ideas of this kind as metaphysical.[14] However, whereas I, taking my lead from Laclau, maintain that such metaphysically closed projections are harmless, Wellmer, as we shall see, regards them as pernicious, arguing that they give rise to problems of meaning and motivation.

Utopian ideas such as the ideal speech situation are not just metaphysical in the sense of being beyond the constraints of human existence; in addition they are closely linked to the notion of redemption. By "redemption" I mean the making good of present (and possibly past)[15] deficiency: the idea of redemption refers to a condition in which all relevant obstacles to human flourishing would finally be removed. Clearly, therefore, it has an emancipatory dimension: in the projected condition of redemption, human beings would be released from present suffering. Equally, it has a connotation of perfection: the idea of redemption conjures a state of complete sufficiency, a condition in which all salient deficiencies would once and for all have been overcome. In short, the utopian dimension of critical social theory consists in its evocation of the society that would be best for human beings. Not best in the sense of being the most adequate to our present needs and interests (for our present perceptions of our needs and interests might be distorted) but best in the transcendent, absolute sense of "incapable of being bettered." We might also say that critical social theory is concerned to criticize forms of social imperfection and that criticism of imperfection presupposes a more or less determinate idea of perfection. Thus, Rousseau's criticisms of a society in which social relations are governed by *amour propre* project the idea of a social condition in which human beings would relate to each other and to their own subjectivities freely and virtuously, without the corrupting dependence on the opinions of others. Or again, Marx's criticisms of a society characterized by alienated labor conjure the idea of a social condition in which the essential powers of the individual would be genuinely self-confirming. In each case, criticism of socially produced deficiency evokes an idea of perfect sufficiency in terms of the perfect realization of human potentials.

It is easy to see why such idealizing, metaphysical projections are cause for concern. When the good society is presented as a condition of redemption and, as such, beyond the constraints of human existence, bad utopianism and finalism seem difficult to avoid. Bad utopianism seems inevitable because the good society is presented as a condition beyond history, unattainable by human effort, thus apparently denying the importance of transformative agency. Finalism seems inevitable because the projected condition is characterized by closure, thus apparently denying the creativity and freedom of human will, the finitude of human knowledge, and the contingency of human life and history.

It appears, therefore, that even formal conceptions of the good society have a metaphysical, redemptory aspect that awakens fears of bad utopianism and finalism. Even when they specify no more than the structural requirements of the good society, leaving decisions regarding its material substance to historically situated agents who must respond to specific experiences and exigencies, they evoke a condition of redemption, removed from the constraints of human existence, in which all relevant obstacles to human flourishing would once and for all have been overcome. This has led Wellmer to reject approaches to the question of context-transcending validity that rely on idealizing projections of any kind, proposing instead a pragmatic approach that dispenses entirely with regulative ideas. This pragmatic approach has two key components. The first component is its insistence on the context-transcending character of claims to validity.[16] The second component is its rejection of any sort of specification, whether formal or more substantive, of the content of the transcendent object to which such claims refer. In conceiving of the transcendent object purely abstractly, Wellmer's idea of truth can be compared to Laclau's conception of the universal as an empty place. As we shall see, it runs up against similar difficulties.

Like Habermas, Wellmer seeks to retain the context-transcending dimension of critical social thinking. Unlike Habermas, however, he rejects context-transcending approaches that rely on idealizing, metaphysical projections. Despite his initial enthusiastic reception of Habermas's linguistic reformulation of the utopian content of critical social theory,[17] he now distances himself from it, primarily on grounds of its reliance on the idea of the ideal speech situation. As indicated, his main reservations regarding ideas of this kind have to do with their metaphysical character.[18] He argues that, by projecting the idea of a social condition beyond the constraints of human life and human history, idealizing projections of the good society give rise to problems of motivation and of meaning.

The problem of motivation has been introduced in chapter 5. We will recall that, in Wellmer's view, regulative ideas such as the ideal speech situation require human beings to strive to attain a social condition whose realization would negate the conditions of finitude that make them human beings in the first place. It seems, therefore, that ideas of this kind can exert a regulative (and hence motivating) force only if knowledge of their paradoxical character is naively ignored or suppressed. The alternative seems to be a cynical detachment from or resignation toward such ideas and, consequently, the loss of their motivating power. In addition, Wellmer holds that there is a problem of meaning.[19] His point seems to be that ideas such as the ideal speech situation project the idea of a communicative community that negates the conditions that make communication necessary and possible: conditions such as inadequate information, interpersonal misunderstandings, linguistic infelicities, and lack of insight. As such they appeal to an idea of communication that is fundamentally alien to human beings.[20] But why does this give rise to a problem of meaning? Although Wellmer does not develop this part of his argument, it can be reconstructed on the basis of his view of pragmatic meaning as elaborated in other contexts.[21]

Wellmer's position, as I understand it, is that Habermas's idea of the ideal speech situation is fundamentally removed from the realm of human experience; therefore, no reasons in support of its claims to validity are available. This makes it strictly speaking unintelligible, for, as we saw in the last chapter, pragmatic meaning is a matter of using linguistic expressions in everyday dealings with others in society, embedding them in utterances to which validity claims are attached, and supporting these claims with reasons, if challenged. In other words, to understand an utterance—a pragmatically situated linguistic expression—is to know how to use it to reach understanding with others (*sich verständigen*) concerning the validity of the claims it raises; this means, in turn, knowing how to support these claims with reasons.[22]

For Wellmer, lack of intelligibility appears to be a problem primarily because it leads to a problem of motivation.[23] His position seems to be that ideas such as the ideal speech situation cannot serve as regulative ideas, and hence cannot exert a motivating power, because they cannot be understood; and they cannot be understood because we are unable to know when a speaker has good grounds to warrant that they are valid.

The discussions in the last chapters provide us with the means for reducing the force of Wellmer's objections regarding meaning and motivation. The crucial issue in each case is whether ideas of the good society raise claims that can be assessed intersubjectively as valid or invalid; I suggest that the difficulties Wellmer discerns on the levels of meaning and motivation arise only if we dispute that this is the case. Wellmer appears to hold the view that claims concerning the validity of ideas such as the ideal speech situation are not open to intersubjective evaluation; this may be due to an overly narrow view of the claims raised by ideas of this kind. Although he evidently recognizes the disclosing power of ideas of the good society, he does not acknowledge their claims to provide ethical orientation. But, as we have seen, it is only because they raise claims to provide ethical orientation, together with claims to disclose the ethical object powerfully, that ideas such as the ideal speech situation are open to critical interrogation in public processes of intersubjective deliberation. Wellmer's neglect of the orienting functions of metaphysical ideas may be due in part to his deep appreciation of the disclosing powers of works of art (especially music) and his agreement with Adorno's views concerning the ineffable aspect of aesthetic experience.[24] However, it may also be due to a failure to allow for regulative functions other than adjudication—to a failure to see that metaphysical ideas do not relinquish all of their regulative powers once they give up their role as arbiters of truth. Although Wellmer quite rightly challenges the view that ideas such as the ideal speech situation provide standards for adjudicating matters of validity, he pays too little attention to their capacity to provide ethical orientation, understood in a suitably historical, comparative, open-ended, and concrete manner. In the last chapter, I sketched a model of practical rationality that would be congruent with the antiauthoritarian impulses of contemporary critical social theory, yet allow for rationally backed judgments regarding the claims to validity raised by particular ideas of the good society. A model of this kind would significantly reduce the force of Wellmer's objections. If practical reasoning regarding the merits of the claims they raise is deemed possible in principle,[25] he could no longer object that ideas such as the ideal speech situation are unintelligible. Since what is at issue in such processes of practical reasoning is not the realizability of the projected idea of the good society but its merits from the point of view of disclosure and ethical orientation, he could no longer object that its metaphysical character impinges on its motivating power.

Wellmer's critique of the idea of the ideal speech situation has been influential, fueling suspicion that context-transcending approaches to social criticism cannot be sustained without violating the demands of situated rationality. This is one reason why it is important to show that his objections can be dispelled. For those who remain committed to a context-transcending approach, there is a further reason; this has to do with the difficulties arising from purely abstract conceptions of the transcendent objects to which claims to validity refer. In chapters 5 and 6 I argued that, in critical social thinking, the transcendent ethical object (the universal, the good society, and the like) is *re-presented* in particular imaginative projections. If the transcendent object were not mediated by way of "warmly-coloured" images of the good society (Sorel), the idea of ethically oriented, critical interrogation would make no sense. We might say: such interrogation would have no purchase; there would be no surface on which it could get a grip. The same point can be made from the perspective of motivation: without its embodiment in particular ideas of the good society, it would be difficult to account for the transcendent object's affectively imbued, rational power. Re-presentation of emptiness cannot serve these purposes: an entirely empty object could not serve as a source of illumination and orientation and could not motivate us rationally and affectively in our judgments and actions. Laclau runs up against these difficulties by insisting on the emptiness of the transcendent object; this prevents him from establishing an ethically significant link between it and its historical articulations. In dispensing with regulative ideas and, by extension, utopian projections of the good society, Wellmer encounters the same sort of problems.

Wellmer continues to insist on the context-transcending dimension of social criticism, regarding this as a crucial point of distinction between his approach and Rorty's radically contextualist one.[26] However, he claims that regulative ideas (and, by extension, utopian projections of the good society) are not necessary to establish the reference to truth, justice, and the like that is required for a context-transcending standpoint. In contrast to Rorty, who offers a deflationary account of truth, Wellmer seeks to defend a strong conception that not only takes account of the distinction between truth and justification but attaches central importance to it. He insists that the truth predicate plays an essential role in our practices of justification; indeed, that it is constitutive for our practices of making claims and justifying them.[27] In addition to playing an essential role on the level of the implicit knowledge that forms a backdrop for practices of justification,[28] it expresses a normative attitude toward propositions that is inherently context transcending. Clearly, this part of his argument is crucial for our present purposes. For, Rorty accepts that there is a semantic difference between truth and justification; indeed, he even acknowledges a pragmatic difference, recognizing that the term "truth," on occasion, serves a cautionary function. However, he vehemently disputes that the concept of truth expresses a context-transcending perspective that is an indispensable part of our socially critical and politically engaged practices. In contrast to Rorty, Wellmer seeks to defend a conception of truth with "normative substance"; in contrast to Habermas (and Apel)[29] he wants to do so in a way that avoids metaphysical projections such as those entailed by references to idealized standards of validity or to properties of objectively valid reasons.[30]

In his endeavor to elaborate a context-transcending conception of truth that avoids idealizing projections, Wellmer draws on Robert Brandom's explication of the difference between truth and justification. This relies on the thesis of a difference between the perspective of a speaker vis-à-vis her own reason giving and the perspective of that same speaker vis-à-vis another speaker's reason giving. It may be noted that Brandom accepts that his perspectival approach has to be able to accommodate a notion of context-transcending validity, acknowledging that a central challenge facing it is how to make sense of the emergence of an objective notion of the correctness or appropriateness of claims and the applications of concepts. The difficulty he sees is the ontological disparity between concepts and the objects they apply to: "For concepts are essentially perspectival, yet if they are to be objectively true or false of objects, these objects must be understood as nonperspectival in a strong sense."[31] On the other hand, there is "no bird's-eye view above the fray of competing claims from which those that deserve to prevail can be identified."[32] Brandom concludes, nonetheless, that it is possible to account for the ineliminable difference between truth and justification without an appeal to nonperspectival facts.[33] His solution is to reconstrue objectivity as consisting in a kind of perspectival form, rather than in a nonperspectival or cross-perspectival content.[34]

It is also noteworthy that Brandom acknowledges the representational dimension of concepts. In his view, concepts are ultimately answerable to the world for their correct application; they are answerable, that is, not to what you or I or all of us *take* to be the case but to what *is* the case.[35] Rorty regards this as a kind of flirtation with something like the "bird's-eye view above the fray of competing claims"[36] and thinks that Brandom—whose "heart is certainly in the right place"—should drop the notions of "answering" and "representing" completely.[37] He does not see that this would make Brandom's account of the perspectival difference between truth and justification seriously incomplete, indeed, that it would deflate this difference and render it insignificant. For, a speaker's perception that claims, though justified, may not be true, makes sense only if we attribute to her an orientation toward an idea of context-transcending validity. This may not be a problem for Rorty, who sidelines the concept of truth, relegating the use of the truth predicate to certain relatively unimportant formal-semantic and pragmatic functions. But Brandom, unlike Rorty, asserts the need for a reference to context-transcending validity as an indispensable element of our practices of reason giving. For this reason, he cannot lightly abandon his position that a perspectival approach to the question of truth requires the assumption of an objective world independent of human descriptions and interpretations.

Wellmer finds Brandom's thesis of a perspectival difference fruitful, interpreting it in the following way: whereas a speaker who regards her own claims as justified must also regard them as true, she may acknowledge the subjective justification of another speaker's view of his claims as true, without herself having to accept them as true.[38] Wellmer draws the further implication that, if a speaker holds something as reasoned truth—as true on the basis of good reasons—she also regards it as *meriting* agreement: truth is transsubjective. By this I take him to mean that a speaker who supports her convictions with arguments also seeks to reach an understanding with others concerning the validity of her convictions and presumes that their validity is not determined by the (individual or shared) subjective positions of the parties involved.[39] This fits well with Wellmer's insistence that what makes a reason a good reason is not determined by the outcome of an argumentation but rather manifests itself in the fact that it compels us to agree with it. As he puts it: "The concept of a 'good reason' is tied irreducibly to the perspective of the person who is compelled 'by good reasons.'"[40] To be sure, Wellmer leaves open the question of what makes a reason a good reason. In this regard, his substantive thesis is a negative one: he confines himself to the claim that it is not discursively reached agreement that makes a reason a good reason and does not say anything positive about what determines its quality.[41] Rather than specifying conditions for the soundness of reasons, he pursues an alternative strategy. Like Brandom, he shifts the focus of attention from content to disposition: he leaves aside the question of the content of "transsubjective" validity, concentrating instead on the attitudes (and feelings) of speakers who are concerned with it. Thus, instead of specifying the criteria that a sound reason must satisfy, he makes explicit the subjective assumptions underlying the behavior of reason givers, in particular, their attitudes toward their own reason giving and toward the reason giving of other speakers and their feelings of being compelled by a reason. He writes: "One cannot describe from a metaperspective which 'qualities' reasons must have in order to be *really* good reasons. To call reasons 'good' is not an ascription of an 'objective' quality, rather it is the adoption of an attitude with normative consequences."[42]

It is one thing to claim that no metaperspective—no bird's-eye view—is available from which the conditions of transsubjective validity could be specified once and for all. Such a metaperspective is clearly incompatible with the antiauthoritarian impulses of contemporary critical social theory. But it is another thing to claim that the speakers themselves dispense with the very idea of a transcendent object; were they to do so, it would be hard to make sense of the perspectival difference between truth and justification to which Brandom and Wellmer attach such significance. If the speakers themselves did not assume the existence of a transcendent object that is not reducible to any subjective or intersubjective standpoint, their perception that claims, though justified, may not be true would be inexplicable. Furthermore, from the point of view of the participants, the practice of argumentation, which according to Wellmer aims at transsubjective validity, would be pointless. For this reason, we must suppose that Wellmer agrees with Brandom regarding the need to posit an object that is not reducible to subjective perceptions. In other words, like Brandom, he must hold the view that the thesis of a perspectival difference between truth and justification implies a subjective orientation toward validity in a context-transcending sense. Presumably, this is what he has in mind when he refers to "transsubjective truth."

The difficulty, however, is that Wellmer stops short of telling us how his idea of transsubjective truth should be understood. As indicated, his argument proceeds negatively in this regard: he confines himself to an insistence that what makes a reason a good reason is *not* the fact that it is accepted as such (even if acceptance is won in a process of argumentation that satisfies the demanding requirements of Habermasian discourse). To be sure, it is hardly surprising that he refrains from specifying the positive conditions that reasons must meet if they are to be valid in a context-transcending sense—were he to do so, he would undermine his own clearly expressed position that no vantage point beyond history and context is available that would permit us to determine the content of truth.[43]

Nonetheless, Wellmer needs to provide a more differentiated account of how justified propositions stand in relation to truth. In its present form, his perspectival approach relegates all justified propositions to the same basket so far as their truth content is concerned. The only basis on which propositions may be distinguished is justifiability: whether or not they meet with approval from speakers in appropriate contexts of justification. But in Wellmer's conception justifiability tells us nothing positive about truth content, we know only that justifiability is not the same as truth. In the end, therefore, we seem to be left with a choice between authoritarianism, decisionism, or conventionalism: either some authority tells us whether propositions are valid, or we decide ourselves on contingent grounds, or we appeal to the procedures for determining validity, or to the standards of validity, that happen to be already socially established. Thus, by construing the idea of truth purely abstractly, Wellmer runs up against difficulties similar to those encountered by Laclau. Like Laclau, he runs up against problems on the level of justification, for he is unable to provide a satisfactory account of the distinction between justified and unjustified validity claims. Moreover, like Laclau he faces problems on the level of motivation, for he is unable to account for the feeling of being compelled by reasons, which he himself acknowledges as a component of the idea of truth. Finally, like Laclau he runs up against the problem of how to allow for cognitive learning processes, for his perspectival approach seems to posit a gap between truth and justification that is historically and contextually invariable.

Despite similar weaknesses in their accounts of the relation between the transcendent object and its particular articulations, Laclau's idea of hegemonic democracy does have one significant advantage over Wellmer's conception: its emphasis on the material—pictorial—character of representations. I have argued in previous chapters that it is their re-presenting, pictorial aspect that permits a critical interrogation of the kind I propose. If the transcendent object were not articulated in the form of more or less determinate representations of the good society, there would be no set of propositions, norms, and principles with which we could critically engage. Unlike Laclau, however, Wellmer is staunchly opposed to regulative ideas.[44] This makes him hostile to any attempt to articulate the concept of truth in the form of more or less concrete representations. Since he extends his argument regarding truth claims to claims to moral validity, it is likely that he would be equally hostile to attempts to articulate the good society in the form of more or less concrete representations; the good society, consequently, would have to be conceived purely abstractly: as Butler's "non-place" or as Laclau's "empty place." But, as we have seen, from the point of view of critical social theory, the consequences are troubling. Since an empty object cannot serve as a source of illumination and orientation, a theory guided by such an object would fail to impact ethically on the reason and affects of human agents. Rather than successfully escaping the problems that have plagued utopian thinking in critical social theory, therefore, Wellmer's proposal to dispense with idealizing projections would result in a critical social theory too abstract to engage the rational and affective capacities of the human beings to whom it is supposed to appeal and, in consequence, unable to stimulate them to engage in transformative social thinking or action. Ironically, therefore, his rejection of regulative ideas leads to bad utopianism.[45]

Wellmer could avoid bad utopianism by accepting an interpretation of regulative ideas as idealizing projections whose fictive status can openly be acknowledged and by adopting a model of practical rationality that allows for a critical evaluation of the claims raised by such ideas; this would require, in turn, a more differentiated view of the validity claims they raise, specifically, a recognition of their claim to provide ethical orientation. To make sense of their claim to provide ethical orientation (in a context-transcending sense of "ethical"), he would have to posit a transcendent, "transsubjective" object that is not entirely empty. This would, of course, have implications for his critique of the metaphysical aspect of ideas such as the ideal speech situation. Rather than regarding the metaphysical aspect of such ideas as a flaw that could be eradicated without cost to critical social theory, he would have to acknowledge it as an integral part of its critical enterprise.

I have argued that the problems of motivation and meaning that Wellmer connects with regulative ideas arise only on an impoverished understanding of the kind of claims to validity raised by such ideas, combined with the absence of a model of practical rationality appropriate for the purposes of assessing such claims. If Wellmer accepts the possibility of intersubjective evaluation of the claims to validity raised by regulative ideas, his worries about meaning and motivation become less pressing. For this reason, I argued that we should construe the validity claims raised by ideas of the good society as claims to provide better ethical orientation, and to disclose the ethical object more powerfully, than rival conceptions; I then made the case for a model of practical reasoning concerning such claims that is suitably historicist, comparative, open-ended, and concrete. By allowing for the critical interrogation of the claims to validity raised by regulative ideas in public processes of intersubjective deliberation that are open-ended, inclusive, and fair, we can significantly reduce the force of Wellmer's objections to validity-oriented thinking that is guided by regulative ideas. This also allows us to avoid the problem of bad utopianism, understood as the problem of rational motivation that arises when the critical diagnoses and emancipatory projections offered by a given critical social theory fail to connect with the constellations of reasons shaping the particular identities of its addressees.

It also helps to resolve the problem of finalism. The crux of this problem is closure, understood as a denial of the finitude of human knowledge, the contingencies of human life and history, and the creativity and freedom of human will. Closure in the finalist sense amounts to a curtailment of the process of history. However, interpreting regulative ideas in the way I propose enables critical social theory to avoid this kind of curtailment. Here, it may help to recall our earlier distinction between harmless metaphysical closure and pernicious ideological closure. In chapter 5 I argued that metaphysical closure does not necessarily lead to ideological closure, suggesting moreover that, in the case of regulative ideas, ideological closure can be avoided by making two key moves: a self-conscious acknowledgment of their fictive character, coupled with their connection to validity claims that are inherently open to contestation. Finalist closure, too, can be avoided by making these moves. By making the first move, we avoid the closure arising when utopian projections are interpreted as blueprints that can be implemented to bring about the projected good society. By making the second move, we avoid the closure arising when a particular idea of the good society is presented as unquestionably valid, irrespective of historical experience and the constraints and opportunities of specific sociocultural contexts.

It could be argued, however, that this addresses only one part of the problem of finalist closure. Even if it is accepted that representations of the good society are pictures rather than blueprints and that they raise claims to validity that are inherently open to interrogation, it could be objected that some representations of the good society evoke the idea of a social condition that is fundamentally at odds with the dynamic understanding of claims to validity advocated in the foregoing. This is the kind of objection that Laclau directs against Habermas's utopian idea of a communicatively rationalized lifeworld. As indicated in chapter 4, Laclau, like many poststructuralists, is hostile to Habermasian approaches to critical social theory. Whereas Butler's hostility seems to be directed primarily against Habermasian conceptions of rational agency, Laclau is suspicious of the normative ideal of reconciliation guiding Habermasian conceptions of deliberative democracy, claiming that such conceptions presuppose the "possibility of a final reconciliation, of . . . rational consensus, of a fully inclusive 'we.'"[46] As I see it, this criticism contains two separate objections. The first objection is that Habermasian models of practical reasoning project the idea of a good society in which the contestation of the validity of norms, principles, and so on would have come to an end. This objection is tied to Laclau's criticism of the "apodictic" reasoning he sees as characteristic of Habermas's conception of political deliberation. Laclau holds that apodictic reasoning, which implies that the indisputable validity of norms and principles can be demonstrated, should be replaced by "non-foundationalist" forms of argumentation; these are described as inherently pluralist and open-ended and as allowing us to reason about the verisimilitude (rather than truth) of the available political choices.[47] In my view, this objection is no longer applicable to Habermas's theory of argumentation in general; however, it continues to constitute a valid objection to his account of moral argumentation. I want to suggest, in consequence, that it calls upon Habermas to modify his account of moral reasoning in ways that would bring it into line with his account of argumentation in the domain of truth, and to develop his account of legal and political deliberation accordingly.

The second objection is that Habermasian conceptions of deliberative democracy are guided by ideals of harmony and reconciliation. I want to suggest that the valid intuition expressed by this objection is accommodated if we deal with the first objection. Apart from that, the second objection is not sustainable, for it implies an understanding of democratic activity that is out of step with the context-transcending aspect of Laclau's own account of hegemonic struggles.

The first objection is that Habermasian models of practical reasoning imply that truth—the universal, the ethical, justice, and the like—is attainable and can be shown to have been attained. If I understand Laclau correctly, he sees an intimate connection between the thesis of the attainability and demonstrability of truth and the content of the idea of the good society projected by Habermasian kinds of critical social thinking. Let us recall, once again, our discussion in chapter 5 in which I argued that representations of the good society have a metaphysically closed character that is unavoidable but harmless. The important point for our present purposes is that representations of the good society, although they all share this metaphysically closed character, are different in other respects. In particular, they differ regarding the normative content of the idealized social condition they evoke. Thus, Honneth's idea of a good society in which there would be full recognition of all three dimensions of the ethical personality is evidently different from Habermas's idea of a communicatively rationalized lifeworld that would exist in a relation of harmony with the functionalist demands of the economic and administrative systems; Laclau's idea of a social condition of ceaseless conflict and permanent suspicion, in which there would be never-ending contestation of claims to hegemony, evidently differs from both of these.

As I see it, Laclau's objection is directed against the *content* of the idea of the good society evoked by Habermasian models of practical deliberation, not against the harmless metaphysical closure it shares with all ideas of the good society, including his own. His objection to its content is direted, at least in part, against its static quality. He contends that Habermasian models of practical deliberation project the idea of a social condition in which there would be no further contestation of the validity of propositions, norms, or principles once their validity had been established in a deliberative procedure. Laclau appears to find the projected idea of the good society unacceptable on account of its closed quality. From his point of view we might say that Habermas construes human flourishing too statically: he sees conflict, suspicion, and contestation as obstacles to human flourishing.

Such an objection has some force. A more dynamic idea of the good society, and a correspondingly dynamic idea of human flourishing, would fit better with the dynamic model of practical reasoning I have advocated in the foregoing. It is important to see, however, that the projected, static picture of the good society is the direct result of Habermas's view of moral validity as a consensus concerning the universalizability of a given norm or principle that is reached in a procedure of argumentation that satisfies certain demanding conditions. This view of moral validity is apodictic in the sense that it conceives of moral truth as an object that can be attained by way of moral reasoning in discourse and that can be used as a standard for adjudicating moral disputes. The idea of the good society corresponding to this view of moral validity is one of a social condition in which the prevailing moral norms and principles would result from a public procedure of intersubjective deliberation that is perfectly open, inclusive and fair; in consequence, they would be genuinely universalizable—equally in the interests of all concerned. In the projected social condition, neither the universalizability of the prevailing norms and principles nor the idea that moral validity is a matter of universalizable interests would be open to dispute. This, presumably, is the kind of static picture of the good society to which Laclau and other poststructuralist thinkers object. It can be rendered more dynamic, however, by introducing an ineliminable gap between the transcendent object—in this case, moral validity—and its particular articulations—in this case, the idea of discursively achieved, universalizable interests. This, as we saw, is Laclau's approach to the question of context-transcendent validity. But, as we also saw, Habermas himself follows this path in the case of nonmoral truth, where he allows for a "recalcitrant reality" that always exceeds our descriptions and interpretations. It is this gap that allows for the inherently context-transcending dimension of validity-oriented deliberation, by allowing us to construe even well-justified—verisimilar—propositions as open to public interrogation. In consequence, it allows for a projected idea of the good society in which validity claims would be the subject of permanent public contestation. This implies that Habermas could avoid the objection that the idea of the good society projected by his theory is too static by revising his account of moral validity along the lines of his revised account of truth. This would entail introducing an ineliminable gap between the transcendent moral object and its particular articulations.

A good illustration of the kind of revision that is called for here can be found in Seyla Benhabib's proposal for a communicative utopia in which the accent shifts from consensus to conversation. Like Wellmer, Benhabib fundamentally supports Habermas's communicative reformulation of critical social theory, while at the same time expressing certain reservations. In her book, *Critique, Norm, and Utopia*, she applauds Habermas's endeavor to rescue critical social theory from the theoretical impasse into which Horkheimer and Adorno led it with their *Dialectic of Enlightenment*.[48] To begin with, she praises his achievement in restoring equilibrium between the explanatory and the utopian dimensions of critical social theory.[49] She sees it as one of the great merits of Habermas's theory that it succeeds in mediating these two dimensions: its diagnosis of the pathologies of the present is undertaken in the light of an anticipated future that expresses a potential for emancipation and rationality already implicit in the present.[50]

In addition to praising his theory's integration of explanatory and utopian questions, Benhabib endorses Habermas's communicative vision, regarding it as a more persuasive interpretation of the good society than Adorno's utopian idea of reconciliation between human beings and nature.[51] At the same time, Benhabib seeks to remedy certain weaknesses in this communicative vision.[52] Most relevant for our present purposes is her attempt to explicate more fully the utopian potential of the idea of universalizability that constitutes the heart of Habermas's discourse ethics.[53] As we have seen, discourse ethics defines moral validity (justice) as discursively reached agreement as to the generalizability of norms or principles; since in the moral realm discursively reached agreement means actual agreement among all those affected by the norm or

principle in question, participants in discourse are required to bracket all
particular needs and interests, for otherwise agreement would be impossible;
thus, on the standard reading of Habermas's conception, moral discourses
operate at a high level of abstraction.[54] However, Benhabib identifies a
strand in Habermas's theory of justice that would require need interpretations
to be thematized in moral discourses.[55] She argues, furthermore, that since
needs are always formed within cultural traditions, discursive thematization
of need interpretations would bring about a loosening of the "sedimented
and frozen images of happiness in the light of which we formulate needs
and motives."[56] When this happens, inner nature is moved into a utopian
perspective in the sense that our needs and affects become communicatively
accessible.[57]

Benhabib argues that Habermas suppresses this utopian perspective by
failing consistently to make need interpretations the subject matter of discourses on justice. Although on occasion he speaks of rendering inner nature
fluid and transparent in processes of discursive argumentation—even describing this as a utopian perspective[58]—on the whole he appears to relegate such
reflection on inner nature to aesthetic-expressive discourses; these are concerned not with universalizable matters of justice but with nonuniversalizable
and culturally specific questions.[59] By contrast, Benhabib insists on the relevance of need interpretations in the moral realm, maintaining that it is precisely their cultural specificity and relation to concrete individuals that makes
them properly the subject matter of discourses about justice.

Benhabib envisages moral deliberations in which the interpretation of concrete needs would go hand in hand with deliberation on general issues such
as human rights and the validity of moral norms and principles. In her conception of the good society, two complementary perspectives would be brought
to bear in matters of justice: recognition of the human dignity of the "generalized other" and acknowledgment of the specificity of the "concrete other."[60]
Whereas the standpoint of the generalized other requires us to view each and
every individual as a rational being entitled to the same rights and duties we
would want to ascribe to ourselves, the standpoint of the concrete other
requires us to view each and every rational being as an individual with a concrete history, identity, and affective-emotional constitution. Benhabib insists
that both perspectives are equally important in deliberations on justice. Evidently, therefore, the interpretation of needs she envisages is not simply a
matter of evaluating culturally specific needs from the point of view of their
universalizability, for this would privilege the standpoint of the generalized

other. Nor may the discursive interpretation of needs disregard considerations of universalizability, for to do so would be to privilege the standpoint of the concrete other.

Since in modern pluralist and multicultural societies the perspectives of the concrete and the generalized other are likely to produce conflicting demands, this raises the question of how these can be reconciled. Integrating the two perspectives seems to call for a third perspective that would determine which specific needs deserve to be considered from the point of view of universalizability and which universalizable norms and principles should be rejected as unjust due to their neglect of cultural specificity. The danger, of course, is that this third perspective would be a bird's-eye view or, as Benhabib puts it, an "Archimedean center from which the moral philosopher pretends to be able to move the world."[61] Benhabib holds that Habermas's discourse ethics succumbs to this danger when it makes an idealized consensus the arbiter of disputes in matters of moral validity. By doing so, discourse ethics does not merely project the idea of a third perspective from which the correct balance between generalizable and particular interests would be visible; it presupposes the possibility of attaining such a perspective and of implementing it in deliberations in order to legislate as to the correctness of their outcome. Against this kind of "legislative universalism," Benhabib proposes an "interactive" version, which construes moral deliberations as conversations in which the willingness to reason from the other's point of view is paramount.[62] Although in Benhabib's moral conversations, as in Habermas's moral discourses, participants are guided by the idea of "the general interest," in contrast to Habermas's conception this idea is not the object of a substantive consensus but a regulative idea.[63]

In the terms of our discussion in the foregoing, we could say that, in Benhabib's account, the idea of the general interest re-presents the third perspective, which reconciles the requirements of universalizability and particularity.[64] With this she opens the gap between the transcendent object and its historical articulations that I have argued is vital for the context-transcending dimension of critical social theory. The result is a picture of the good society that gives a more prominent place to conflict and division than Habermas's conception. For, in the projected good society, moral norms and principles would be the subject of permanent critical interrogation that assesses their claims to validity, whereby these processes of assessment would involve critical interrogation of the idea that moral validity is a matter of reconciling universalizability and particularity.

To be sure, Benhabib's model of interactive universalism is underdeveloped. Its main limitation is that it fails to clarify what is meant by a "regulative idea." The context-transcending aspect of such ideas—their orientation toward a transcendent object that always exceeds particular representations of it—is not discussed. This context-transcending aspect is noticeably absent from her account of moral conversations, resulting in a lack of clarity regarding their cognitive aspect: it is unclear why certain outcomes should be regarded as better than others, in a context-transcending, cognitive sense.[65] If Benhabib gives up the context-transcending aspect of moral argumentation, her conception is open to the accusation of radical contextualism and the various problems associated with it. To avoid this accusation, therefore, she must acknowledge that her account of practical deliberation relies on a reference to a transcendent object that is articulated by particular regulative ideas (for example, the idea of the general interest) in constitutively inadequate ways. This would also require her to reconsider the appropriateness of the term "postmetaphysical" to describe her approach to validity.[66] Subject to clarification along these lines, Benhabib's account of moral reasoning is helpful; it illustrates well that giving up a legislative view of moral validity allows for a picture of a communicative utopia that is vibrant and dynamic, characterized not by harmony and reconciliation but the ongoing contestation of validity claims.

Interestingly, Habermas has himself made a partial move in the direction indicated by Benhabib. There is some evidence in *Between Facts and Norms* that he has responded to the interventions of Benhabib and other sympathetic critics concerning the role of consensus in his theory.[67] In this book Habermas gives an account of public deliberation in the domains of law and politics in which the emphasis is on process rather than outcome. In addition, he seems to have given up the "legislative" view of validity to which Benhabib objects: he seems prepared to accept that the ideal speech situation does not have the status of an ideal rooted in the universal presuppositions of argumentation that could be realized approximately;[68] moreover, that it is not possible to identify deviations from the ideal. Criticizing what he calls "essentialist misunderstandings" of the idea of the ideal speech situation, he refers to it as a "projection" and as a "thought experiment"—indeed, as a "methodological fiction"—that helps to make us aware of the scarcity of the resources on which the processes of deliberative opinion and will formation depend.[69] Similarly, in another essay written around the same time, he refers to the idealizing presuppositions of discourse as a "regulative idea";[70] in an interview given in the late 1980s, too, he emphasizes the regulative (as opposed to legislative) functions of the idea of the ideal speech situation, albeit warning against an overly hasty assimilation of his conception with Kant's notion of a regulative idea.[71]

There are a number of indications, therefore, that in the case of legal-political validity Habermas has given up the position that the idea of a consensus reached under conditions of the ideal speech situation could be applied as a standard for settling disputes of a normative kind. However, like Benhabib's conception of moral conversation, Habermas's conception of legal-political discourses requires further elaboration. In particular, like Benhabib's, his conception suffers from a lack of clarity regarding its cognitive dimension. To be sure, unlike Benhabib, Habermas makes clear that public deliberations in the areas of law and politics are guided by a concern for the right answer, distinguishing this right answer both from the answer that wins due to the exercise of power and from the compromise that results from fair bargaining processes.[72] In the same vein he attributes to the discourse principle "the *cognitive sense* of filtering reasons and information, topics and contributions, in such a way that the outcome of a discourse enjoys a presumption of rational acceptability. . . ."[73] Further evidence of his concern to maintain a connection between public deliberation and validity in a context-transcending sense is the claim that majority rule bears an internal relation to the search for truth.[74] However, he fails to elucidate how the context-transcending, cognitive moment of legal-political validity is to be understood. As we have seen, he makes sense of the context-transcending aspect of truth claims through reference to the idea of a recalcitrant reality; in order to make sense of the context-transcending aspect of legal-political claims, he needs to posit some equivalent transcendent object. In addition, of course, he needs to show that there is no conflict between positing a transcendent object and his commitment to a postmetaphysical approach to critical social theory.

It is not at all clear, however, that Habermas is prepared to allow for a transcendent legal-political object that functions as the equivalent of the recalcitrant reality posited in his account of truth. I have suggested that the account of legal-political validity that he offers in *Between Facts and Norms* pushes him in this direction. In addition, I have drawn attention to some important concessions that he has made concerning the status of the idea of the ideal speech situation. However, Habermas has not so far made the crucial move that would be required: he has not conceded that the idea of the ideal speech situation, qua regulative idea, merely *re-presents* a transcendent object to which it is constitutively inadequate. It is surely significant, moreover, that he explicitly refuses to make this move in the case of claims to moral validity. Although, as we know, Habermas has given up the view that truth can be defined as the outcome of an idealized procedure of discourse, he continues to defend the need for a constructivist account of moral validity.[75]

Habermas's reluctance to give up the position that a consensus reached under idealized conditions defines moral validity appears to stem from a worry about the dangers of "ontologizing interests": his apprehension that a nonconstructivist position would require us to assume the existence of a realm of generalizable interests that could be discovered by a disinterested observer. Habermas objects that appeal to an ahistorical—transcendent—idea of a realm of generalizable interests is no longer possible since, under the conditions of a secularized modernity, interests have to be conceived of as subject specific and as emerging only in concrete situations.[76] This is why he insists that generalizable interests have to be constructed by way of the exchange of arguments in moral discourse. It is important to see, however, that Habermas can give up his constructivist view of moral validity, yet retain his view that moral validity is context transcending, without ontologizing interests. The crucial point to recognize is that the idea of a realm of generalizable interests is merely a particular representation of moral validity: it is not moral validity itself. At first glance it may look as though positing a realm of generalizable interests in the moral realm is the counterpart to positing a recalcitrant reality in the realm of truth.[77] In chapter 5, however, we interpreted the recalcitrant reality that must be posited in order to make sense of the claim to truth of empirical propositions as an "impossible object"—as a transcendent object that always exceeds its particular representations; Habermas's idea of the ideal speech situation is, I proposed, one such representation. Correspondingly, the idea of a realm of generalizable interests should be seen, not as the transcendent moral object itself, but as a particular, constitutively inadequate, representation of it. In other words: the idea of generalizable interests should be understood as merely a particular articulation—re-presentation—of the idea of moral truth. As a representation of truth it serves functions of disclosure and orientation; accordingly, it may be described as a regulative idea. Regulative ideas, I suggested, have an imaginary, fictive character. Thus, the idea of a realm of generalizable interests is an imaginative projection: it does not imply that this realm is attainable by human beings. For this reason, Habermas does not commit himself to the position that access to a realm of generalizable interests is possible if he gives up his constructivist view of moral validity, yet continues to maintain a context-transcending position. To be sure, giving up his constructivist view would require him to acknowledge the contestable character of his view that moral validity is a matter of generalizing interests.[78]

In sum, the idea of a realm of generalizable interests, like the idea of the ideal speech situation, is cause for concern only when understood as the transcendent object itself, as opposed to a particular representation of it. If, following my suggestion, it is interpreted as a regulative idea, and if this in turn is interpreted as a fiction with disclosing and orienting functions, the idea of a realm of generalizable interests allows us to make sense of the context-transcending aspect of moral deliberation without either ontologizing interests or succumbing to a legislative universalism in which an idealized agreement serves as a criterion for adjudicating moral disputes.

If we adopt the understanding of regulative ideas that I have proposed, therefore, there seems to be no good reason for Habermas's reluctance to revise his account of moral validity along the lines of his revised account of truth, and to elaborate his account of legal-political validity along the same lines. The advantage of doing so, as we have seen, is that it would allow for an idea of the good society that is more vibrant and dynamic than the static picture currently projected by his account of moral deliberation, enabling him to avoid the accusation, leveled against him by Laclau and other poststructuralist thinkers, that his communicative utopia is harmonistic and reconciliatory. Revising his moral theory along the proposed lines would have a further advantage: it would enable him to avoid the position that the realm of morality is produced in moral discourse, which leads to the counterintuitive position that moral insight is acquired only through the discursive exchange of arguments. Since, as we have seen, the hostility of poststructuralists to Habermasian conceptions of democracy is based in part on a perceived tendency to overinflate the importance of argumentation in bringing about cognitive and social transformation, this, too, might help to reduce their antipathy. As it stands, Habermas's account of moral validity is open to this objection.

On Habermas's constructivist account of moral validity, only those shifts in perception that take place in moral argumentation are morally salient. This is because moral reality—the moral world—is made by us: the realm of morality is itself generated in discourse.[79] As he puts it: in the case of moral validity, the very domain of validity has to be *produced*.[80] If, as he implies, moral reality has no independence of argumentation, it follows that the acquisition of moral insight is possible only in argumentation. For Habermas, as we know, moral insight is insight into the generalizability of interests. A given person can come

to see that her interests are not, as she had previously thought, truly generalizable only by way of the intersubjective exchange of reasons. Habermas cannot
lightly give up this position: were he to do so, conceding that moral insight can
be acquired in nonargumentative ways, he would be obliged to concede that
morality is not purely constructed and, consequently, to relinquish his constructivist conception of moral validity.

However, as Albrecht Wellmer observes with regard to revisions in collective
moral matrices, these "do not as a rule take place only in the medium of
argumentation, but under the *pressure* of a struggle for recognition and under
the *influence* of new experiences."[81] His point might also be applied to shifts in
individual moral perception: these, too, generally occur as a result of new
experiences prompted by encounters with different cultures and different
species, or arising out of new life situations, or as a result of ecological and
technological developments.

To conclude, by bringing his account of moral validity into line with his
theory of truth, Habermas's critical social theory would not only project an
idea of the good society whose dynamic content would fit well with the antiauthoritarian model of critical social thinking I have advocated in the foregoing and would, moreover, be more acceptable to poststructuralist social critics;
in addition, it would be able to offer a more plausible account of how moral
insight is generated and a correspondingly richer account of cognitive and
social transformation.

It is important to note, however, that even the revised model of moral deliberation does not dispense with ideas such as harmony and reconciliation. The
second objection I identified in Laclau's criticism of Habermasian conceptions
of deliberative democracy is directed against the view that reconciliation is the
inherent telos of democratic activity. By contrast, Laclau makes a plea for a
notion of democratic activity that is characterized by permanent conflict and
contestation. However, it is one thing to envision a good society in which there
would be permanent contestation of validity claims; it is another thing to
suggest that democratic political struggles are not oriented by a desire for
harmony and reconciliation. If they were not, it would be hard to make sense
of Laclau's conception of political representations as incarnations of an impossible transcendent object that are characterized by self-sufficiency and self-
transparency (it is for this reason that they may be described as "metaphysically
closed"). On this conception, the ethical ideas orienting political struggles
project the idea of a condition of perfection, a state in which the salient

obstacles to human flourishing would have been overcome. To be sure, this condition of perfection can be represented dynamically as a condition in which there is permanent contestation of validity claims, as opposed to the more static condition projected by Habermas's idea of moral deliberation; nonetheless, as a metaphysically closed representation of a transcendent object, it, too, has harmonistic connotations. Thus, not only is Laclau's emphasis on social conflict and division readily compatible with the view that social struggles are guided by ideas of harmony or reconciliation; his account of political representation commits him to such a view.

In this chapter, I have explored the implications of my reflections on context-transcending validity for the utopian dimension of critical social theory. My reflections imply, first, that utopia is *re-presented* in the form of particular pictures of the good society; these pictures, whose imaginary, fictive status must be acknowledged, have a propositional content that can be articulated in the form of validity claims that are open to intersubjective assessment. Such representations contrast with the purely abstract relation to the transcendent object advocated by Wellmer. The abstract utopian thinking that would result from Wellmer's approach to context-transcending validity gives rise to bad utopianism for, by failing to allow for the rational assessment of the claims to validity raised by utopian projections, it fails to allow for their resonance with the constellations of reasons shaping the subjectivities of those addressed; as a result it leads to a problem of rational motivation. My reflections imply, second, that utopian thinking is always characterized by metaphysical closure; however, this should be seen, not as a flaw to be eradicated, but as an integral part of thinking about the good society.

I suggested, in addition, that the advocated approach to context-transcending validity enables us to deal with certain problems that have plagued the utopian dimension of critical social theory. By connecting representations of the good society with validity claims that are open to intersubjective assessment, we grant them an affectively imbued, rationally motivating power. This enables us to avoid the problem of bad utopianism, understood as a problem of rational motivation. By conceiving of representations of the good society as pictures rather than blueprints, and by acknowledging their inherent contestability and revisability, we can avoid the problem of finalism, for by conceiving of them in this way, we allow for the finitude of human knowledge, make room for the contingencies of human life and history, and accommodate the creativity of human free will. Lastly, by espousing models of practical rationality in which validity is construed as inherently context transcending, we favor representations of the good society in which there is permanent contestation, rearticulation, and reenactment of normative ideas; this enables critical social theory to avoid the "morally repulsive visions of a closed world" that led Isaiah Berlin to denounce utopian thinking and that give grounds for poststructuralist suspicion of Habermasian conceptions.

8

Theory and Praxis

In this book my principal aims have been to argue that ideas of context-transcending validity are necessary for the purposes of critical social thinking and democratic politics and to demonstrate that they are not incompatible with the claims of situated rationality. Against critics such as Rorty, I have argued that a reference to context-transcending validity is required for the purposes of cross-cultural and transhistorical criticism; I then endeavored to show that context-transcending validity and situated rationality are not fundamentally incongruent but can exist in a relationship of productive tension.

In order to maintain this relationship of productive tension I have recommended a two-step justificatory strategy. The first step entails social criticism on a context-immanent level; here, the theorist exposes the discrepancies between certain deep-seated, normative intuitions and expectations and the possibilities for realizing them that are available within a particular sociocultural context. The second step entails social criticism on a context-transcending level; here, the theorist claims that the deep-seated, normative intuitions and expectations she identifies are the result of historical learning processes and constitute ethical progress in a context-transcending sense.

For the purposes of this second step I propose a conception of context-transcending validity as a transcendent object that is articulated in the form of regulative ideas; these ideas are imaginative projections whose fictive character can openly be acknowledged without compromising their functions of ethical disclosure and orientation. In critical social thinking, regulative ideas take the form of particular representations of the good society or, in Laclau's terminology, "political representations." These representations of the good society give a point to the theorist's critical interrogation of social reality.

Moreover, by virtue of their material, pictorial aspect they have a semantic content that can be articulated in the form of claims to validity and, accordingly, subjected to rational interrogation. This means that ideas of the good society can be accepted or rejected on the basis of good reasons and can exert a rationally motivating power.

Furthermore, I have argued that, if critical interrogation is to operate in ways congruent with the antiauthoritarian impulses of contemporary critical social theory, it must be tied to public processes of open-ended, inclusive, and fair argumentation; moreover, that such argumentation should, in addition, be construed as operating in a historicist, comparative, and concrete manner and that its interlocking affective and intellectual components should be recognized.

Our discussion has centered on questions of normative validity. This could be seen as symptomatic of a fixation on problems of philosophical justification that distracts from the proper concerns of critical social theory. A view of this kind was articulated some time ago by Nancy Fraser.[1] For Fraser, the qualities that distinguish a critical from an uncritical theory of society are more political than philosophical: the strength of a critical theory resides more in its power to illuminate the struggles and wishes of the age than in the soundness of its philosophical justifications. Her inspiration here is the 1843 definition of critical philosophy offered by Karl Marx as the "self-understanding . . . by our age of its struggles and wishes."[2] Indeed, this definition of critical social theory does seem to call less for convincing philosophical justifications than for enlightening explanations of the causes of social oppression.[3] If we add to this Marx's famous remark in his eleventh thesis on Ludwig Feuerbach: "the philosophers have only interpreted the world, in various ways; the point is to change it,"[4] the resulting picture of the tasks of a critical social theory looks, at first glance, quite different from the picture presented in the foregoing. Whereas in the picture I have painted, the figures in the foreground are "nonauthoritarian justification" and "affectively imbued, rational motivation," these are replaced in Marx's picture by "enlightening explanation," and "transformative social action."

An overemphasis on questions of normative validity seems to threaten the connection between critical social theory and praxis. By "praxis" I mean intentionally guided, rationally based human activity aimed at changing the social order for the better. Transformative social activity of this kind, which aims at remedying social evils, seems to presuppose an explanation of their causes as well as explanations of the ways in which they are disseminated and perpetuated. It appears, therefore, that in order to secure its connection with praxis, critical social theory requires less a model of normative justification than an appropriate explanatory model. Since critical social theories that lose their connection with praxis are open to the accusation of ethical authoritarianism, this kind of objection must be taken seriously.

We have seen in chapter 3 that, by disconnecting theory from praxis, *Dialectic of Enlightenment* ends up offering a critical perspective that is ethically authoritarian. Due to their thesis that a repressive instrumental rationality has pervaded every part of the social order including the consciousness of its inhabitants, Horkheimer and Adorno are unable to appeal to the intuitions and expectations already contained within existing social reality for rational support for their views. At most they can point to a latent emancipatory interest: to something like the "somatic moment" of resistance to which Adorno subsequently refers in *Negative Dialectics*.[5] One result of this is a loss of motivating power: the critical diagnosis offered by Horkheimer and Adorno cannot be acted upon intentionally by anyone who hears it. This opens their theory to the charge of ethical authoritarianism, for it calls for a kind of social change whose necessity cannot be endorsed on the basis of good reasons by those whose lives it is supposed to improve and that cannot be brought about by way of their intentionally guided activity. As we saw in chapter 3, the thesis of the all-pervasiveness of instrumental rationality opens their theory, in addition, to the charge of epistemological authoritarianism, for it restricts the possibility of valid knowledge to the epistemically privileged social critic and denies the contestability of his critical diagnosis, and corresponding emancipatory projection of a good society, in public processes of interrogation.

In view of the antiauthoritarian self-understanding of contemporary critical social theory it is noteworthy that a version of Horkheimer and Adorno's thesis has made a reappearance in the current debates on globalization. In their book *Empire*, already mentioned in chapter 4, Michael Hardt and Antonio Negri offer a critique of globalizing capitalism that is strikingly similar to *Dialectic of Enlightenment*'s critique of a totalizing instrumental rationality. Both books make use of the concept of immanence to describe the governing principle of the capitalist orders of their times, and both advance the thesis that repressive power now extends deep into the consciousness of the inhabitants of these orders. Both books offer persuasive descriptions and penetrating analyses of what is wrong with these orders. And, both books share the same ultimate weakness: by disconnecting the possibility of social change for the better from the intentionally guided, rationally backed activity of human beings, they stand accused of ethical authoritarianism.

In *Dialectic of Enlightenment* "enlightenment" is characterized by the principle of immanence: the explanation of every event as repetition.[6] Horkheimer and Adorno maintain that "enlightenment proclaims the arid wisdom that holds that there is nothing new under the sun"; enlightenment is totalitarian since, for it, "the process is always decided from the start."[7] In *Empire*, Hardt and Negri make similar claims for contemporary processes of globalizing capitalism. The concept of "Empire" refers to the new kind of imperial global order emerging from these processes. The authors describe the passage from modernity to the new imperial global order in terms of the realization of the principle of immanence, understood as the idea that there is no "outside"; Empire is the fullest articulation to date of this principle.[8] Empire signifies the breaking down of all boundaries, spatial and temporal. Its rule operates by way of global flows and exchanges and its power is distributed in networks. The surface of imperial sovereignty is smooth, there is no place of power; power is both everywhere and nowhere.[9] The social institutions of Empire are fluid processes in which subjectivities are generated and "corrupted." In short, Empire operates on "the plane of immanence."[10]

Hardt and Negri see a deep affinity between imperial globalization and capitalism. It is not just that capitalism thrives on the smooth surfaces of imperial rule and profits from the overcoming of national and other boundaries: imperial globalization and capitalism are conceptually connected. The authors maintain that the principle of immanence is intrinsic to the very concept of capital.[11] The capitalist market has always run counter to any division between inside and outside:[12] the tendency to create an imperial world market is directly given in the concept of capital itself.[13] This is why the new imperial global order does not merely provide a congenial context for the expansion of capitalism, it is the logical product of capitalism's internal dynamics. The conceptual connection between imperial globalization and capitalism means, in their view, that emancipation requires fundamental, revolutionary change in the economic structure itself:[14] any attempt to construct a "Counter-Empire" and find new ways of living in the world requires more than political regulation of the excesses of capitalism, it requires capitalism's overcoming. It is important to note that the kind of revolutionary change they envisage will not be the result of intentional human agency but an explosion—or, rather, implosion—resulting from the contradictions between the inherent productive energies of human beings ("the multitude") and the expropriation of these energies through the dynamics of the laws of capitalism.[15]

For our present purposes, the most interesting aspect of Hardt and Negri's analysis is that it leads them to sever the connection between critical social theory and praxis. They do so on the basis of two kinds of arguments: a social-theoretical one and an ethical one.

Hardt and Negri's thesis that revolutionary change is not dependent on intentionally guided, transformative social action derives much of its force from their view of the ways in which the negative effects of globalizing capitalism are disseminated and perpetuated. In their account of Empire, the exercise of social control is completely immanent: social control is internalized and distributed by way of the brains and bodies of citizens. Moreover, it flows in circuits and networks of relations of domination.[16] These relations of domination shape the production of subjectivities and their ways of being in the world. Since oppression is immanent to the very production of subjectivities, emancipatory social transformation requires changes in the regimes and practices of production.[17] But such change is impossible without revolutionary change: that is, nonintentionally guided change, in which capitalism collapses due to its own internal contradictions. The immanence of power dissemination and perpetuation means that political change will be insufficient: even a radical democratization of the market—for instance, one that encompasses redistribution of wealth, reorganizing of work practices, and redressing of imbalances in social status—will fail to remedy its dominating effects. So long as social domination is stamped on the brains and bodies of subjectivities and reproduced by their ways of being in the world, democratization is futile: democratization may lead to greater involvement in political decision making, but without revolutionary changes in the regimes and practices of production, it remains the involvement of dominated subjectivities whose decisions reproduce the relations of domination that produced these subjectivities in the first place.

Hardt and Negri's social-theoretical argument is reinforced by an ethical one. In their view, social change for the better is not just impossible without revolutionary change; it is ethically undesirable.

The authors object to the notion of intentional agency on ethical grounds. Their objection is connected with a celebration of immediacy, which is linked in turn with a normative view of human freedom that emphasizes vitality, unconstrained desire, and spontaneous creativity and productivity. In their account of subjectivity, all forms of mediation threaten the spontaneity and vitality of subjectively embodied productivity and are, accordingly, inimical to human freedom. Since intentional agency entails the mediation of will by (purposive) reason, it constitutes a threat of this kind. The externalization of human subjectivity in the form of a transcendent political authority is rejected for similar reasons. Not surprisingly, therefore, the authors are hostile to all modern conceptions of political organization, in particular to those involving representation, delegation, or any other kind of alienation of power.[18] However, it is hard to see how they could find any mode of political organization acceptable, for they all seem to entail some kind of externalization of authority and, hence, constraint on spontaneous creative productivity.

Like *Dialectic of Enlightenment, Empire* relies on a number of powerful rhetorical devices that lend force to its critique of globalizing capitalism.[19] In both cases, moreover, the rhetoric serves arguments that tap into existing worries and seem to cast light on negative aspects of contemporary reality. Like *Dialectic of Enlightenment* in its time, *Empire* articulates matters that, today, are of deep concern to many people. Just as, for example, Horkheimer and Adorno's critique of the culture industry spoke to many people disturbed by the manipulative and repressive effects of the U.S. music and film industries of the mid-twentieth century, Hardt and Negri's rejection of political authority speaks to many people distressed by the failure of contemporary democratic politics to deal with the new forms of injustice, suffering, and oppression resulting from current processes of globalization (for example, the ever-widening gap between the rich and the poor, new forms of social exclusion and subordination, and irreparable damage to the earth's ecosystem).[20]

However, like Horkheimer and Adorno's, Hardt and Negri's argument is overstated. Their critique of globalizing capitalism clearly resonates with contemporary worries that its negative effects cannot be regulated and controlled by democratic politics, at least in their current forms. But if they were right that dominating power permeates every aspect of subjectivity (unlike Adorno, they leave no room even for latent resistance in the form of a "somatic moment"), their critique would be unable to find any such resonance. Moreover, Hardt and Negri end up in the same unwelcome position as Horkheimer and Adorno. Like the latter, Hardt and Negri offer a critical diagnosis and corresponding emancipatory projection that can neither be accepted as valid on the basis of good reasons nor acted upon intentionally by those they address. This disconnection of theory and praxis opens their theory to the accusation of ethical authoritarianism. Equally, of course, their theory is open to the accusation of epistemological authoritarianism for, like Horkheimer and Adorno, they set themselves up in a position of epistemic privilege: only they and similarly privileged social critics have access to the truth about contemporary processes of globalizing capitalism, and their critical diagnosis and emancipatory projection cannot be challenged on the basis of good reasons in public processes of interrogation.

As the examples of *Dialectic of Enlightenment* and *Empire* show, disconnecting critical social theory from praxis has authoritarian consequences. Thus, if it is correct that a sundering of theory and praxis results from the kind of approach to critical social theory I have advocated in the foregoing, I shall certainly have to reconsider my argument. However, closer examination suggests that this is not the case. If we recall the salient features of the model of rational justification I have proposed, we can see that this model is sufficient for the purpose of securing the link between theory and praxis. No additional explanatory component is required. To be sure, the connection it secures between theory and praxis rearticulates the term "praxis" as it was understood by Marx and by many of his followers in the Left-Hegelian tradition. Whereas for Marx, praxis was understood as transformative social action whose concrete content was supplied in advance by his theory's explanation of social evils, it must now be understood as transformative social activity whose concrete content is a matter for deliberation among those concerned, taking into account the constraints and opportunities of the particular sociocultural contexts in which they find themselves. Only a conception of praxis along these lines is congruent with the antiauthoritarian impulses of contemporary social theories.

This point can be illustrated by returning to the picture of the tasks of a critical social theory that I have attributed to Marx in his writings of the 1840s. As we have seen, his picture foregrounds "enlightening explanation" and "transformative social action." However, if we look at it more closely, we can see that, for Marx, critical social theory secures its link with praxis by way of a conception of explanation that is epistemologically authoritarian. In this phase of his praxis philosophy,[21] Marx advocates reliance on a "materialist method" in which the theorist's illumination of the "struggles and wishes" of the age expresses a potential for social change for the better whose validity, underwritten by the dynamics of history, is verifiable through the findings of the empirical sciences. The advocated materialist method starts from premises "that are not arbitrary ones, not dogmas, but real premises . . . [that can] be verified in a purely empirical way."[22] These premises relate to real human beings, to their production of the means of subsistence, and to their organization of the relations of production.

The important point for our present purposes is that, in adopting the materialist method, Marx affirms the view that his critical diagnosis of what is wrong with capitalist society can be verified scientifically.[23] The materialist method does not only explain the sources of the normative deficits of the capitalist social order and the mechanisms whereby these deficits are distributed and reproduced; it specifies the action necessary in order to overcome them; moreover, the validity of its proposals for action is secured by the validity of the theory's explanations, which, underwritten by the inherent rationality of the historical process, can be verified empirically. Evidently, therefore, the concept of praxis corresponding to this view of theory describes a kind of transformative social action whose content is determined in advance by the theorist's descriptions and explanations.

In the foregoing, however, I have made the case for an understanding of critical social theory whose claims to validity are not empirically verifiable scientific facts; rather they are contestable claims that are subject to assessment in public processes of inclusive, open-ended, and fair argumentation in a suitably historicist, comparative, and concrete manner. If we draw out the implications of this model of rational justification for social theory, we can see that its correlate is a model of social analysis whose normatively guided descriptions of the deficits of a particular social order, and normatively guided explanations of how these deficits are distributed and reproduced,[24] are not empirically verifiable propositions; rather they take the form of claims to validity that, like the theory's guiding ideas of the good society, are subject to assessment in public processes of inclusive, open-ended, and fair argumentation in a suitably historicist, comparative, and concrete manner.

These models of rational justification and social description and explanation call for a rearticulation of the concept of praxis. The appropriate model is no longer transformative social action whose content is predetermined by the theorist's descriptions and explanations; rather it is transformative social activity by autonomous agents concerned with the concrete possibilities for change for the better that are available in particular sociocultural contexts; this concern entails willingness on the part of such agents to join in deliberations with others in order to ascertain the possibilities that are available, which they evaluate with the help of multiple theoretical and empirical studies, drawing on their own experiences and analyses and anticipating future social, technological, and ecological developments. To be sure, deliberations of these kinds must also concern themselves with explanations; without adequate explanations of how the identified social evils are distributed and reproduced, it would be impossible even to consider possibilities for eliminating or alleviating them. However, it is important to see that, on the model of critical social theory I propose, the need for explanations arises once the theory has succeeded in motivating praxis: in contrast to the model I attributed to Marx, social explanation is not needed in order to set in train praxis, but only once the theory has already exerted a motivating power. In other words, the motivating power of a particular critical social theory is not determined by its ability to offer convincing explanations of the social evils it diagnoses; moreover, the need for such explanations arises on the level of praxis once the theory's critical perspective, and corresponding emancipatory projection of a good society, have motivated autonomous agents to act with a view to bringing about social change for the better; such agents must themselves decide, in deliberation with others, what change means in the circumstances in question and what possibilities for change are available.

In sum, in order to motivate praxis in a nonauthoritarian sense, critical social theory does not have to provide explanations of the social evils it identifies. For the purposes of praxis in this sense, it is sufficient that, on the level of normative validity, it evokes an idea of the good society that permits a critical perspective on the existing social order and, on the level of social theory, provides a conceptual apparatus for describing the social order in such a way that a diagnosis of what is wrong with it is possible. It is important to see that the normative and the social-theoretical levels are intimately connected. The theory's guiding idea of the good society provides the conceptual resources for its social-theoretical analyses of a particular social order, with the aim of allowing that order's normative deficits to come into view. It is these analyses that prompt—or fail to prompt—human agents to engage in praxis.

As indicated, this is not to deny that critical social theories are fundamentally concerned with social explanation. It is merely to deny that the motivating power of critical social theories is determined by their explanatory abilities. On my account, explanation occupies a different place in critical social theory to the one traditionally allocated to it: in the theory-praxis relationship it belongs to the side of praxis rather than theory; moreover, it is construed in a nonauthoritarian way as a set of contestable validity claims. These conclusions suggest a further one: it may be that critical social theories do not merely need to relocate explanation to the side of praxis rather than theory and to affirm the nonauthoritarian epistemological status of their explanations; they may need, in addition, to reconsider their view of the proper object of their explanations. I want to propose that, in light of the complexity of contemporary social orders and their multiple and multifaceted interdependencies, an explanation of the ways in which dominating power is disseminated and perpetuated may be more fruitful than an explanation of the sources of this power.

In the Left-Hegelian tradition, at least, critical social theories have tended to understand their task as entailing an explanation of the causes of the social evils they identify. Moreover, their explanations have tended to depend on a single grand theory, in the sense of a theory that offers a structural account of the social order it criticizes and traces its normative deficits back to key features of the structure. Thus, Marx explains the causes of the normative deficits of nineteenth-century capitalism in terms of the structure of its social order, tracing these deficits back to the capitalist mode of production. Similarly, Habermas explains the causes of the normative deficits of twentieth-century capitalism in terms of the structure of its social order, tracing these deficits back to the colonization of the communicatively regulated domains of the "lifeworld" by the functionalist rationality of the economic and administrative systems. Against such attempts to offer a grand explanation of the causes of the normative deficits of a particular social order, the complexity of contemporary social orders and their multiple and multifaceted interdependencies raises the question of whether grand explanations are still possible today (if, indeed, they ever were). It could be argued that a more fruitful line of enquiry for contemporary critical social theories is to endeavor to explain the ways in which dominating power is distributed and reproduced in a particular social order, leaving aside the question of the origins of such power.

The need for further reflection on these explanatory issues is evident in a recent debate between Axel Honneth and Nancy Fraser. Although their dispute centers on their rival conceptions of the good society and the appropriate strategy for justifying these conceptions, questions concerning the place of explanation in critical social theory, and the proper object of such explanations, emerge as an interesting subtext.

In their book *Redistribution or Recognition: A Political-Philosophical Exchange*, Fraser and Honneth offer conflicting views as to how the project of a critical social theory should be renewed today.[25] To be sure, as the two theorists acknowledge, their views share a great deal in common. Both theorists position themselves within the Left-Hegelian tradition, affirming that tradition's commitment to a

critical method that proceeds by way of a dialectics of immanence and transcendence.[26] Moreover, like Honneth's, Fraser's critical social thinking appears
to be guided by an idea of the good society that is held to be valid in a context-
transcending sense.[27] Notwithstanding these important points of agreement,
however, their views of critical social theory diverge in a number of respects.
The most obvious differences are on a normative level, where they disagree as
to which particular picture of the good society is valid and as to the kind of
justification that is appropriate. Less obvious, but most interesting for our
present purposes, are their different views as to the place that social explanation should occupy in critical social theory.

On a normative level, as we saw in chapter 3, Honneth evokes the idea of
a social condition in which full recognition of the three aspects of ethical personality would be possible.[28] We have also seen that justification of this normative idea takes the form of (what I have called) a two-step strategy: with the
first step, he looks to empirical studies of a historical, sociological, and psychoanalytical kind for support for his hypothesis; with the second step, he seeks to
justify the validity of the three expectations of recognition through reference
to the normative ideas of social inclusiveness and individuality, which are held
to be valid in a context-transcending sense.[29] By contrast, Fraser evokes the
idea of a social condition of "participatory parity" in which it would be possible for human beings to interact with each other on an equal footing; participatory parity is held to entail two equally important requirements: first,
distribution of material resources in a way that ensures independence and
"voice" and, second, institutionalized patterns of cultural value that express
equal respect for all inhabitants of the social order in question as well as an
equal opportunity for achieving social esteem.[30] Fraser pursues two complementary lines of argument in justifying this guiding idea. One argument is
conceptual: she maintains that the idea of participatory parity is simply an
elucidation of the core intuition of the modern liberal concept of equal
autonomy and moral worth.[31] The other argument is historical: she argues that
the idea of participatory parity is the outcome of a broad, multifaceted historical process that has, over time, enriched the meaning of liberal equality,
expanding both its scope and substance.[32]

As we have seen, in critical social theory the normative and the social-
theoretical levels are intimately connected. On the normative level, theorists
evoke ideas of the good society that permit critical perspectives on the existing
social order. These ideas of the good society provide them with the conceptual
resources they require for their analyses at the social-theoretical level; here they

endeavor to describe the social order in such a way that its normative deficits come into view. Accordingly, Fraser's and Honneth's different conceptions of the good society translate into correspondingly different conceptual frameworks for social analysis. In other words, the differences between their respective social-theoretical frameworks are determined by the differences between their respective conceptions of the good society. But over and above the social-theoretical differences that are determined by the differences in their normative conceptions, Honneth and Fraser hold different views as to the place of social explanation in the critical enterprise. Honneth describes his theory of recognition as a "moral grammar" and acknowledges that his theory has no explanatory component; by contrast, Fraser seems concerned to retain the explanatory component at the center of her critical social theory.[33] As we shall see, their positions have various strengths and weaknesses.

Honneth characterizes his critical social theory as a "moral grammar of social conflict."[34] A moral grammar as he understands it seeks to uncover the general structural features of social interaction in a particular social order: "to uncover the normative principles that . . . structure communication processes from within."[35] Thus, Honneth's grammatical analyses seek to show how social interaction within the capitalist social order is normatively structured by three expectations of recognition. On the normative level, these expectations are supposed to provide a basis for the criticism of actual institutions and practices within capitalism, and for evaluating the validity of protests articulated in its social struggles. On the social-theoretical level, his grammatical reflections supply conceptual tools for describing certain modes of interaction *as* failures of recognition. Here, however, they reach their limit. A moral grammar of social conflict can neither enlighten us as to how failures of recognition are distributed and reproduced nor indicate how they could be remedied. For these purposes, a moral grammar would have to be supplemented by explanatory theories that purport to throw light on the specific ways in which failures of recognition come about in the contemporary capitalist social order.[36]

In his exchange with Fraser, Honneth acknowledges the limited scope of his theory, stating that his attempt to reconstruct the recognition order of modern capitalist societies is not connected with any explanatory aims.[37] However, it is not clear whether Honneth's "more modest"[38] approach to critical social theory is due to deliberate reticence or to an inability to provide the kinds of explanations that social change for the better requires. On the one hand, it could be reticence. In the foreground of the social-theoretical part of his debate with Fraser, Honneth places the question of which categorical tools are the most promising for reviving critical social theory's claim to "at once appropriately articulate and morally justify the normative claims of social movements."[39] Passages such as these could be read as evidence of his more modest ambitions. On this reading, he does not deny the need for explanations of the failures of recognition he identifies; he has simply opted to confine himself to articulating the moral grammar of social struggles in the contemporary capitalist order, and to showing how the claims to validity they raise may be justified. On the other hand, it could be incapacity. He admits on occasion that he is unable to outline in any satisfactory way an explanatory model that would avoid the functionalist pitfalls of Marx's and Habermas's approaches,[40] and adequately take into account the requirements of normative justification.[41] This admission is coupled with hints as to the kinds of explanatory models he would *not* find congenial.[42] Passages such as these could be read as evidence of a valid intuition: there is at least room for conjecture that Honneth's "more modest" approach, together with his admission that he can think of no satisfactory explanatory model, testify to his valid intuition that the pursuit of explanations of the causes of social evils is not a fruitful path for contemporary critical social theory. However, not only does Honneth fail to articulate this intuition; if he has it, he appears to suppress it on occasion, declaring his commitment to the importance of grand theory.

Thus, in the jointly written introduction to their exchange, Honneth professes to share with Fraser the aim of theorizing capitalist society as a totality. With Fraser, he rejects what he perceives as the current tendency among friends and colleagues who identify with the tradition of critical social theory to assume a disciplinary division of labor: to assign moral theory to the philosophers, social theory to the sociologists, and political analysis to the political scientists. Against this kind of division of labor both Fraser and Honneth affirm their commitment to a grand theory, maintaining that "critique achieves both its theoretical warrant and its practical efficacy only by deploying normative concepts that are also informed by a structural understanding of contemporary society, one that can diagnose the tensions and contextualize the struggles of the present."[43] Honneth's attestation to the importance of grand theory, which, as we have seen, seeks to provide grand explanations, is quite out of keeping with the modest aims of his "moral grammar of social conflict" and is, in my view, inadvisable under contemporary conditions of social complexity.

I have suggested that there may be good reasons for the absence of an explanatory component in Honneth's theory; however, his lack of attention to questions of "practical efficacy" is harder to justify. Certainly, one would expect some discussion of questions concerning the relation of theory to praxis. Not only does he not engage with such questions, a number of his remarks in this regard are ambiguous. An example here is his assertion that critical social theory must allow "the anticipation of points of departure for normative improvements."[44] Although such remarks can be made to fit with the view of the connection between theory and praxis I have proposed in the foregoing, they are equally compatible with the Marxist view that I have criticized. On my view, we will recall, the theorist's guiding idea of the good society provides conceptual resources for describing social reality in such a way that the "points of departure for normative improvements" become visible; by illuminating social reality in a convincing way, the theorist motivates autonomous agents to act with a view to bringing about social change for the better; crucially, however, the theorist leaves open the question of what change for the better means in particular circumstances, and what possibilities for action are available. On Marx's view, by contrast, the meaning of social change for the better is supplied in advance by the critical social theorist, and the kinds of actions to be undertaken in order to bring it about are specified.

Although it is most unlikely that Honneth would subscribe to this authoritarian view of the relation between theory and praxis, his remark on the need to anticipate "points of departure for normative improvements" is compatible with it. Furthermore, this remark, which expresses Honneth's commitment to the view that the theorist's emancipatory, critical perspective must be anchored in the subjective experiences and normative expectations of the inhabitants of the social order in question, is reminiscent of many formulations in Marx's writings of the 1840s. In the 1843 essay cited earlier, for example, Marx states: "We do not . . . set ourselves opposite the world with a doctrinaire principle, saying: 'Here is the truth, kneel down here!' It is *out of the world's own principles* that we develop for it new principles."[45] To be sure, as we know, Honneth endorses Marx's emphasis on the immanence of social criticism, while distancing himself from Marx's belief that the inherent rationality of the historical process guarantees the validity of the "world's own principles," which can then be verified by empirical science.[46] However, although we know that he does not agree with Marx regarding the basis for the validity of the theorist's standpoint, we do not know where he stands vis-à-vis Marx on the question of the relation of theory to praxis. In view of the dangers of an authoritarian understanding of the concept of praxis, and given his own reference to "practical efficacy," some clarification of his position in this regard is called for.

In contrast to Honneth's theory, where the question of social explanation is simply left aside, in Fraser's theory it is a central component.[47] There are a number of clear indications that she holds the view that explanation is one of the core tasks of critical social theory, for instance, where she describes its task as conceptualizing types of injustice, *their causes, and their remedies.*[48] Accordingly, her "perspectival dualist" approach[49] is supposed to provide the framework not just for social-theoretical description but also for an explanation of the causes of social subordination: its guiding aim is to "investigate how precisely institutionalized patterns of cultural value interact with capitalist economic dynamics to *generate* maldistribution and misrecognition."[50] This understanding of the tasks of critical social theory is also evident in her critique of Honneth's theory, for she attributes to it explanatory intentions, suggesting that in his work, the concept of recognition is supposed to capture the normative deficits of contemporary society, the social processes that generate them, and the political challenges facing those seeking emancipatory change.[51] Indeed, this is the basis for her main objection against Honneth, which is that he overextends the concept of recognition, depriving it of critical force.[52]

Although I have argued that explanation is not necessary in order to secure the link between theory and praxis, I have also argued that critical theories must recognize the importance of social explanation as an integral part of deliberation among those concerned to act to bring about social change for the better. This leaves open the question of whether the theorist herself should offer hypotheses regarding the dissemination and perpetuation of the social evils she identifies or leave it up to others to do so.[53] In the first case, her hypotheses would feed into deliberations among those concerned to act to bring about social change for the better; the theorist's expertise would lend more weight to her contributions than to contributions that are less well-informed theoretically and empirically; nonetheless, they would still be contestable on the basis of good reasons. In the second case, the theorist would confine herself to providing an illuminating description of the normative deficits of a particular social order, abstaining from any kind of speculation as to how they are disseminated and perpetuated. Both positions are, of course, quite different to the Marxist one. Here, the validity of the normative claims of the theory, together with the validity of the theory's explanations, are guaranteed by the inherent rationality of the historical process and can be verified by empirical science; moreover, the remedies are supplied in advance by the theory.

Evidently, therefore, the mere assumption that social explanation is a core component of the critical enterprise does not commit Fraser to the authoritarian, Marxist position.[54] Either of the two positions mentioned above is open to her. Although Fraser does not engage directly with these issues, there are some indications that she would favor the first position. In her discussion of the question of the institutional arrangements necessary in order to ensure the conditions for participatory parity, she calls for a position midway between monologism and proceduralism.[55] The monological stance, as she describes it, gives the theorist the task of drawing substantive conclusions on matters of justice, which are verifiable by the rational enquirer (Fraser associates this stance with Plato but it could just as easily be associated with Marx). The proceduralist stance, by contrast, makes such substantive conclusions a matter for deliberation among those concerned. For Fraser, the monological stance is insensitive to context, pays no attention to the plurality of value orientations, and disregards the requirement of political legitimacy, whereby citizens should be able to see themselves as the authors of the laws to which they are subject. However, she sees a danger that the proceduralist stance will dissolve into empty formalism, resulting in an abstract insistence on procedure that has little to say about justice. The shortcomings of each stance leads Fraser to advocate an appropriate division of labor between theorist and citizenry: the theorist can help to clarify the range of options available in matters of justice; the citizens deliberate among themselves as which of these options are preferable.

With some modification, Fraser's position would fit well with the conception of social explanation that I have advocated in the foregoing. Modification is necessary because Fraser's characterization of the theorist's task is at times infelicitous. On occasion, it has authoritarian overtones, implying that the theorist's input into deliberation is not a matter for inclusive, open-ended, and fair debate. Thus, she refers to the theorist's task as "delimiting the range of permissible options," suggesting that, when it comes to deciding which options are compatible with the requirements of justice, the theorist has a privileged position.[56] Congruence with the conception I have proposed would require Fraser to relinquish the view that the theorist has authority in matters of justice, and to avoid formulations that suggest she attributes to her such authority. Subject to modification along these lines, Fraser's view of the theorist's role in matters relating to the institutionalization of justice could form the basis for a suitably nonauthoritarian conception of social explanation.

However, if Fraser favors the first position, whereby explanation remains a core component of critical social theory, she might be well advised to modify her commitment to grand theory; such a theory, we will recall, not only provides the conceptual apparatus for describing the normative deficits of a particular social order, it also offers a grand explanation of these deficits. This takes the form of a structural account of the order in question, which traces the identified normative deficits back to key features of the structure. As indicated, there is reason to suspect that explanatory theories of such grand design are no longer convincing today. It is probably no accident that Fraser's attempt to argue that society is structured by two mutually irreducible, yet practically entwined principles—the economic and the cultural—runs into problems. On the one hand, she seeks to avoid the essentialism of "substantive dualist" accounts, which equate these two principles with actual social domains. To avoid this, she advocates a "perspectival dualist" approach, whereby the economic and the cultural dimensions merely constitute two analytically distinct perspectives on the social order. On the other hand, she seems unable to avoid formulations in which these two perspectives are described as "*ordering* principles" or "*orders* of subordination," implying that they do constitute two distinct modes of social integration and reproduction and, hence, two distinct social domains.[57] By relinquishing her aspiration to offer a grand explanation of the normative deficits of the contemporary capitalist social order, Fraser could avoid this difficulty without compromising the critical power of her theory.

One of the main points of her perspectival dualist approach is to show that dominating power is distributed and reproduced by way of multiple and multifaceted interconnections of both an economic and a cultural kind. Her principal objection to substantive dualism is that it overlooks the interpenetration of the two dimensions, disregarding the facts that the economic order is always permeated with interpretations and norms and that the cultural order is always permeated by economic interests.[58] But to make this point, Fraser does not need to make any grand claims about the structure of the capitalist social order: she can leave open the question of whether the structure of society is governed by two distinct ordering principles or, indeed, give up a structural approach entirely.

I have suggested that the complexity of contemporary social orders and their multiple and multifaceted interdependencies undermines the assumption that one grand theory would be able to explain the causes of social evils. In view of this complexity and interdependency, I proposed a distinction between social-theoretical explanations of the causes of dominating power and social-theoretical explanations of the ways in which such power is distributed and reproduced. Although often combined in a single theory, these two kinds of explanations are not dependent on one another. An illustration of their mutual independence can be found in an essay by Fraser in which she criticizes the gender bias of Habermas's theory of communicative action.[59]

In the essay in question, mentioned at the start of this chapter, Fraser argues that the gender bias of the theory of communicative action makes it blind to the ways in which flows of influence between social institutions (such as the workplace, welfare institutions, and the family) are mediated by key social roles (such as the client and consumer) that are gendered roles. Since Habermas fails to notice that these mediating social roles are gendered, he fails to notice that they are channels, not just for the dominating effects of functionalist rationality but for the dominating effects of repressive and subordinating modes of communicative action as well. Consequently, he misses the multi-directionality of the process of social domination, underplaying the complexity of the social mechanisms that lead to the reification of interpretations. For the same reason, he misses the need for changes in the repressive and subordinating modes of communicative action that are channeled between the family, workplace, and welfare institutions by way of gendered roles. Fraser's critique of Habermas's gender bias is forceful because it shows effectively that his theory neglects the complex ways in which dominating power is perpetuated and disseminated in contemporary capitalist societies. However, her critique does not entail allegiance to any particular view of the causes of dominating power in contemporary capitalist social orders; hence, it does not require an acceptance of Habermas's thesis that the causes of dominating power can be traced back to the encroachment of the functionalist rationality of the economic and administrative systems into the communicatively regulated domains of the lifeworld.[60]

From this we can see that explanations of the ways in which dominating power is distributed and reproduced do not presuppose any particular explanation of the sources of dominating power; certainly, they do not presuppose any grand explanation. Given the difficulties into which her endeavor to supply a grand explanation lead her, Fraser—like Honneth—might be better advised to give up her commitment to grand theory and to concentrate on providing illuminating accounts of the multiple and complex ways in which dominating power is disseminated and perpetuated in the contemporary capitalist order.

With two caveats, therefore, our discussion has endorsed the view that social-theoretical explanation is part of the critical enterprise. The first caveat is that such explanation has to be construed in a nonauthoritarian way: *pace* Marx, the validity of the social theorist's explanations are not guaranteed by the process of history and cannot be verified by empirical science. This has implications for the concept of praxis. It implies that the concrete content of praxis—the actions that have to be undertaken in order to bring about change for the better—is a matter for deliberation among those who have been motivated to act to this end by the critical diagnosis, and corresponding emancipatory projection of the good society, offered by a given critical social theory. The second caveat is that grand explanations may no longer be appropriate. Rather than attempting to explain the normative deficits of a particular social order as the result of key features of that social order, contemporary critical social theory might be better advised to endeavor to describe the various complex ways in which dominating power is distributed and reproduced in the social order in question.

Guided by ideas of the good society, critical social theories seek to make the world a better place. Our discussion has cast light on how they endeavor to do so. It has enabled us to see that they aim to show us what is wrong with the social orders we inhabit, evoke images of alternative, better, social orders, convince us that their critical diagnoses and emancipatory projections are right (this entails making us feel that they are right), and, on the basis of this conviction, motivate us to explore possibilities for action that could bring about social change for the better. The words from Rousseau with which we started our discussion still seem appropriate as a motto for this endeavor: "Man is born free; and everywhere he is in chains." But we are now in a better position to interpret their meaning for those engaged in the critical enterprise today.

Our discussion has shown that, for contemporary critical social theories, the freedom toward which Rousseau points must be interpreted as autonomy: the freedom to form and pursue one's conceptions of the good on the basis of reasons one can call one's own. Such freedom does not have to be the sole emancipatory point of a particular critical social theory, nor does it have to be posited as its highest good. I have argued, nonetheless, that if critical social theories wish to live up to their own antiauthoritarian aims, they must acknowledge autonomy as a core component of their enterprise. In the concluding pages of *Between Facts and Norms*, Habermas expresses a thought of this kind. He suggests that autonomy is the "dogmatic core" of critical social theory: dogmatic in the "harmless" sense "that for us, who have developed our identity in [a particular] form of life, it cannot be circumvented."[61] To be sure, even when described as harmless, the word "dogmatic" strikes a discordant note.

Our discussion has suggested that dogmatism is never harmless, for it impedes learning experiences and blocks the creative rearticulation and reenactment of the concepts in question. Indeed, I have argued that it is precisely in order to allow for such creative rearticulation and reenactment that we must be open to the possibility of learning through cross-cultural encounters and engagement with the historical past and that, to conceptualize this, a concept of context-transcending validity is necessary. Although I endorse Habermas's suggestion that contemporary critical social theories must acknowledge their commitment to the ideal of autonomy, I want to emphasize the importance of rearticulating and reenacting this ideal when the limitations of its existing interpretations are exposed.

Furthermore, our discussion has clarified the role of theory in releasing human subjects from the social chains that bind them and prevent them from flourishing as members of a projected good society. Critical social theories seek to release human subjects from the *psychological* chains that bind them by means of the illuminating power of their critical diagnoses and emancipatory projections—they aim to enlighten them as to the social obstacles that impede their flourishing as human subjects and as to the concrete ways in which these obstacles are actualized and reproduced. However, critical social theories cannot release human subjects from their *social* chains since, for this, transformative social action is necessary. Such action, if effective, enables human subjects to free themselves from the social chains that bind them: the practical efficacy of critical social theories consists in their ability to stimulate processes of emancipation that are self-emancipation.

Notes

Introduction

1. J. J. Rousseau, "The Social Contract" in his *The Social Contract and Discourses*, ed. and trans. G. D. H. Cole (London: Dent, 1973), pp. 163–278 (*Du contrat social*, 1762).

2. In tracing critical social theory back to Rousseau, I am in agreement with Axel Honneth's normative account of the history of social philosophy in his "Pathologien des Sozialen. Tradition und Aktualität der Sozialphilosophie," in A. Honneth, ed., *Pathologien des Sozialen: Die Aufgaben der Sozialphilosophie* (Frankfurt am Main: Fischer, 1994), pp. 9–69.

3. In situating critical social theory within the evaluative horizon of Western modernity, I do not wish simply to presume that this form of modernity is superior to other forms. I follow S. N. Eisenstadt in confining myself to the thesis that it is distinctive; I also follow Eisenstadt in recognizing "the great variability of the symbolic, ideological and institutional responses to it [Western modernity—M. C.], of the ways in which different civilizations and societies interpret different symbolic premises of modernity and different modern institutional patterns and dynamics." Introduction to S. N. Eisenstadt, ed., *Patterns of Modernity*, vol. 1 (London: Frances Pinter, 1987), pp. 1–11 (here, p. 5).

4. There is an evident resonance between this formulation of the idea of autonomy and Immanuel Kant's view of enlightenment as presented in his well-known 1784 essay, "Answer to the Question: What Is Enlightenment?" trans. T. Abbott, in I. Kant, *The Basic Writings of Kant*, ed. A. Wood (New York: Modern Library Classics, 2001), pp. 133–142. ("Beantwortung der Frage, Was ist Aufklärung?" in *Was ist Aufklärung? Ausgewählte kleine Schriften*, ed. E. Cassirer [Hamburg: Meiner, 1999].) I outline a conception of ethical autonomy, offering an interpretation of what it means for human subjects to "call reasons their own" in chapter 6 below.

5. F. Nietzsche, *Thus Spake Zarathustra*, trans. T. Common (London: Allen and Unwin, 1967). (*Also sprach Zarathustra* [Ditzingen: Reclam, 1978].) F. Nietzsche, *Beyond Good and Evil*, trans. R. J. Hollingdale (Harmondsworth: Penguin Books, 1973). (*Jenseits von Gut und Böse* [Berlin and New York: De Gruyter, 1988].)

6. Here I am guided by Cornelius Castoriadis's view that every society creates a social imaginary that determines society's values and the institutions that embody them. However, I use the term in a general way without committing myself to other aspects of Castoriadis's account of the social

imaginary. See C. Castoriadis, *The Imaginary Institution of Society* (Cambridge, Mass.: MIT Press, 1987). My use of the term is closer to Charles Taylor's. See C. Taylor, *Modern Social Imaginaries* (Durham, N.C.: Duke University Press, 2004).

7. J. Habermas, "On the Pragmatic, the Ethical, and the Moral Employments of Practical Reason," in his *Justification and Application*, trans. C. Cronin (Cambridge, Mass.: MIT Press, 1993), pp. 1–19. ("Zur pragmatischen, ethischen, und moralischen Gebrauch der praktischen Vernunft," in his *Erläuterungen zur Diskursethik* [Frankfurt am Main: Suhrkamp, 1991], pp. 100–118.) See also M. Cooke, "Realizing the Post-Conventional Self," *Philosophy and Social Criticism* 20, nos. 1–2 (1994): 87–101.

Chapter 1

1. Axel Honneth interprets Hegel's *Philosophy of Right* in this way in his *Suffering from Indeterminacy: An Attempt at a Reactualisation of Hegel's Philosophy of Right*, Spinoza Lectures 5 (Assen: Royal Van Gorcum, 2000). (*Leiden an Unbestimmtheit: Eine Reaktualisierung der Hegelschen Rechtsphilosophie* [Stuttgart: Reclam, 2001].)

2. T. W. Adorno, *Aesthetic Theory*, trans. R. Hullot-Kentor (London: Athlone Press, 1997). (*Ästhetische Theorie* [Frankfurt am Main: Suhrkamp, 1970].)

3. J. Habermas, "What Is Universal Pragmatics?" in his *On the Pragmatics of Communication*, edited and with an introduction by M. Cooke (Cambridge, Mass.: MIT Press, 1998). ("Was heißt Universalpragmatik?" In K.-O. Apel, ed., *Sprachpragmatik und Philosophie* [Frankfurt am Main: Suhrkamp, 1976].)

4. This strain of thought is particularly evident in C. Taylor's *Sources of the Self* (Cambridge: Cambridge University Press, 1989). To be sure, Taylor does not see hermeneutic retrieval of forgotten collective hopes and aspirations as the only valid means of encouraging people to change or modify their current ideas relating to human flourishing; he also draws attention to the importance of poetic disclosure. See chapter 6 below. Cf. also M. Cooke, "Argumentation and Transformation," *Argumentation* 16 (2002): 79–108.

5. J. Butler, *Antigone's Claim: Kinship between Life and Death* (New York: Columbia University Press, 2000). See also chapter 4 below.

6. Michael Rosen regards the thesis that consciousness is systematically determined by society for the purposes of its own self-preservation as the problematic core of the concept of ideology. See M. Rosen, *On Voluntary Servitude* (Cambridge: Polity Press, 1996).

7. Adorno's definition of ideology as "objectively necessary, yet false consciousness" nicely encapsulates this view. See Th. W. Adorno, "Beitrag zur Ideologielehre," in his *Soziologische Schriften I* (Frankfurt am Main; Suhrkamp, 1972), pp. 457–477, here, p. 465, my translation.

8. J.-J. Rousseau, "A Discourse on the Origin of Inequality," in his *The Social Contract and Discourses*, pp. 44–113. ("Discours sur l'origine et les fondements de l'inégalité parmi les hommes," 1754.)

9. K. Marx, "The German Ideology," in D. McLellan, ed., *Karl Marx: Selected Writings* (Oxford: Oxford University Press, 1977). ("Die Deutsche Ideologie," in K. Marx and F. Engels, *Werke*, Bd. 3 [Berlin: Dietz Verlag, 1969].)

10. The system's interests may, of course, express the interests of a transhistorical collective subject such as Hegel's *Geist* or a materialist equivalent.

11. In the 1960s, Habermas was still sufficiently convinced of the usefulness of the concept of ideology to publish a book with "ideology" in its title: *Technik und Wissenschaft als Ideologie* (Frankfurt am Main: Suhrkamp, 1968).

12. His distance from the notion of ideology critique is evident since the publication of his *The Theory of Communicative Action*, vol. 2, trans. T. McCarthy (Boston: Beacon Press, 1987), pp. 354–355. (*Theorie des kommunikativen Handelns*, vol. 2 [Frankfurt am Main: Suhrkamp, 1981].)

13. Habermas, *The Theory of Communicative Action*, vol. 2, p. 354.

14. Ibid., p. 355.

15. This is evident in the contributions by J. Heath, T. Kelly, M. Rosen, and J. Bohman in *Constellations* 7, no. 3 (2000). Kelly and Heath emphasize the epistemological and moral problems with which the concept of ideology is connected. By contrast, Rosen sees the supposition that consciousness is systematically determined by society for the purposes of its own self-preservation as more problematic (see also his *On Voluntary Servitude*). Interestingly, only Bohman makes a serious attempt to rehabilitate the concept of ideology as a form of false consciousness that serves to maintain an unjust or irrational social system (but see my comments on an earlier version of Bohman's thesis in M. Cooke, *Language and Reason: A Study of Habermas's Pragmatics* (Cambridge, Mass.: MIT Press, 1994), pp. 149–50. Among thinkers in other traditions, by contrast, there seems to be renewed interest in the concept of ideology. See A. Norval, "The Things We Do with Words—Contemporary Approaches to the Analysis of Ideology" (review essay), *British Journal of Political Science* 30 (2000): 313–346.

16. At least in its modern usage, the concept of "progress" implies the openness of history—an idea that is itself a core element of the normative horizon of modernity. See R. Koselleck, *Vergangene Zukunft* (Frankfurt am Main: Suhrkamp, 1979). For this reason, the terms "beneficial transformation" and "progress" are not, strictly speaking, synonyms. Since, for our present purposes, nothing turns on this issue, I shall use them interchangeably in the following.

17. Cf. R. Rorty, *Philosophy and the Mirror of Nature* (Princeton, N.J.: Princeton University Press, 1979), pp. 5–7. Rorty uses the term "linguistic turn" to refer to a process that "started as the attempt to produce a nonpsychologistic empiricism by rephrasing philosophical questions as questions of 'logic.'" The initial aim was to restate philosophical points about the nature and extent of human knowledge as remarks about language. Ibid., pp. 257–258; cf. also pp. 161–162 and pp. 165–212.

18. Alessandro Ferrara posits coherence and depth as two of the four normative requirements of authentic identity. A. Ferrara, *Reflective Authenticity* (London and New York: Routledge, 1998).

19. In the following I follow Axel Honneth in using the term "Left-Hegelian" to describe the tradition of critical social thinking more commonly described as the "Frankfurt School" tradition. The advantage of the term, and the reason I use it here, is that it makes explicit the Frankfurt School's concern to rearticulate the critical social thinking of Hegel, as interpreted above all by Marx and Lukács. See A. Honneth, "Eine Soziale Pathologie der Vernunft: Zur intellektuellen Erbschaft der Kritischen Theorie," in C. Halbig and M. Quante, eds., *Sozialphilosophie zwischen Kritik und Anerkennung* (Münster, Hamburg, Berlin, Wien, and London: LIT Verlag, 2003).

20. In this tradition, Ernst Bloch describes critical thinking as a "venturing beyond" that grasps the new as something that is mediated in what exists, but demands an extreme effort of will in order to be revealed. E. Bloch, *The Principle of Hope*, vol. 1, trans. N. Plaice, S. Plaice, and P. Knight (Oxford: Blackwell, 1986), p. 4. (*Das Prinzip Hoffnung* [Frankfurt am Main: Suhrkamp, 1959].)

21. A. Ferrara makes a similar point in his *Justice and Judgment* (London: Sage, 1999), pp. 3–4. Cf. also S. Benhabib, *Situating the Self* (London and New York: Routledge, 1992).

22. T. Kuhn, *The Structure of Scientific Revolutions* (Chicago: University of Chicago Press, 1962). In the general sense it has acquired over the past forty years, I take the term "paradigm shift" to refer to changes in the intellectual and normative frameworks that shape identities and institutions in historically and culturally specific sociocultural contexts. To be sure, since Kuhn was primarily concerned with changes in scientific thought, the concept should be applied in nonscientific fields with caution.

23. Habermas, who defends a context-transcending position, accuses radically contextualist approaches such as Rorty's of collapsing the distinction between the strategic and nonstrategic uses of language. J. Habermas, "Richard Rorty's Pragmatic Turn," in his *On the Pragmatics of Communication*, pp. 343–382. ("Wahrheit und Rechtfertigung: Zu Richard Rortys pragmatischer Wende," in J. Habermas, *Wahrheit und Rechtfertigung* [Frankfurt am Main: Suhrkamp, 1999], pp. 230–270.) Rorty replies in his "Response to Habermas," in R. Brandom, ed., *Rorty and His Critics* (Oxford: Blackwell, 2000), p. 58.

24. These objections to a radically contextualist critical approach are tailored to discursive—argumentation-based—models of social criticism. However, as I point out in chapter 4 below, there are equivalent objections to nonargumentative models of social criticism.

Chapter 2

1. See R. Rorty, "Solidarity or Objectivity," in *Post-Analytic Philosophy Today*, edited by J. Rajchman and C. West (New York: Columbia University Press, 1985), pp. 11–12.

2. R. Rorty, "Putnam and the Relativist Menace," *Journal of Philosophy* 90, no. 9 (1993): 443–461 (here, pp. 451–452).

3. Rorty does now accept that the term "truth" has the cautionary function of pointing out that "justification is relative to an audience and that we can never exclude the possibility that some better audience might exist, or come to exist, to whom a belief that is justifiable to us would not be justifiable." R. Rorty, *Truth and Progress*, Philosophical Papers, volume 3 (Cambridge: Cambridge University Press, 1998), p. 22. Nonetheless, he continues to dispute that there is a need for ideas such as truth in practices of social criticism and democratic politics.

4. See, for example, R. Rorty, "Habermas and Lyotard on Postmodernity," in R. Bernstein, ed., *Habermas and Modernity* (Cambridge: Polity Press, 1985), pp. 161–175 and Habermas's response to it in the same volume (pp. 192–216).

5. Rorty, *Truth and Progress*, p. 12. Rorty discusses the question of universal validity at length in his "Sind Aussagen universelle Geltungsansprüche?" *Deutsche Zeitschrift für Philosophie* 40, no. 6 (1994): 975–988 and in his "Universality and Truth," in Brandom, *Rorty and His Critics*.

6. Rorty, *Truth and Progress*, p. 12.

7. Rorty, "Universality and Truth," p. 2.

8. Ibid., p. 24. Cf. R. Brandom's introduction to *Rorty and His Critics*, pp. ix–xx (here, p. xi).

9. Rorty has used the term "ironist" to refer to the type of person who faces up to this contingency. See R. Rorty, *Contingency, Irony, and Solidarity* (Cambridge: Cambridge University Press, 1989), p. xv.

10. R. Rorty, "Feminism and Pragmatism," in R. B. Goodman, ed., *Pragmatism: A Contemporary Reader* (London: Routledge, 1995), pp. 125–148 (here, p. 128).

11. Rorty, *Truth and Progress*, pp. 303–304.

12. Ibid., p. 304.

13. Rorty, "Response to Habermas," p. 60. Cf. also Rorty, "Feminism and Pragmatism," p. 128. Here, Rorty cites Darwin, and contemporary Darwinians such as Richard Dawkins and Daniel Dennett, approvingly.

14. Thus, in an essay on feminism and pragmatism, Rorty characterizes pragmatist feminists as "utopians" who aim to invent new languages, new beings, and new social structures that are better than the ones presently available (see below). Rorty, "Feminism and Pragmatism," p. 128.

15. Accordingly, Rorty does not "much care whether democratic politics are an expression of something deep, or whether they express nothing better than some hopes which popped from nowhere into the brains of a few remarkable people (Socrates, Christ, Jefferson, etc.) and which, for unknown reasons, became popular." Rorty, "Universality and Truth," p. 14.

16. R. Brandom, "Vocabularies of Pragmatism: Synthesizing Naturalism and Historicism," in *Rorty and His Critics*, pp. 156–183 (here, p. 170). Brandom sees Rorty as identifying a category of interests that can be described in these terms. Rorty appears to accept his reading: R. Rorty, "Response to Robert Brandom," *Rorty and His Critics*, pp. 183–190 (esp. p. 184).

17. To be sure, the human impulse to create and invent comes to the fore only under certain social conditions.

18. Picking up on one of Rorty's own statements, we could say that human beings tend to ask *why* it is sometimes a bad thing to "block the road of inquiry" and other times an excellent thing to do. See Rorty, "Response to Habermas," p. 63.

19. This view has evident affinities with Charles Taylor's attribution of an interest in "strong evaluation" to human beings, in Taylor, *Sources of the Self*. See chapter 6 below.

20. Cf. Rorty, "Response to Habermas," p. 56.

21. Cf. Habermas, "Rorty's Pragmatic Turn," pp. 373–374.

22. Rorty, *Truth and Progress*, p. 132. Again, cf. Brandom's introduction to *Rorty and His Critics*, p. xi.

23. Rorty, *Truth and Progress*, p. 4.

24. Rorty makes a sharp distinction between "poetry" and democratic politics (Nietzsche and Heidegger are "poets" for Rorty). Autonomy, in the sense of self-creation, is the domain of poetry and its vocabulary is fundamentally private. By contrast, the vocabulary of justice is public and shared, a medium for argumentative exchange. Rorty, *Contingency, Irony, and Solidarity*, pp. xiv–xv. I return to this point below.

25. Ibid., p. 3. (My emphasis.)

26. Ibid., pp. 3–4.

27. Rorty, "Universality and Truth," p. 2.

28. R. Rorty, *Essays On Heidegger and Others*, Philosophical Papers 2 (Cambridge: Cambridge University Press, 1991), p. 12.

29. Rorty, *Contingency, Irony, and Solidarity*, p. xiv. Rorty's distinction between public and private has been subjected to much criticism. For a critique of his distinction that succinctly presents the main objections, see N. Fraser, "Solidarity or Singularity: Richard Rorty between Romanticism and Technocracy," in *Reading Rorty*, ed. A. Malachowski (Oxford: Basil Blackwell, 1990), pp. 303–321.

30. Rorty, *Contingency, Irony, and Solidarity*, p. xiv.

31. Rorty, "Universality and Truth," p. 2. See also his *Contingency, Irony, and Solidarity*.

32. Rorty, "Universality and Truth," p. 11.

33. Ibid., p. 19.

34. Ibid., p. 21.

35. Rorty, "Essays on Heidegger and Others," p. 20.

36. It is interesting that Rorty himself generally makes use of a "soft" model of argument. For instance, he draws provocative comparisons and makes use of analogies and historical narratives in order to encourage us to rethink our philosophical commitments to certain epistemological positions. A good example here is his provocative description of the realism versus antirealism debate as a "downmarket version of the nineteenth-century debate between those who did not want to let go of religion and those who thought that, now that we knew how things work, we could forget God." See R. Rorty, "Response to Williams," *Rorty and His Critics*, pp. 213–219 (here, p. 217).

37. Rorty, "Universality and Truth," p. 8.

38. Ibid., p. 27, note 23.

39. Ibid., p. 23. Rorty does consider it possible and important to make a distinction between violent and nonviolent attempts to change people's minds (ibid., p. 20). Presumably, however, this distinction makes sense only from the internal perspective of the agents engaged in this endeavor.

40. Rorty, "Feminism and Pragmatism," p. 131. (My emphasis.)

41. Ibid., p. 140.

42. Rorty, "Universality and Truth," p. 26, note 11. Here, Rorty defends Castoriadis against Habermas and Apel, without noticing that his support for Castoriadis's notion of instituting the social imaginary is at odds with his own private-public distinction.

43. Ibid., p. 2. The utopian motif is evident throughout the essay (explicitly, p. 30, note 67). Elsewhere he expresses this utopian motif negatively; philosophical inquiry should be driven by concrete fears of regression rather than abstract hopes of universality. The memory of how parochial our ancestors have been, and fear that our descendents will find us equally so, should encourage us to strive for a critical rather than dogmatic attitude and a global rather than parochial perspective (Rorty, "Response to Habermas," pp. 60–61). Brandom characterizes Rorty's position here as a "meliorist substitute for the supposed need to orient and motivate criticism by a univer-

salist vision of how things always already in the end ought to be for creatures such as ourselves" (Brandom, "introduction" to *Rorty and His Critics*, p. xvi). By contrast, I see it as a (negative) utopian idea that is, as such, guided by idealizing projections (see chapter 7 below).

44. Brandom, "Vocabularies of Pragmatism: Synthesizing Naturalism and Historicism," p. 179. In his response to Brandom, Rorty claims to be in enthusiastic agreement with the sections of Brandom's essays from which this quotation is taken: Rorty, "Response to Robert Brandom," p. 184.

45. Rorty, "Response to Robert Brandom," p. 189.

46. Ibid., pp. 187–188.

47. Habermas, "Rorty's Pragmatic Turn," pp. 353–354. ("Wahrheit und Rechtfertigung: Zu Richard Rortys Pragmatischer Wende," pp. 241–243.)

48. See Rorty, *Philosophy and the Mirror of Nature*, esp. pp. 315–356.

49. Rorty, "Response to Habermas," p. 63, note 1.

50. Here Rorty refers to the work of Thomas Kuhn. See Kuhn, *The Structure of Scientific Revolutions*.

51. A. Ferrara makes a similar point in his *Reflective Authenticity*, pp. 151–152.

52. Of course, this is by no means an exhaustive list of contemporary critical social thinkers in whose work there is an interesting tension between contextualism and context transcendence, or an interesting attempt to negotiate this tension. An intriguing recent attempt to construe the idea of normative validity in the wake of the linguistic turn can be found in Alessandro Ferrara's theories of reflective authenticity and justice as reflective judgment. With these theories, Ferrara sets out to establish normative foundations for critical social thinking that would be at once universal in reach and sensitive to history, contingency, and plurality. See Ferrara, *Reflective Authenticity* and *Justice and Judgment*. See my review of Ferrara's theory of reflective authenticity (*Reflective Authenticity: Rethinking the Project of Modernity* by Alessandro Ferrara), in *Constellations* 5, no. 4 (1998): 572–575. I discuss various aspects of the theory in M. Cooke, "Between 'Objectivism' and 'Contextualism': The Normative Foundations of Social Philosophy," *Critical Horizons* 1, no. 2 (2000): 193–227 and M. Cooke, "An Evil Heart: Moral Evil and Moral Identity," in *Rethinking Evil*, ed. M.-P. Lara (Berkeley, Calif.: University of California Press, 2001), pp. 163–186 (esp. pp. 171–174).

Chapter 3

1. Here I disregard the strand of critical social theory that, influenced by the elements of economic determinism in Marx's thinking, construes emancipation as the inevitable result of the development of capitalism. I assume, for reasons outlined in chapter 6 below, that change for the better depends on the critical thought and action of autonomous human agents. In chapter 8 I consider the challenge to this view issued by M. Hardt and A. Negri in their book, *Empire* (Cambridge, Mass.: Harvard University Press, 2000).

2. See chapter 1 above, note 19.

3. I describe it in these terms in Cooke, "Between 'Objectivism' and 'Contextualism.'"

4. Cf. A. Honneth, "The Social Dynamics of Disrespect: On the Location of Critical Theory Today," *Constellations* 1, no. 2 (1994): 255–269.

5. M. Horkheimer and T. W. Adorno, *Dialectic of Enlightenment*, trans. J. Cumming (London: Allen Lane, 1973). (*Dialektik der Aufklärung* [Amsterdam: Querido, 1947].) For a succinct account of the theoretical impasse into which Horkheimer and Adorno lead critical social theory, see A. Wellmer, "Reason, Utopia, and the Dialectic of Enlightenment," in Bernstein, ed., *Habermas and Modernity*, pp. 35–66.

6. In his subsequent writings, Adorno struggles to find ways of reasserting the immanent moment of critical social theory. In *Negative Dialectics*, for example, he advocates an "immanent method" that, rather than securing the rationality of a given object by the progressive movement of history, makes it an inherent property of the object itself. On this account, each object (e.g., social structure or idea) has a set of properties inherent to it, to which we have access only through the mediation of language and concepts. This "conceptuality" always exceeds its actual, historical manifestations or interpretations. Criticism is a matter of releasing the energy in the "forcefield" of conceptualization in which every object is located by exposing the reifying tendencies of particular conceptions of an object. It proceeds by way of negative dialectics, constantly disrupting attempts at closure on the part of a repressive identity logic that aims at the subsumption of all particular objects under general concepts, resulting in an annihilation of particularity. It is evident, however, that from the point of view of critical social theory, Adorno's "immanent method" cannot replace an account of historical progress: it can, at best, complement it. Without an accompanying account of what constitutes cognitive or social change for the better, critical social thinking would be unable to account for why the immanent method is useful—why negative dialectics, by releasing the energy in an object's forcefield, is part of an emancipatory critical endeavor. See T. W. Adorno, *Negative Dialectics*, trans. E. B. Ashton (London: Routledge and Kegan Paul, 1973). (*Negative Dialektik* [Frankfurt am Main: Suhrkamp, 1966].)

7. Honneth, "The Social Dynamics of Disrespect," p. 255.

8. N. Fraser and A. Honneth, *Redistribution or Recognition? A Political-Philosophical Exchange* (London: Verso, 2003), pp. 238–241. (*Umverteilung oder Anerkennung? Eine politisch-philosophische Kontroverse* [Frankfurt am Main: Suhrkamp, 2003].)

9. Honneth, "The Social Dynamics of Disrespect," p. 257.

10. Honneth, "Eine Soziale Pathologie der Vernunft."

11. Adorno, *Negative Dialectics*.

12. See J. Habermas, *The Theory of Communicative Action*, vol. 1, trans. T. McCarthy (Boston, Mass.: Beacon Press, 1984), pp. 386–399. (*Theorie des kommunikativen Handelns*, vol. 1 [Frankfurt am Main: Suhrkamp, 1981]); Honneth, "The Social Dynamics of Disrespect"; Fraser and Honneth, *Redistribution or Recognition?*, pp. 238–241.

13. In the 1960s, Habermas attempted to overcome the shortcomings he perceived in the Frankfurt School tradition of thinking by making a number of conceptual distinctions, most notably between instrumental rationality and communicative rationality. However, he did not yet challenge the subject–object model of cognition and action directly.

14. See the work by Habermas cited in note 12 above and Habermas, *The Theory of Communicative Action*, vol. 2.

15. Honneth's principal reservations are set out clearly in "The Social Dynamics of Disrespect."

16. This theory is set out most systematically in Habermas, *The Theory of Communicative Action*, vols. 1 and 2.

17. See M. Cooke, *Language and Reason: A Study of Habermas's Pragmatics* (Cambridge, Mass.: MIT Press, 1994), esp. pp. 150–162.

18. See my critical remarks in *Language and Reason*, pp. 157–162.

19. In Habermas's writings, the term "lifeworld" refers to the totality of the network of communicative actions in a given society. See J. Habermas, "Actions, Speech Acts, Linguistically Mediated Interactions, and the Lifeworld," in his *On the Pragmatics of Communication*, pp. 215–255. ("Handlungen, Sprechakte, vermittelte Interaktionen, und Lebenswelt," in J. Habermas, *Nachmetaphysisches Denken* [Frankfurt am Main: Suhrkamp, 1988].) See also Cooke, *Language and Reason*, pp. 5–8.

20. This could be called the utopian content of his theory of communicative action. See chapter 7 below and J. Habermas, "The New Obscurity: The Crisis of the Welfare State and the Exhaustion of Utopian Energies," in his *The New Conservatism: Cultural Criticism and the Historians' Debate*, trans. and ed. S. W. Nicholsen (Cambridge, Mass.: MIT Press, 1991), pp. 48–70 (here, pp. 64–69). ("Die Krise des Wohlfahrtsstaats und die Erschöpfung utopischer Energien," in *Die Neue Unübersichtlichkeit* [Frankfurt am Main: Suhrkamp, 1985].) Cf. also Cooke, *Language and Reason*, pp. 38–50.

21. In addition to the colonization of communicative reason by functionalist reason, Habermas mentions a second "pathology" of social life under the conditions of late capitalism: cultural impoverishment due to the ever-increasing divorce between the specialist cultures (science, law and morality, and art) from everyday communicative action. However, not only does Habermas have less to say about this second pathology, his account of its status is unclear. On the one hand, he often treats it as a pathology of late capitalist society that is quite distinct from that of the colonization of the lifeworld. On the other hand, he sometimes describes it as a pathology that results from the colonization of the lifeworld. See my critical comments in Cooke, *Language and Reason*, pp. 142–147.

22. The second volume of his *The Theory of Communicative Action* is subtitled "The Critique of Functionalist Reason."

23. Habermas, *The Theory of Communicative Action*, vol. 2, p. 117.

24. Ibid., p. 150. Cf. Cooke, *Language and Reason*, pp. 133–135.

25. Habermas, "The New Obscurity," p. 65. It is worth noting that, with his thesis of the colonization of the communicatively regulated domains of social life by functionalist modes of social reproduction, Habermas satisfies a condition traditionally deemed crucial to any convincing critical social theory: he claims that the social obstacles to human flourishing he identifies are caused by certain historically contingent features of the social order he criticizes. In other words, his theory has the explanatory component traditionally deemed necessary if a critical social theory is to have motivating power. I return to this point in chapter 8 below.

26. Habermas identifies postmetaphysical thinking as one of the most important philosophical impulses of the twentieth century. See J. Habermas, *Postmetaphysical Thinking*, trans. M. W. Hohengarten (Cambridge, Mass.: MIT Press, 1992). (*Nachmetaphysisches Denken* [Frankfurt am Main: Suhrkamp, 1988].)

27. For a brief account of the postmetaphysical aspects of Habermas's notion of communicative rationality, see Cooke, *Language and Reason*, pp. 38–43.

28. J. Habermas, "Toward a Reconstruction of Historical Materialism," in his *Communication and the Evolution of Society*, trans. T. McCarthy (London: Heinemann, 1979), pp. 130–177, here, pp. 138–141. ("Zur Rekonstruktion des historischen Materialismus," in *Zur Rekonstruktion des*

historischen Materialismus [Frankfurt am Main: Suhrkamp, 1976].) J. Habermas, "Philosophy as Stand-In and Interpreter." In his *Moral Consciousness and Communicative Action*, trans. C. Lenhardt and S. W. Nicholsen (Cambridge, Mass.; MIT Press, 1990), pp. 1–20. ("Der Philosoph als Platzhalter und Interpret," in his *Moralbewusstsein und kommunikatives Handeln* [Frankfurt am Main: Suhrkamp, 1983], pp. 9–28.)

29. Habermas, *The Theory of Communicative Action*, vol. 2, pp. 382–383. See also chapter 7 below.

30. See J. Habermas, *Between Facts and Norms*, trans. W. Rehg (Cambridge, Mass.: MIT Press, 1996), pp. 445–446. (*Faktizität und Geltung* [Frankfurt am Main: Suhrkamp, 1992].)

31. M. Cooke, "Habermas, Autonomy, and the Identity of the Self," *Philosophy and Social Criticism* 18, nos. 3–4 (1992): 269–291. See also my account of autonomy in chapter 6 below.

32. This is the main thesis of Habermas "Philosophy as Stand-In and Interpreter." See also Cooke, *Language and Reason*, pp. 1–3.

33. "Rational reconstruction" is described by Habermas as a nonfoundationalist justificatory strategy: see J. Habermas, "What Is Universal Pragmatics?" in his *On the Pragmatics of Communication*, pp. 21–103. ("Was heißt Universalpragmatik?" in K.-O. Apel, ed., *Sprachpragmatik und Philosophie* [Frankfurt am Main: Suhrkamp, 1976].)

34. Of course, empirical evidence is always selected and assessed from a position informed by a complex interconnection of theoretical and normative considerations.

35. See Cooke, *Language and Reason*, esp. pp. 29–38.

36. One of Habermas's clearest statements of the role formal pragmatics plays in justifying his theory of communicative action can be found his writings on discourse ethics. See J. Habermas, "Discourse Ethics: Notes on a Program of Philosophical Justification," in his *Moral Consciousness and Communicative Action*, pp. 42–115, esp. pp. 82–98. Here, the universalist character of his formal-pragmatic hypotheses is evident, for example, when he states that "the principle of universalization . . . is implied by the presuppositions of argumentation *in general*" (p. 86, my emphasis). It is not clear exactly how this statement is to be understood. On occasion, he suggests that certain of the strong idealizations on which his theory depends are the result of sociocultural learning processes; these learning processes, which come about for historically contingent reasons, can be seen as developing the inherent logic of normative intuitions that are features of communication in all sociocultural contexts and historical epochs. However, this qualification merely increases his burden of proof, for he now has to show not only that the normative intuitions in question are a feature of communication in general but also that there is an inherent logic to their development along the reflexive and universalist lines he describes. In his writings of the 1970s and 1980s Habermas held the view that reconstructive theories of individual moral development of the kind proposed by Lawrence Kohlberg could help him in this regard, while acknowledging that the difficulties involved in developing any such theory on a sociocultural level were considerable (see Habermas, *Communication and the Evolution of Society*). Since then, however, he has made no attempt to develop the required theory of sociocultural learning and has, moreover, expressed reservations about a number of fundamental aspects of Kohlberg's theory (see J. Habermas, "A Philosophico-Political Profile," in his *Autonomy and Solidarity*, ed. Peter Dews, London: Verso [1986], pp. 149–189, here, p. 168, and J. Habermas, "Lawrence Kohlberg and Neo-Aristotelianism," in his *Justification and Application*, pp. 113–132). For these reasons, I leave aside this complication in the following.

37. Cooke, *Language and Reason*, pp. 31–34. S. Benhabib makes a similar point with regard to the idealizing presuppositions guiding moral argumentation in her *Situating the Self*, p. 32.

Notes

38. See Cooke, *Language and Reason*, esp. pp. 150–162.

39. See, for example, Habermas, *Theory of Communicative Action*, vol. 1, p. 240; Habermas, "A Reply," in A. Honneth and H. Joas, *Communicative Action* (Cambridge, Mass.: MIT Press, 1991), p. 226. ("Entgegnung," in Honneth and Joas, *Kommunikatives Handeln* [Frankfurt am Main: Suhrkamp, 1986], pp. 327–405.) See also Cooke, *Language and Reason*, pp. 39–43.

40. Habermas, *Postmetaphysical Thinking*, pp. 115–148.

41. See Cooke, *Language and Reason*, esp. pp. 84–94. I argue that the substance of Habermas's thesis is correct, requiring only minor qualification.

42. Habermas, *The Theory of Communicative Action*, vol. 1, part 4. A number of commentators have drawn attention to problems arising from Habermas's reliance on a notion of functional rationality. See, for example, T. McCarthy, "Complexity and Democracy: The Seducements of Systems Theory," in his *Ideals and Illusions* (Cambridge, Mass.: MIT Press, 1991), pp. 152–180.

43. I make this point in Cooke, *Language and Reason*, pp. 145–146.

44. This is the kind of "congruence argument" I advocate in M. Cooke, "Five Arguments for Deliberative Democracy," *Political Studies* 48, no. 5 (2000): 947–969 (esp. pp. 954–968).

45. I make the case for a two-step justificatory strategy in Cooke, "Beyond 'Objectivism' and 'Contextualism.'" It may be noted that in the present discussion I have modified my view of what the second step entails.

46. Habermas, "Discourse Ethics"; J. Habermas, "Remarks on Discourse Ethics," in his *Justification and Application*, pp. 19–112. ("Erläuterungen zur Diskursethik," in his *Erläuterungen zur Diskursethik*.)

47. Habermas, "Remarks on Discourse Ethics," pp. 75–76.

48. Ibid. Here, Habermas responds to Charles Taylor's theses regarding the motivating force of moral sources in his *Sources of the Self*.

49. J. Habermas, "Exkurs: Transzendenz von innen, Transzendenz ins Diesseits," in his *Texte und Kontexte* (Frankfurt am Main: Suhrkamp, 1991), pp. 127–156, here, p. 144. To be sure, questions of socialization raise thorny problems. Habermas sometimes hints at these, for example, when he points to the dependency of what we understand as morality on socialization into traditions that owe much to the Judaeo-Christian religions; here, he points to the problem of how the semantic energies of such religions can be renewed in secular society in ways congruent with postmetaphysical thinking (see J. Habermas, "Metaphysics after Kant," in his *Postmetaphysical Thinking*, pp. 10–27, here, p. 15). ("Metaphysik nach Kant," in his *Nachmetaphysisches Denken*.)

50. Habermas, "Discourse Ethics," pp. 91–102. I draw attention to the limitations of this argument in Cooke, *Language and Reason*, pp. 26–27.

51. I discern evidence of an implicit acknowledgment of the limited justificatory power of formal pragmatics in Habermas's recent metatheoretical writings, in particular in the "weak" naturalist argument he outlines in his *Truth and Justification*, trans. B. Fultner (Cambridge, Mass.: MIT Press, 2003), pp. 1–49. (*Wahrheit und Rechtfertigung* [Frankfurt am Main: Suhrkamp, 1999].)This argument aims to shed light on the question of how we can uphold a conception of objectivity notwithstanding the multiplicity and contingency of world-generating grammars. Habermas acknowledges his theory's reliance on the assumption that human beings unavoidably conceive of the progress of

history as the possibility of learning. I regard this as a definite step in the right direction. See my discussion in M. Cooke, "Socio-Cultural Learning as a 'Transcendental' Fact: Habermas's Postmetaphysical Perspective," *International Journal of Philosophical Studies* 9, no. 1 (2001): 63–83 and Cooke, "Beyond 'Objectivism' and 'Contextualism.'"

52. See J. Habermas, "A Genealogical Analysis of the Cognitive Content of Morality," in his *The Inclusion of the Other*, ed. C. Cronin and P. de Greiff (Cambridge, Mass.: MIT Press, 2000), pp. 3–46, here, p. 45. ("Eine genealogische Betrachtung zum kognitiven Gehalt der Moral," in *Die Einbeziehung des Anderen* [Frankfurt am Main: Suhrkamp, 1996], pp. 11–64.)

53. See J. Habermas, "Historical Materialism and the Development of Normative Structures," in his *Communication and the Evolution of Society*, pp. 94–129.

54. J. Habermas, *The Philosophical Discourse of Modernity*, trans. F. Lawrence (Cambridge, Mass.: MIT Press, 1987). (*Der Philosophische Diskurs der Moderne* [Frankfurt am Main: Suhrkamp, 1985].)

55. See note 36 above. Indeed, it is open to the further objection that its reconstructions of moral competence have a gender bias: they fit the patterns of socialization and corresponding moral competences typical of the male inhabitants of modernity, overlooking the quite different patterns of moral socialization, and corresponding competences, of its female inhabitants. See Habermas's reply to his feminist critics in *Moral Consciousness and Communicative Action*, pp. 175–184. Cf. C. Gilligan, *In a Different Voice: Psychological Theory and Women's Development* (Cambridge, Mass.: Harvard University Press, 1982).

56. See Habermas, *Between Facts and Norms*, pp. 9–27. Admittedly, his discussion in these pages does not expressly affirm the need for a formal-pragmatic justificatory strategy that makes universalist claims. It could be read as affirming the merits of a reconstructive approach to normative political theory, while leaving open the question of whether or not such an approach entails universalist claims. On p. 109 of the same work, however, Habermas does explicitly endorse the formal-pragmatic justification of the moral principle of universalizability that he conducted in his earlier work.

57. See especially Habermas, *Between Facts and Norms*, chapters 7 and 8.

58. See my discussion in M. Cooke, "The Weaknesses of Strong Intersubjectivism: Habermas's Conception of Justice," *European Journal of Political Theory* 2, no. 3 (2003): 281–305. I return to this issue in chapter 7 below.

59. J. Rawls, *Political Liberalism* (New York: Columbia University Press, 1993), esp. lecture 3, pp. 89–129.

60. J. Habermas, "Reconciliation through the Public Use of Reason: Remarks on John Rawls's Political Liberalism," *Journal of Philosophy* 92, no. 3 (1995): 109–131 (here, p. 110). Reprinted in Habermas, *The Inclusion of the Other*, pp. 49–73. ("Versöhnung durch öffentlichen Vernunftgebrauch," in *Die Einbeziehung des Anderen*, pp. 65–94.)

61. The concept of *political* constructivism is elaborated in Rawls, *Political Liberalism*, esp. lecture 3, pp. 89–129.

62. J. Rawls, "The Idea of Public Reason Revisited," *The University of Chicago Law Review* 64, no. 3 (1997): 765–807 (here, p. 766).

63. J. Rawls, "Kantian Constructivism in Moral Theory," *Journal of Philosophy* 72, no. 9 (1980): 518–519.

64. Rawls, *Political Liberalism*, p. 127.

65. Ibid., p. 119.

66. Ibid., p. 94.

67. Ibid., pp. 126–129. See also Rawls, "The Idea of Public Reason Revisited," pp. 787–794.

68. Rawls, *Political Liberalism*, p. 3.

69. Ibid., p. 129.

70. Ibid., p. 4.

71. See M. Cooke, "Are Ethical Conflicts Irreconcilable?" *Philosophy and Social Criticism* 23, no. 2 (1997): 1–19.

72. See Cooke, "Five Arguments for Deliberative Democracy," pp. 959–965.

73. The problem of radical contextualism is particularly evident in Rawls's attempt to develop a "law of peoples" out of liberal ideas of justice. See J. Rawls, *The Law of Peoples* (New York: Basic Books, 1993).

74. Habermas, "Reconciliation through the Public Use of Reason" (esp. pp. 119–126).

75. The main ideas guiding Honneth's critical social theory are set out in his *Struggle for Recognition*, trans. J. Anderson (Cambridge, Mass.: MIT Press, 1995). (*Kampf um Anerkennung* [Frankfurt am Main: Suhrkamp, 1992].) In this, and in many shorter pieces, he clarifies his own guiding intuitions through comparison and contrast with Habermas's critical social theory. See Honneth, "The Social Dynamics of Disrespect," pp. 260–266; Honneth, "Moralbewußtsein und soziale Klassenherrschaft: Einige Schwierigkeiten in der Analyse normativer Handlungspotentiale," in A. Honneth, *Das Andere der Gerechtigkeit* (Frankfurt am Main: Suhrkamp, 2001), pp. 110–129; Fraser and Honneth, *Redistribution or Recognition?*, pp. 246–247.

76. Honneth, "The Social Dynamics of Disrespect," pp. 264–266. Cf. Honneth, *Das Andere der Gerechtigkeit*, pp. 111–112.

77. Honneth refers to the Left-Hegelian "*fixation* on the concept of interest" in Fraser and Honneth, *Redistribution or Recognition?*, p. 136 (my emphasis).

78. Honneth, "The Social Dynamics of Disrespect," pp. 264–265.

79. Ibid., pp. 261–264; Honneth, "Eine Soziale Pathologie der Vernunft," note 47. Honneth's objection is directed against Habermas's theory of communicative action. He is in my view correct to discern functionalist tendencies in this theory. It is less clear, however, that the objection can be leveled against Habermas's later writings. In particular, *Between Facts and Norms* makes room for the articulation of subjective experiences of suffering in ethical-political discourses.

80. Honneth, "Eine Soziale Pathologie der Vernunft," note 47.

81. Honneth, "Eine Soziale Pathologie der Vernunft."

82. Honneth emphasizes the importance of taking account of the subject's own normative expectations. In this respect, his approach is clearly congruent with the ethical aspect of the notion of

situated reason. In contrast to Habermas, however, Honneth does not attach importance to the subject's capacity to *argue* the validity of her normative expectations; in other words, rational accountability is not a central ingredient of Honneth's conception of autonomous agency (cf. chapter 4 below, note 6).

83. Honneth, "The Social Dynamics of Disrespect," p. 261.

84. Honneth, "Grounding Recognition: A Rejoinder to Critical Questions," *Inquiry* 45, no. 4 (2002): 499–519 (here, pp. 514–515). Here, Honneth is responding to Kauppinen, who describes Honneth's theory, in evident analogy with Habermas's, as "reconstructive internal critique," in the sense of a critique that seeks to make implicit standards explicit. See. A. Kauppinen, "Reason, Recognition, and Internal Critique," *Inquiry* 45, no. 4 (2002): 479–498 (here, pp. 484–485).

85. Even in *Struggle for Recognition*, Honneth drew heavily on the support of psychoanalytic theory, in particular, on object relations theory. Nonetheless, in this and in other shorter pieces published about the same time he also emphasized the importance of historical and sociological studies to support his claim that certain expectations relating to recognition are universal presuppositions of communicative action. In his recent articles, by contrast, we find fewer references to historical and sociological data and increasing appeal to the evidence of psychoanalytic theories.

86. As indicated, there is some evidence in his recent work that Habermas is moving back from this position to a more situated view of communicative rationality.

87. Honneth admits that in his *Struggle for Recognition* he had not worked out whether the three modes of mutual recognition should be thought of as invariant anthropological features or as the contingent results of historical processes. Honneth, "Grounding Recognition," p. 501.

88. Fraser and Honneth, *Redistribution or Recognition?*, pp. 136–137.

89. Ibid., pp. 138–150.

90. In his *Struggle for Recognition*, Honneth identified not "accomplishment" but "solidarity" as the category of recognition corresponding to self-esteem; see pp. 92–130. The move away from the idea of solidarity to that of accomplishment is just one of a number of modifications of his theory that Honneth has undertaken in the past decade. Another modification is his explicit acknowledgement in recent texts that his three normative categories of recognition are historically and culturally specific features of communicative action, and not universal ones (see note 87 above). Yet another modification is his increased reliance on the theoretical support of psychoanalysis rather than sociology or history (see note 85 above).

91. This might be seen as further evidence of Habermas's cognitivist bias.

92. Fraser and Honneth, *Redistribution or Recognition?*, pp. 144–145, 150, and 263.

93. Ibid., p.143.

94. Ibid., pp. 264–265.

95. Honneth, "Grounding Recognition," p. 517.

96. Fraser and Honneth, *Redistribution or Recognition?*, p. 263.

97. See note 6 above.

98. Honneth, "Grounding Recognition," p. 517.

99. Here Honneth's debt to Hegel is evident. See A. Honneth, *Suffering from Indeterminacy: An Attempt at a Reactualisation of Hegel's Philosophy of Right*, Spinoza Lectures 5 (Assen: Royal Van Gorcum, 2000). (*Leiden an Unbestimmtheit: Eine Reaktualisierung der Hegelschen Rechtsphilosophie* [Stuttgart: Reclam, 2001].)

100. Honneth, "Grounding Recognition," pp. 509–511 and 517–518. Cf. Fraser and Honneth, *Redistribution or Recognition?*, pp. 256–265.

101. It is not clear whether Honneth uses the terms "ethical" and "moral" interchangeably here or whether he intends to distinguish moral from ethical learning processes.

102. In an exchange with Finnish critics, Honneth has begun to address these questions. However, although he has clarified the important question of where he stands on the issue of value realism, he has said little as yet about where he stands on the issue of moral or ethical realism (see note 101 above), or more generally, ethical validity. In this critical rejoinder, Honneth merely mentions the problem of accounting for the specifically moral character of his three normative expectations of recognition. However, his response to Laitinnen, in which he rejects a strong value realism, suggests that he is likely to reject a strong moral realism as well. See Honneth, "Grounding Recognition," esp. pp. 513–517. Cf. his discussion of McDowell's moral realism: A. Honneth, "Between Hermeneutics and Hegelianism: John McDowell and the Challenge of Moral Realism," in N. Smith, ed., *Reading McDowell: On Mind and World* (London: Routledge, 2002), pp. 246–265.

103. There is an evident contrast here with Habermas's elaboration of a theory of moral validity ("discourse ethics") as an integral part of his critical social theory.

104. Honneth, "Social Dynamics of Disrespect," p. 262.

105. Again, it is not clear how we should interpret the term "moral" here (see note 101 above).

106. Honneth, "Social Dynamics of Disrespect," p. 262.

107. Fraser and Honneth, *Redistribution or Recognition?*, pp. 1, 89.

108. Ibid., pp. 114–117.

109. Ibid., pp. 120–122.

110. Nancy Fraser makes this point in Fraser and Honneth, *Redistribution or Recognition?*, p. 8.

111. See, for example, Fraser and Honneth, *Redistribution or Recognition?*, pp. 130–134.

112. A. Honneth, "Invisibility: On the Epistemology of Recognition," *The Aristotelian Society* 75 (2001): 111–126.

113. A. Honneth, "Facetten des vorsozialen Selbst: Eine Erwiderung auf Joel Whitebook," *Psyche* 55 (2001): 790–802.

114. In chapter 6 I point out that this contextual dimension is cause for concern only for those who hold that knowledge of a reality independent of our descriptions, interpretations, and evaluations is possible.

115. Fraser and Honneth, *Redistribution or Recognition?*, pp. 245–246.

116. Ibid., p. 125 (cf. "Anerkennung oder Umverteilung?" pp. 147–148 [my emphasis, my translation]). The published English translation leaves out the words "all" and "completely." This difference between the original and the published translation is possibly indicative of a concern on Honneth's part to eradicate the last traces of foundationalism from his theory.

Chapter 4

1. Hardt and Negri, *Empire*. I return to Hardt and Negri's critique of contemporary globalizing capitalism in chapter 8 below.

2. Ibid., p. 353.

3. Ibid., p. 354.

4. Ibid.

5. Butler's objections seem to be directed primarily against Habermasian conceptions of rational agency; Laclau's objections seem to be directed primarily against the alleged harmonistic and reconciliatory aspects of Habermasian models of social criticism and democratic politics.

6. By contrast, Honneth appears not to connect agency with the capacity for argumentative reasoning. His general definition of autonomy or self-realization is: "every human being's interest in being able to freely determine and realize his own desires and interests" (Honneth, "Grounding Recognition," p. 516). Although he makes second-order reflection ("strong evaluation") one of the core components of autonomy, he does not, in contrast to Habermas, connect this with rational accountability. See A. Honneth, "Decentered Autonomy: The Subject after the Fall" in his *The Fragmented World of the Social*, trans. J. Farrell, ed. C. W. Wright (New York: State University of New York Press, 1995), pp. 261–271. ("Dezentrierte Autonomie" in *Zur Verteidigung der Vernunft gegen ihre Liebhaber und Verächter*, ed. C. Menke and M. Seel [Frankfurt am Main: Suhrkamp, 1993], pp. 149–164.) His views on democratic deliberation are less clear. On occasion, at least, he seems to endorse a view of public reasoning that is close to Habermas's. See Honneth, "Between Hermeneutics and Hegelianism," esp. pp. 258–263.

7. In chapter 8 I take up the question of overemphasis on justificatory issues from another angle, asking whether it leads to a disconnection of theory from praxis.

8. Poststructuralist theory is, of course, deeply influenced by the writings of Michel Foucault, one of the most provocative critical social theorists of the twentieth century. In view of this, it may be wondered why I do not devote more space to Foucault's thinking in this chapter or, indeed, elsewhere in the book. However, since there are already a number of excellent attempts to consider Foucault's work from the vantage point of Left-Hegelian critical social theory, and considerably fewer attempts to consider the work of Butler or Laclau from this perspective, I have decided to focus on these theorists' writings, which seem to me to make interesting and productive use of some of Foucault's most important ideas. For an interesting exchange between Left-Hegelian critical social theory and Foucauldian poststructuralism, see D. Couzens Hoy and T. McCarthy, *Critical Theory* (Oxford: Blackwell, 1994). For commentaries on Foucault from a Left-Hegelian perspective, see N. Fraser, *Unruly Practices* (London and New York: Routledge, 1989) and A. Honneth, *Critique of Power*, trans. K. Baynes (Cambridge, Mass.: MIT Press, 1991). (*Kritik der Macht* [Frankfurt am Main: Suhrkamp, 1985]).

9. In the preface to the second edition of *Hegemony and Socialist Strategy*, jointly written by Laclau with Chantal Mouffe (London: Verso, 2001), readers are told that "poststructuralism is the terrain where we have found the main source of our theoretical reflection and, within the post-

structuralist field, deconstruction and Lacanian theory have had a decisive importance in the formulation of our approach to hegemony" (p. xi). Butler's affiliation with poststructuralism is made especially clear in her "Contingent Foundations: Feminism and the Question of 'Postmodernism,'" in J. Butler and J. Scott, eds., *Feminists Theorize the Political* (New York: Routledge, 1992), pp. 3–21.

10. The label "Habermasian" is used, for example, by Laclau (with Mouffe) in the preface to the second edition of their *Hegemony and Socialist Strategy*, p. xvii and by Butler in her "Was ist Kritik? Ein Essay über Foucaults Tugend," *Deutsche Zeitschrift für Philosophie* 50, no. 1 (2002): 249–265 (here, p. 251) and in her "Restaging the Universal: Hegemony and the Limits of Formalism," in J. Butler, E. Laclau, and S. Žižek, *Contingency, Hegemony, Universality* (London: Verso, 2000), pp. 11–43 (pp. 3, 38).

11. Though some of Laclau's and Butler's critical remarks on Habermas could be read as criticism of his foundationalism, this does not seem to be the main focus of their objections. See, for example, E. Laclau, "Identity and Hegemony: The Role of Universality in the Constitution of Political Logics," in Butler, Laclau, and Žižek, *Contingency, Hegemony, Universality*, pp. 44–89, here, p. 82 and Butler, "Restaging the Universal," p. 15.

12. In addition, Laclau's silence with regard to the status of his own idea of hegemonic democracy could be interpreted as evidence of a latent foundationalism. Cf. S. Žižek, "Class Struggle or Postmodernism? Yes, Please!" in Butler, Laclau, and Žižek, *Contingency, Hegemony, Universality*, pp. 90–135, esp. p. 106.

13. See chapter 6 below and also M. Cooke, "Habermas, Feminism, and the Question of Autonomy," in P. Dews, ed., *Habermas: A Critical Reader* (Oxford: Blackwell, 1999), pp. 178–210, esp. 180–184.

14. J. Butler, "Dynamic Conclusions," in Butler, Laclau, and Žižek, *Contingency, Hegemony, Universality*, pp. 263–280, here, pp. 278–279.

15. Butler, "Restaging the Universal," p. 40.

16. Ibid., p. 13. Butler in fact refers to "the normative and optimistic moment" of *hegemony*; however, her formulation seems equally applicable to critical social thinking as she conceives it.

17. Butler, "Dynamic Conclusions," p. 277.

18. Butler, "Restaging the Universal," p. 12.

19. Ibid., pp. 12–13.

20. For Butler, all forms of identity—for example, the identity of individual subjects—are constituted differentially. That is, their constitution produces a constitutive outside that can never become fully inside or immanent. On the incompletion of what she calls the subject position, see Butler, "Restaging the Universal," p. 12.

21. Butler, "Dynamic Conclusions," p. 268.

22. Ibid., p. 269.

23. For Butler, the contingency of norms refers to their variable and limited cultural operation. The contingency of transcendental rules and functions, by contrast, refers to the lack of any final ground for their operation. See Butler, *Antigone's Claim*, pp. 44–45.

Notes

24. It is likely that Butler also objects to Habermas's prioritization of argumentative forms of social criticism and democratic politics. I come back to this point in chapter 6 below.

25. Butler regards the notion of critique developed in the work of Foucault as particularly fruitful in this regard. See her "Was ist Kritik?"

26. J. Butler, "Competing Universalities," in Butler, Laclau, and Žižek, *Contingency, Hegemony, Universality*, pp. 136–181 (here, pp. 177–178). This links her with Adorno (see chapter 3 above, pp. 42–43).

27. Ibid., p. 177.

28. Similarly, Butler holds that anomalous linguistic responses to offensive speech acts can rearticulate or restage the speech act in a way that counters its offensive call. See J. Butler, *Excitable Speech: A Politics of the Performative* (London and New York: Routledge, 1997).

29. Butler, *Antigone's Claim*, p. 182.

30. For an account of kinship rules as threshold rules, see Butler, *Antigone's Claim* (esp. pp. 16–17). For Butler's understanding of transcendental rules, see her "Competing Universalities," pp. 145–148.

31. Butler, "Competing Universalities," p. 138.

32. Butler, "Restaging the Universal," pp. 37–39.

33. Ibid., pp. 5–43.

34. Ibid., p. 15.

35. Butler, "Was ist Kritik?", pp. 250–251. Cf. Butler, *Excitable Speech*, pp. 86–89.

36. Butler, "Restaging the Universal," pp. 38–41. See also Butler, *Excitable Speech*, p. 90.

37. Butler, "Restaging the Universal," pp. 36–38. Butler refers to Spivak's "A Translator's Preface" and afterword to Mahasweta Devi, *Imaginary Maps* in D. Landry and G. MacLean, eds., *The Spivak Reader* (New York: Routledge, 1996).

38. H. Bhabha, *The Location of Culture* (New York: Routledge, 1996).

39. Butler, "Restaging the Universal," p. 41.

40. Butler, *Excitable Speech*, p. 89.

41. Butler, "Competing Universalities," pp. 167–169.

42. Ibid., p. 168.

43. Ibid., pp. 168–169.

44. Butler, "Restaging the Universal," p. 39.

45. Butler, *Excitable Speech*, p. 89.

46. E. Laclau and C. Mouffe, "Post-Marxism without Apologies," *New Left Review* 166 (1987): 79–106 (here, p. 86). Cf. Laclau, "Identity and Hegemony," p. 85.

47. Laclau and Mouffe, "Post-Marxism without Apologies," pp. 96–97.

48. Laclau and Mouffe, *Hegemony and Socialist Strategy*, pp. xv, 176, and 184.

49. Ibid., p. 125.

50. Ibid., pp. 125–126.

51. Butler, "Restaging the Universal," p. 12.

52. Laclau and Mouffe, *Hegemony and Socialist Strategy*, p. 104.

53. Ibid., pp. 110–111.

54. Ibid., pp. 111–112.

55. J. Derrida, "Structure, Sign, and Play in the Discourse of the Human Sciences," in his *Writing and Difference*, trans. A. Bass (London: Routledge, 1978), pp. 278–293 (here, p. 280). ("La structure, le signe, et le jeu dans le discours des sciences humaines," in J. Derrida, *L'écriture et la différence* [Paris: Seuil, 1967], pp. 409–429.)

56. Laclau and Mouffe, *Hegemony and Socialist Strategy*, p. 113.

57. Laclau, "Identity and Hegemony," pp. 64–73. Cf. J. Torfing, *New Theories of Discourse: Laclau, Mouffe, and Žižek* (Oxford: Blackwell, 1999), pp. 54–57.

58. Laclau, "Identity and Hegemony," p. 69. To be sure, in this passage Laclau does not make an explicit link between subjective motivation and a desire for the transcendent ethical object; however, I interpret his remarks on the shift from a search for ultimate meaning to a concern with truth, which he sees as a decisive change within the history of psychoanalysis, in this vein. I deal with the specifically ethical character of the transcendent object of desire in the course of my discussion.

59. This is a difficulty with Butler's view of the subject as entirely constructed by way of multiple social and political discourses. See Cooke, "Habermas, Feminism, and the Question of Autonomy," pp. 180–184. Despite her intriguing analysis of the formation of subjectivity in *The Psychic Life of Power: Theories in Subjection* (Stanford, Calif.: Stanford University Press, 1997), Butler has not yet resolved the problem of intentionality.

60. Butler, "Restaging the Universal," p. 37; Laclau, "Identity and Hegemony," p. 58.

61. Laclau, "Identity and Hegemony," p. 57.

62. E. Laclau, "Structure, History, and the Political," in Butler, Laclau, and Žižek, *Contingency, Hegemony, Universality*, pp. 182–212 (here 211–212).

63. On the centrality of the concept of "articulation," see Laclau and Mouffe, *Hegemony and Socialist Strategy*, pp. 85–89.

64. Here, Laclau refers to Marx's essay "Contribution to the Critique of Hegel's Philosophy of Law: Introduction," in K. Marx and F. Engels, *Collected Works*, vol. 3 (London: Lawrence and Wishart, 1975), pp. 186–187. Quoted in Laclau, "Identity and Hegemony," p. 45.

65. Laclau, "Identity and Hegemony," p. 55.

66. Laclau and Mouffe, *Hegemony and Socialist Strategy*, p. x.

67. E. Laclau, "Constructing Universality," in Butler, Laclau, and Žižek, *Contingency, Hegemony, Universality*, pp. 281–307 (here, p. 304).

68. Laclau and Mouffe, *Hegemony and Socialist Strategy*, p. xiii; Laclau, "Constructing Universality," pp. 301–305; Laclau, "Identity and Hegemony," pp. 54–56.

69. Laclau and Mouffe, *Hegemony and Socialist Strategy*, p. x.

70. Laclau, "Identity and Hegemony," p. 56.

71. Ibid., pp. 55–56. The same holds for their correlates, representations of the "notorious crime" that prevents society from reaching its fullness.

72. E. Laclau, "The Death and Resurrection of the Theory of Ideology," *Journal of Political Ideologies* 1, no. 3 (1996): 201–220 (here, p. 211).

73. Laclau notes the similarities between his conception of chains of equivalences and Butler's idea of cultural translation. Laclau, "Structure, History, and the Political," p. 193.

74. Laclau and Mouffe, *Hegemony and Socialist Strategy*, pp. 183–184.

75. Laclau acknowledges affinities between his thinking and Sorel's on a number of occasions. See his "Identity and Hegemony," pp. 83–84 and Laclau, "The Death and Resurrection of the Theory of Ideology," pp. 215–218.

76. G. Sorel, *Reflections on Violence*, trans. T. E. Hulme (New York: AMS Press, 1975), pp. 164–165. (Réflexions sur la violence [Paris: Marcel Rivière et Cie, 1972].)

77. Ibid., p. 22.

78. Ibid., p. 135.

79. I. Berlin makes this point in "George Sorel" in his *Against the Current* (Oxford: Clarendon Press, 1981), pp. 296–332. With his emphasis on unconstrained vital activity, Sorel is a typical representative of the nineteenth-century zeitgeist that produced what is now called "Lebensphilosophie."

80. E.g., Laclau, "Identity and Hegemony," pp. 71, 78.

81. Ibid., pp. 83–84.

82. Ibid.

83. Laclau, "The Death and Resurrection of the Theory of Ideology," p. 216. Laclau also notes that the political trajectory of Sorel himself is an example of the contingency of the content of myth: "he passed from being a theoretician of revolutionary syndicalism to allying himself with a faction of the monarchist movement, and ended his career by supporting the Third International."

84. Laclau, "Constructing Universality," p. 285. In view of his remarks here it is strange that Laclau explicitly compares his idea of a chain of equivalence to Butler's idea of cultural translation (see note 73 above).

85. Laclau regards it as "self-defeating." However, he pursues a somewhat different line of argument against (what I call) "radical contextualism." His main argument is that restricting the range

of applicability of normative categories requires the theorist to "specify contexts, something she can do only through a metacontextual discourse which would have to have transcendental aprioristic validity." Laclau, "Constructing Universality," p. 286.

86. Thomas Brockelman offers a very different reading of this aspect of Laclau's work, attributing to him (and Mouffe) a conventionalist position that insists on the nonexistence of external truth in relation to society. See T. Brockelman, "The Failure of the Radical Democratic Imaginary," *Philosophy and Social Criticism* 29, no. 2 (2003): 187–212. Whereas Brockelman may be correct to read Laclau's earlier work in this way, I regard it as a misinterpretation of his more recent work.

87. Laclau, "Constructing Universality," pp. 285–286.

88. Ibid., p. 295. He assures his readers that he intends to restore the correct balance between the two dimensions in future works.

89. Laclau, "Identity and Hegemony," p. 80.

90. Ibid., p. 81.

91. This is just another way of describing the hegemonic relation. See Laclau, "Identity and Hegemony," p. 81.

92. Ibid.

93. Laclau and Mouffe, *Hegemony and Socialist Strategy*, p. 168.

94. S. Žižek, *The Ticklish Subject: The Absent Centre of Political Ontology* (London: Verso, 1999), p. 174, quoted in Laclau, "Identity and Hegemony," pp. 79–80. Laclau rejects this accusation.

95. This is deliberate. Laclau chastises Rawls, Habermas, and Levinas for failing to resist the temptation to introduce some normative content into the ethical moment. See Laclau, "Identity and Hegemony," pp. 81–82.

96. Ibid., pp. 82–86.

97. Ibid., p. 82.

98. Ibid., p. 85.

99. Ibid.; cf. also p. 57.

Chapter 5

1. Our discussion of Butler showed that these questions (whether a gap is needed and, if so, how it should be construed) are as relevant for her theory as for the theories of Rorty, Habermas, or Honneth.

2. By positing an invariable gap between an empty transcendent ethical object and its particular representations, Laclau also raises a question concerning the source of ethical motivation: as we saw in the last chapter, Laclau's account is ambiguous as to whether it is the transcendent object or its particular representations that exerts an affective pull. If he attributes it to the former, it is unclear how an empty object can have motivating power; if he attributes it to the latter, it is unclear why we should regard the motivation as ethical.

3. In referring to ideological closure in the following, I do not attempt to consider what an adequate definition of ideology might be. I should clarify, however, that I am in agreement with Butler's view that removing normative contents from the realm of critical interrogation constitutes (one form of) ideological closure.

4. Laclau, "The Death and Resurrection of the Theory of Ideology," pp. 201–220.

5. Ibid., pp. 202–203.

6. Ibid., p. 203.

7. Ibid., p. 212; cf. also p. 220, note 8.

8. Ibid., p. 205.

9. Ibid.

10. Ibid., p. 220, note 7.

11. Ibid., p. 205–206.

12. Ibid., p. 201 (abstract).

13. Ibid., p. 202.

14. Ibid., p. 212.

15. Ibid., p. 203.

16. See chapter 4 above, pp. 92–93.

17. To be sure, since his early essay on truth, "Wahrheitstheorien," in H. Fahrenbach, ed., *Wirklichkeit und Reflexion* (Pfüllingen: Neske, 1973), reprinted in J. Habermas, *Vorstudien und Ergänzungen zur Theorie des kommunikativen Handelns* (Frankfurt am Main: Suhrkamp, 1984), Habermas does not often refer explicitly to the idea of the ideal speech situation. By the mid-1980s, there were already clear signs that he was unhappy about using the term. Indeed, on a number of occasions, he claimed to regret ever having used it, referring to it as "too concrete" and "open to misinterpretation." See Habermas, *Autonomy and Solidarity*, p. 163. (*Die Neue Unübersichtlichkeit* [Frankfurt am Main: Suhrkamp, 1985], pp. 228–229 and J. Habermas, *Die Nachholende Revolution* [Frankfurt am Main: Suhrkamp, 1990], pp. 131–132.) In the early 1990s he warns against "essentialist" misunderstandings of the concept (see *Between Facts and Norms*, p. 323). Nonetheless, it is evident from his subsequent writings on truth and justification—see his *Truth and Justification*—that the idea of an ideal speech situation continues to play an important role in his theory.

18. His essay "Wahrheitstheorien" marks the first significant step in this endeavor.

19. See Habermas, *Postmetaphysical Thinking.*

20. Habermas explicitly compares his view of (moral) validity to the constructivist approach of John Rawls. See J. Habermas, "Rightness versus Truth," in his *Truth and Justification*, pp. 237–275, p. 261, note 35; Habermas, *Between Facts and Norms*, p. 156. (*Faktizität und Geltung*, p. 194; the English translation deviates significantly from the German original on this point.) However, there is at least one important difference between Habermas's and Rawls's constructivism: unlike Rawls, who views normative political validity as constructed by way of processes of public reasoning that are

essentially "monological," Habermas insists that the exchange of reasons of argumentation is a vital part of the process of construction. See Cooke, "Five Arguments for Deliberative Democracy," 954–967.

21. Although Habermas continues to define moral validity (justice) as the outcome of an idealized moral discourse, there are some indications that he no longer holds a constructivist account of legal-political validity. In chapter 7 below I point to these indications and discuss the differences between the ideas of validity apparently at work in his theory of law and politics, on the one hand, and in his theory of justice, on the other.

22. C. Lafont, "Realismus und Konstruktivismus in der kantianischen Moralphilosophie—das Beispiel der Diskursethik," *Deutsche Zeitschrift für Philosophie* 50, no. 1 (2002): 39–52. Wellmer makes a similar point in "Ethics and Dialogue" in his *The Persistence of Modernity*, trans. D. Midgley (Cambridge, Mass.: MIT Press, 1991), pp. 113–231, esp. pp. 160–168. (*Ethik und Dialog* [Frankfurt am Main: Suhrkamp, 1986].)

23. I look at Wellmer's objections in detail in chapter 7 below.

24. I use the term "regulative idea" in a general sense throughout these chapters, leaving aside the complexities of Kant's view of regulative ideas and academic discussions of these complexities. Moreover, I confine my discussion to their features and functions in critical social thinking. Cf. Joel Whitebook's discussion of regulative ideas in J. Whitebook, *Perversion and Utopia* (Cambridge Mass.: MIT Press, 1996), pp. 174–175.

25. I. Kant, *The Critique of Pure Reason* (New York: Macmillan, 1956), pp. 152–153, cited by Žižek in his "Holding the Place," in Butler, Laclau, and Žižek, *Contingency, Hegemony, Universality*, pp. 308–329, here, pp. 317–318. Žižek claims that Kant's reasoning with regard to the necessity of human imperfection is reproduced almost exactly by Laclau in his account of the contamination of emancipation by power (and, more generally, the constitutive inadequacy of representations of the universal).

26. Žižek, "Holding the Place," p. 317. This is Žižek's comment on Laclau's "secret Kantianism," but it seems to apply equally to Habermas.

27. See Laclau, "Identity and Hegemony," pp. 81–82.

28. Habermas, "Rorty's Pragmatic Turn," pp. 343–382, esp. pp. 365–366.

29. Ibid., pp. 369–373. See also M. Cooke, "Habermas on Meaning and Truth," *European Journal of Philosophy* 9, no. 1 (2001): 1–23, esp. pp. 9–15.

30. Habermas, "Rorty's Pragmatic Turn," p. 367.

31. Ibid., pp. 364, 370–372.

32. Ibid., pp. 370–372.

33. J. Habermas, "Introduction: Realism after the Linguistic Turn," in his *Truth and Justification*, pp. 1–49, here, pp. 42–43; cf. also Habermas, "Rightness versus Truth," esp. 254–256. The German word usually used by Habermas is "unverfügbar" (see *Wahrheit und Rechtfertigung*, pp. 56–57 and pp. 293–294).

34. It also provides a reason to query his continued allegiance to a constructivist view of morality (see chapter 7 below, pp. 185–186).

35. Other well-known proponents of this view of truth are Karl-Otto Apel and Hilary Putnam (in his work of the early 1980s). See K.-O. Apel, *Towards a Transformation of Philosophy*, trans. G. Adey and D. Frisby (London: Routledge and Kegan Paul, 1979). (*Transformation der Philosophie* [Frankfurt am Main: Suhrkamp, 1973].) H. Putnam, *Reason, Truth, and History* (Cambridge: Cambridge University Press, 1981).

36. On occasion, Habermas has himself referred to truth as a regulative idea. See Habermas, *Die Nachholende Revolution*, pp. 131–132. See also J. Habermas, "From Kant's 'Ideas' of Pure Reason to the 'Idealizing' Presuppositions of Communicative Action: Reflections on the Detranscendentalized 'Use of Reason,'" in his *Truth and Justification*, pp. 83–130, esp. pp. 91–109. He also describes the idea of the ideal speech situation that emerges from the idealizing presuppositions of discourse as a regulative idea. See Habermas, "Remarks on Discourse Ethics," p. 51; cf. also p. 55. Some remarks in his *Between Facts and Norms* also support my suggestion that the idea of the ideal speech situation should be interpreted as a regulative idea (see chapter 7 below, pp. 182–183).

37. In addition to the problem of motivation, which is the main focus of my discussion here, it also raises the question of how the metaphysically closed aspect of regulative ideas can be made to fit with Habermas's commitment to postmetaphysical conceptions of truth and justice.

38. See note 24 above.

39. Interestingly, Laclau seems prepared to accept Žižek's characterization of his conception of political representation as similar to the Kantian notion of a regulative idea. To be sure, he makes a distinction between his and Kant's conceptions on the basis that, for Kant, the content of the regulative idea is given once and for all, from the very beginning, and that, for him, the (ethical) object of investment is constantly changing; moreover, he strongly disputes the objections of cynicism and naivety that, as we have seen, Žižek directs against the Kantian notion. See Laclau, "Structure, History, and the Political," pp. 195–196. Cf. Žižek's reply in "Holding the Place," pp. 316–317.

40. Evident exceptions are truth claims for which it makes no sense to postulate a difference between truth and justification, for example, simple propositions such as "it is raining outside" (when I am standing outside) or "this is a hand" (when I raise it in normal circumstances).

41. See chapter 3 above, note 19.

42. This is the utopian content of Habermas's idea of communicative rationality. See Cooke, *Language and Reason*, pp. 44–45.

43. Below I shall suggest that the space vacated by truth and its equivalents cannot be construed as entirely empty.

44. I owe this point to Kevin Ryan.

45. Laclau does not explicitly extend his account of political representations to his own theory of hegemony. See chapter 4 below, note 12.

46. Žižek, "Class Struggle or Postmodernism?", pp. 110–111; "Holding the Place," pp. 310–311. I leave aside the question of whether Žižek's postulate of an originary trauma is useful in the context of radical democratic (or critical social) thinking.

47. This would explain Laclau's evident lack of enthusiasm for Žižek's idea of an originary trauma.

48. H. Vaihinger, *The Philosophy of "As If,"* trans. C. K. Ogden (London: Routledge and Kegan Paul, 1968). (*Die Philosophie des als ob* [Berlin: Reuther and Reichard, 1911].)

49. W. Iser, *The Fictive and the Imaginary: Charting Literary Anthropology* (London and Baltimore: John Hopkins University Press, 1993). (*Das Fiktive und das Imaginäre*, Frankfurt am Main: Suhrkamp, 1991.)

50. As is well known, Nietzsche takes this point further, famously remarking that the most erroneous judgments are the most indispensable, since "without granting as true the fictions of logic, without measuring reality against the purely invented world of the unconditional and self-identical . . . mankind could not live." Nietzsche, *Beyond Good and Evil*, p. 17. However, we can accept Vaihinger's point concerning the usefulness of fictions without committing ourselves to Nietzsche's thesis concerning their indispensability.

51. Vaihinger, *Philosophy of "As If,"* p. viii; cf. also p. 99.

52. Ibid., pp. 98–99.

53. Ibid., p. 268.

54. Ibid., p. 99.

55. U. Beck, W. Bonss, and C. Lau, "The Theory of Reflexive Modernization," *Theory, Culture, and Society* 20, no. 2 (2003): 1–33 (here, p. 19).

56. Ibid., pp. 24–26.

57. From our discussion in the last chapter we will recall that Laclau prefers to speak of the verisimilitude rather than truth of political representations.

58. Vaihinger considers only the orientating functions of fictions, disregarding their disclosing functions ("the object of the world of ideas as a whole is not the portrayal of reality . . . but rather to provide us with an instrument for finding our way about more easily in the world"). See Vaihinger, *The Philosophy of "As If,"* p. 15. This disregard for the function of disclosure is connected with his view of the nonexistence of the transcendent reality that many fictions purport to represent. For Vaihinger, it is most probable that no such reality exists. See also pp. 100–108; cf. his approving references to Kant's "theoretical non-theism," pp. 319–320.

59. J. Derrida, "Force of Law: The 'Mystical Foundation of Authority,'" in D. Cornell, M. Rosenfeld, and D. G. Carlson, eds., *Deconstruction and the Possibility of Justice* (New York and London: Routledge, 1992), pp. 3–67 (here, pp. 25–26).

60. Adorno quoted in Wellmer, "Ethics and Dialogue," in his *The Persistence of Modernity*, p. 177.

61. Taylor, *Sources of the Self*, p. 419. Taylor's distinction between Romantic and post-Romantic epiphanies is relevant here. He maintains that, in contrast to Romantic epiphanies, post-Romantic epiphanies do not portray anything clearly; the locus of epiphany shifts from what is portrayed to within the work itself.

62. A. Munro, "The Moon in the Orange Street Skating Rink," *The Progress of Love* (London: Chatto and Windus, 1987), p. 160.

63. Habermas has a tendency to make this mistake. I criticize his neglect of the disclosing function in everyday linguistic communication in Cooke, *Language and Reason*, pp. 79–84. Cf. also N.

Kompridis, "Heidegger's Challenge and the Future of Critical Theory," in Dews, ed., *Habermas: A Critical Reader*, pp. 118–150.

64. See, for example, A. Wellmer, "Truth, Semblance, Reconciliation" in his *The Persistence of Modernity*, pp. 113–231 (here, pp. 4–7). ("Wahrheit, Schein, Versöhnung," in his *Zur Dialektik von Moderne und Postmoderne* [Frankfurt am Main: Suhrkamp, 1985], pp. 12–14.)

65. Adorno quoted in Wellmer, "Truth, Semblance, Reconciliation," p. 7.

66. The idea of "navigation points" fits well with Charles Taylor's attempts to understand the human predicament in terms of finding or losing orientation in moral space. See Taylor, *Sources of the Self*, pp. 27–59.

67. Habermas, *Justification and Application*, p. 54. In the same section, he also uses the word "picture" to refer to his normative idea of a porous public sphere.

68. Taylor regards the inseparability of what is manifested from its embodiment as central to the very concept of an epiphany, irrespective of differences between the Romantic and post-Romantic understanding of this idea. See Taylor, *Sources of the Self*, pp. 419–420.

Chapter 6

1. Habermas maintains that validity must be understood in epistemic terms as justification or "validity that is proven for us." The German word that best captures this sense of validity is "Geltung." See his approving discussion of C. S. Peirce's epistemic conception of validity in Habermas, *Between Facts and Norms*, p. 14.

2. Cf. J. Habermas, "Remarks on the Concept of Communicative Action," in G. Seebaß and R. Tuomela, eds., *Social Action* (Dordrecht: Reidel, 1985), pp. 163–164. ("Erläuterungen zum Begriff des kommunikativen Handelns," in J. Habermas, *Vorstudien und Ergänzungen zur Theorie des kommunikativen Handelns* [Frankfurt am Main: Suhrkamp, 1984].)

3. Nor, of course, may a particular critical social theory understand its own utterances as expressions of subjective preference, for this would be at odds with its claims to be critical; at a minimum, the possibility of critique presupposes the availability of evaluative standards that are not purely subjective.

4. L. Wittgenstein, *On Certainty*, trans. D. Paul and G. E. M. Anscombe (Oxford: Blackwell, 1969), §99; cf. also §97. (*Über Gewissheit* [Frankfurt am Main: Suhrkamp, 1997].)

5. Ernst Tugendhat, too, places particular emphasis on the idea of autonomy when endorsing the thesis of an intimate link between validity and argumentation under the conditions of modernity. See E. Tugendhat, *Probleme der Ethik* (Stuttgart: Reclam, 1984), pp. 108–131.

6. Nietzsche, *Beyond Good and Evil*, esp. chapter 1, "On the Prejudices of Philosophers."

7. I see this as the core intuition behind Rousseau's and Kant's conceptions of moral autonomy. It has its correlate in the political domain in a concept of political autonomy as the freedom to bind one's will to laws that one is able to see as one's own.

8. Elsewhere I have argued that much feminist opposition to the ideal of autonomy can be construed as an opposition to particular interpretations of the ideal. See M. Cooke,

"Questioning Autonomy: The Feminist Challenge and the Challenge for Feminism," in R. Kearney and M. Dooley, eds., *Questioning Ethics* (London and New York: Routledge, 1999), pp. 258–282.

9. H. Frankfurt, "Freedom of the Will and the Concept of a Person," in G. Watson, ed., *Free Will* (Oxford: Oxford University Press, 1982).

10. C. Taylor, *Philosophical Papers* 2, (Cambridge: Cambridge University Press, 1985); Taylor, *Sources of the Self*.

11. C. Taylor, "Responsibility for Self," reprinted in Watson, ed., *Free Will*.

12. Taylor, *Sources of the Self*, chapters 1–4.

13. Ibid., pp. 92–93. I return to Taylor's idea of moral sources below.

14. Joseph Raz makes a similar point with regard to autonomous choice in his *The Morality of Freedom* (Oxford: Clarendon Press, 1986), pp. 372–375.

15. B. Berofsky, *Liberation from Self: A Theory of Personal Autonomy* (New York and Cambridge: Cambridge University Press, 1995), p. 105.

16. Berofsky makes tacit use of the distinction between moral worth and ethical worth. His position, as I understand it, is that actions and judgments have moral worth when they conform to some objective standard of moral validity and have ethical worth when they involve a subjective orientation toward a subjectively defined conception of the good. Important for our present purposes is his rejection not just of the link between personal autonomy and morality (pp. 107–138 and 140–181) but also of the link between personal autonomy and (what I call) ethical worth. See Berofsky, *Liberation from Self*, p. 9.

17. Ibid., p. 105.

18. Ibid., pp. 90–1, 77, 79, 182.

19. Ibid., pp. 182–209.

20. Ibid., chapter 10. This chapter, which has the title, "The Value of Autonomy," concentrates on dispelling some feminist objections to the concept of autonomy, and does not engage with the question of why we should regard autonomy as a valuable attribute of agency.

21. As we have seen Berofsky locates objectivity at the core of his conception of autonomy. The capacity for instrumental reasoning is held to be a presupposition of objectivity. Ibid., pp. 9–10.

22. The ideal of self-transparency been called into question by post-Freudian psychoanalytic theory. Theorists such as Julia Kristeva identify, and attach great importance to, a nonlinguistic semiotic realm that is rationally opaque. See J. Kristeva, "The System and the Speaking Subject" and other essays in T. Moi, ed., *The Kristeva Reader* (New York: Columbia University Press, 1986).

23. P. Ricoeur, *Oneself As Another*, trans. K. Blaney (Chicago: University of Chicago Press, 1992), p. 22. (*Soi-même comme un autre* [Paris: Seuil, 1990].)

24. Ibid., pp. 21–23.

25. The classic text on possessive individualism is C. B. McPherson, *The Political Theory of Possessive Individualism: Hobbes to Locke* (Oxford: Clarendon Press, 1962).

26. J. Cohen, "Democracy, Difference, and the Right to Privacy," in S. Benhabib, ed., *Democracy and Difference* (Princeton, N.J.: Princeton University Press, 1996), pp. 187–217; J. Cohen, *Regulating Intimacy* (Princeton, N.J.: Princeton University Press, 2002).

27. Equally, Cohen is concerned to show that her conceptualization of privacy rights does not entail a commitment to essentialist or atomistic conceptions of self-identity.

28. Cohen, *Regulating Intimacy*, p. 56.

29. I make this point in my review essay, M. Cooke, "Making the Case for Privacy Rights," *Philosophy and Social Criticism* 31, no. 1 (2005): 131–143 and in M. Cooke, "Privacy and Autonomy: A Comment on Jean Cohen," in B. Rössler, ed., *Privacies: Philosophical Evaluations* (Stanford, Calif.: Stanford University Press, 2004), pp. 98–112.

30. Cohen, *Regulating Intimacy*, p. 55.

31. Ibid., p. 57.

32. J. Habermas, "Individuation through Socialization: On George Herbert Mead's Theory of Subjectivity," in his *Postmetaphysical Thinking*, pp. 149–204, esp. pp. 184–194. ("Individuierung durch Vergesellschaftung: Zu G. H. Meads Theorie der Subjektivität," in *Nachmetaphysisches Denken*, pp. 187–241.) Cf. Cooke, "Habermas, Autonomy, and the Identity of the Self."

33. See Cooke, "Habermas, Autonomy, and the Identity of the Self" and Cooke, "Realizing the Post-Conventional Self."

34. Indeed, it is also out of tune with the reflexive-procedural model of law advocated by Cohen both as a metaparadigm of law and as a model for the legal regulation of intimacy. See Cooke, "Making the Case for Privacy Rights."

35. As critics of traditional interpretations of the concept of autonomy point out, the view that the human subject is his own ultimate origin is incoherent. It appears to demand that the subject's will, desire, and behavior be governed by his own self, whereby the governing self must be some kind of deeper self, which is in turn guided by a deeper self, and so on ad infinitum. Wolf strongly criticizes the idea of self-origination as part of her critique of the autonomy view of the self in her *Freedom within Reason* (Oxford and New York: Oxford University Press, 1990), pp. 10–14.

36. Berofsky makes this point in *Liberation from Self*, p. 3.

37. This is one of principal objections raised by feminist critics against the deontological tradition of moral theory and the contractarian tradition of political theory. See Cooke, "Questioning Autonomy," pp. 259–260.

38. See Berofsky, *Liberation from Self*, p. 2.

39. See M. Cooke, "A Space of One's Own: Autonomy, Privacy, Liberty," *Philosophy and Social Criticism* 25, no. 1 (1999): 23–53.

40. Rousseau, "A Discourse on the Origins of Inequality."

41. To be sure, there are sociocultural contexts in which the practice of giving reasons publicly is so open to manipulation for strategic purposes that the human subject must seek the erection of barriers to protect her ethical interpretations from abusive forces. However, the concept of autonomy I propose is designed to provide a normative basis for criticizing such sociocultural contexts.

42. In "Questioning Autonomy" I discuss some of the difficulties that face feminist theorists who reject models of agency in which unity and coherence are valued.

43. Foucault's critique of the notion of the sovereign subject has been a major influence on this line of thinking. See M. Foucault, *The Archaeology of Knowledge*, trans. A. M. Sheridan Smith (London: Tavistock, 1972), pp. 11–13. (*L'Archéologie du savoir* [Paris: Gallimard, 1969].)

44. A similar view of subjectivity is offered by Jane Flax (who associates herself with post-modernism rather than poststructuralism). Flax objects to the very term "self," partly because it involves a closure, attaching importance to certain attributes of subjectivity and dismissing other ones, and partly because of its implicit assumption that successful subjectivity is unitary, fixed, homogeneous, and teleological. See J. Flax, *Disputed Subjects* (London: Routledge, 1993), pp. 93–96.

45. J. Butler, "Gender Trouble, Feminist Theory, and Psychoanalytic Discourse," in L. Nicholson, ed., *Feminism/Postmodernism* (New York: Routledge, 1990), p. 324–340.

46. The more fundamental problem seems to be the poststructuralist tendency to treat subjectivity purely as a linguistic effect, reducing the human subject to the systems of meaning in and through which she is constituted. In chapter 4 we saw that Laclau is able to avoid this problem by positing a notion of the subject as prior to the social processes whereby she develops her subjectivity.

47. Butler, "Contingent Foundations: Feminism and the Question of Postmodernism," p. 15.

48. See chapter 4 above, pp. 78–79.

49. See M. Cooke, "Habermas, Feminism, and the Question of Autonomy," in Dews, ed., *Habermas: A Critical Reader*, pp. 178–210 (esp. 190–191).

50. Butler may also object to the privileged position ascribed to rational agency within Habermas's theory of communicative action. In this theory, the exercise of rational agency in public processes of deliberation is given pride of place. Butler, by contrast, emphasizes nonrational and nonverbal modes of actualizing subjectivity. However, it is one thing to seek to redress a per-ceived imbalance in Habermas's work by drawing attention to the multiplicity of ways in which human beings actualize their subjectivities—even to the multiple ways in which they carry out social criticism; it is another to claim that these multiple ways do not include rational agency. If Butler were to make the latter, stronger, claim, she would not only incur a considerable burden of proof; it would further complicate her theory's ability to accommodate the idea of intentional political agency.

51. This is one of the central points made by Habermas in *Between Facts and Norms*. The discourse principle, which is designed to be epistemologically and ethically nonauthoritarian, implies basic rights and democracy. See esp. chapters 3 and 4.

52. Benhabib makes a similar point in *Situating the Self*, esp. pp. 30–38; cf. also, S. Benhabib, *The Claims of Culture: Equality and Diversity in the Global* Era (Princeton and Oxford: Princeton University Press, 2002), p. 39.

53. A. Wellmer, *Sprachphilosophie* (Frankfurt am Main: Suhrkamp, 2004), pp. 250–277. Wellmer also makes the useful point that contestability has a different meaning in different domains of validity: what it means to contest a law of physics differs from what it means to contest a moral principle, which differs again from what it means to contest an aesthetic judgment.

54. C. Taylor, *Philosophical Arguments* (Cambridge, Mass.: Harvard University Press, 1995), pp. 160–161.

55. Žižek, too, appears to endorse this aspect of the Hegelian dialectic, whereby a thing "becomes what it always already was." See Žižek, *Enjoy Your Symptom: Jacques Lacan in Hollywood and Out* (London and New York: Routledge, 1992), p. 184. Adorno also affirms this position, expressing his conviction that every human being, even the most wretched, has a potential that, by conventional bourgeois standards, is comparable to genius. See T. W. Adorno, *Metaphysics: Concept and Problems*, ed. R. Tiedemann, trans. E. Jephcott (Cambridge: Polity, 2000), pp. 132–133. (*Metaphysik: Begriff und Probleme* [Suhrkamp: Frankfurt am Main, 1965].)

56. Taylor, *Sources of the Self*, pp. 72–73.

56. Ibid.

57. Tugendhat, too, makes a plea for a comparative approach to justification. See his *Probleme der Ethik*, chapter 5, esp. pp. 87–108. Overall, the model of practical reasoning he proposes in these pages is very close to Taylor's.

58. I owe this point to Kevin Ryan. Habermas himself emphasizes that his idealized model of discourse has critical force in that it can be used in concrete situations to highlight discrepancies between the norm and reality (see, for example, *Between Facts and Norms*, chapters 7 and 8). He does not, however, discuss the possibility that a consistent pattern of discrepancies between norm and reality may undermine the very intuitions guiding the norm.

59. Other nonargumentative, nonviolent means of persuasion include stories as well as nonrepresentational visual and literary art forms.

60. See below and Cooke, "Argumentation and Transformation," esp. pp. 98–103.

61. My reflections in chapter 7 below suggest that Habermas's account of practical rationality could be developed along the lines proposed above. I acknowledge that, in *Between Facts and Norms*, Habermas suggests an alternative account of practical reasoning; this account presents a discursively achieved consensus not as a guarantee of legal-political validity but as a regulative idea, opening the way for a nonconstructivist account of moral validity. Admittedly, Habermas himself has not pursued this path.

62. Taylor, *Sources of the Self*, esp. chapter 4. The following discussion draws on my discussion of the transformative power of argumentation, and of the connection between cognitive transformation and argumentation, in Cooke, *Argumentation and Transformation*.

63. Taylor, *Sources of the Self*, pp. 95, 53–62 (Taylor does not distinguish between ethical and moral validity). In passages such as these, he seems to affirm a metaphysically based realist position. Cf. N. Smith, *Strong Hermeneutics* (London and New York: Routledge, 1997), esp. pp. 65–75.

64. See chapter 5 above, p. 110.

65. Taylor does not claim that articulation is *necessary* in order to make contact with moral sources; prayer and rituals employing music and visual presentation are examples of forms of expression

that are not mediated by way of articulation yet enable contact with the good. Taylor, *Sources of the Self*, pp. 91–92.

66. Ibid., p. 96.

67. Ibid.

68. Taylor is also sensitive to the importance of nonlinguistic forms of representation (such as painting) in enabling access to moral sources. Ibid., pp. 95–96. See also note 65 above.

69. J. Habermas, "Toward a Critique of the Theory of Meaning," in his *On the Pragmatics of Communication*, pp. 277–306, esp. 277–278. ("Zur Kritik der Bedeutungstheorie," in his *Nachmetaphysisches Denken*, pp. 105–135.)

70. See J. Habermas, "On the Distinction between the Poetic and Communicative Uses of Language," in his *On the Pragmatics of Communication*, pp. 383–401. (Excerpt [in revised translation] of "Exkurs zur Einebnung des Gattungsunterschieds zwischen Philosophie und Literatur," in his *Der Philosophische Diskurs der Moderne* [Frankfurt am Main: Suhrkamp, 1985], pp. 228–247.)

71. R. Jakobson, "Linguistics and Poetics," in T. A. Sebeok, ed., *Style in Language* (Cambridge, Mass.: MIT Press, 1960), pp. 350–377 (here, p. 356).

72. Ibid., p. 358.

73. Ibid.

74. "Poetic function is not the sole function of verbal art but only its dominant, determining function, whereas in all other verbal activities it acts as a subsidiary, accessory constituent." Ibid., p. 356.

75. Habermas, "On the Distinction between the Poetic and Communicative Uses of Language," p. 389.

76. See chapter 5 above, note 63.

77. W. Benjamin, "Theses on the Philosophy of History," in his *Illuminations*, ed. H. Arendt, trans. H. Zorn (London: Pimlico, 1999). (*Illuminationen* [Frankfurt am Main: Suhrkamp, 1955].) Cf. R. Tiedemann, "Historical Materialism or Political Messianism? An Interpretation of the Theses on the Concept of History," in G. Smith ed., *Benjamin* (Chicago: University of Chicago Press, 1983).

78. Horkheimer and Adorno, *Dialectic of Enlightenment*. Cf. A. Honneth, "The Possibility of a Disclosing Critique of Society: The *Dialectic of Enlightenment* in light of Current Debates in Social Criticism," *Constellations* 7, no. 1 (2000): 116–127.

79. This appears to one of Rorty's principal objections to Horkheimer and Adorno's *Dialectic of Enlightenment*. R. Rorty, "The Overphilosophication of Politics," *Constellations* 7, no. 1 (2000): 128–131.

80. Taylor, *Sources of the Self*, p. 97.

81. Ibid.

82. Ibid., pp. 91–92. The failure to confront this problem may be connected with his evident reluctance to tie validity to argumentation, a reluctance that may in turn be due to the difficulties

involved in assessing claims to validity that depend on experiences of disclosure that may not be capable of being articulated as reasons.

83. Cf. M. Kettner, "Gute Gründe: Thesen zur diskursiven Vernunft," in K.-O. Apel and M. Kettner, eds., *Diskursive Rationalität* (Frankfurt am Main: Suhrkamp, 1996), pp. 424–464.

84. See the essays in Habermas, *On the Pragmatics of Communication* and also Cooke, *Language and Reason*, chapter 4.

85. Habermas, *The Theory of Communicative Action*, vol. 1, p. 297.

86. J. Habermas, "Some Further Clarifications of the Concept of Communicative Rationality," in his *On the Pragmatics of Communication*, pp. 307–342 (here, p. 340).

87. Kompridis, "Heidegger's Challenge and the Future of Critical Theory," p. 143.

Chapter 7

1. This definition is close to the one proposed by K. Mannheim in *Ideology and Utopia*, trans. L. Wirth and E. Shiels (London: Routledge, 1991). (*Ideologie und Utopie* [Frankfurt am Main: Klostermann, 1929].) Mannheim defines utopian thinking as "a type of orientation which transcends reality and at the same time breaks the bonds of the existing order" (p. 173). However, in my view, Mannheim's definition overemphasizes the actual transformative effect of utopian thinking (cf. his definition on p. 185).

2. K. Marx and F. Engels, *The Communist Manifesto* (Harmondsworth: Penguin Books, 1967), pp. 114–118. (*Das kommunistische Manifest* [Hamburg: Argument Verlag, 2002].)

3. In consequence, Marcuse regards the concept of utopia as obsolescent, claiming that it refers to projects for social change that are considered impossible whereas "today . . . any transformation of the technical and natural environment is a possibility." H. Marcuse, *Five Lectures: Psychoanalysis, Politics, and Utopia*, trans. J. Shapiro and S. Weber (London: Penguin Press, 1970), p. 62.

4. Albrecht Wellmer raises this objection in "Reason, Utopia, and the Dialectic of Enlightenment," pp. 45–51.

5. One of Sorel's examples of a nonrationalist, imaginative construction is the "myth of the general strike." See Sorel, *Reflections on Violence*, pp. 22–28.

6. Berlin, "Georges Sorel," pp. 331–332.

7. In chapter 4 above I drew attention to a point of divergence between Butler's and Laclau's conceptions of the universal. Whereas Butler conceives of it as a "non-place," as something that manifests itself fleetingly in ephemeral spaces, Laclau conceives it as an "empty place" that is filled temporarily by particular representations, which are constitutively inadequate to their object. However, since Laclau fails to establish an ethically significant relation between this empty place and its historical articulations, in the end his conception converges with Butler's in its postulate of a transcendent object that is purely abstract.

8. See Habermas, "The New Obscurity: The Crisis of the Welfare State and the Exhaustion of Utopian Energies," in his *The New Conservatism: Cultural Criticism and the Historians' Debate*. Habermas advocates a mode of utopian thinking that operates historically and formally; however, he does

not spell out the details of his proposal. For a brief account of the utopian content of his theory of communicative rationality, see Cooke, *Language and Reason*, pp. 38–50.

9. Habermas's conception of autonomy is open to the objection that it is rationalistic: it implies that the rational transparency of subjectivity is possible and desirable. The conception I propose in chapter 6 seeks to avoid this kind of rationalistic interpretation of the idea of autonomous agency.

10. The normative basis for this aspect of Habermas's utopian vision is unclear. See my remarks in chapter 3 above, pp. 53–55, and in Cooke, *Language and Reason*, pp. 144–147.

11. Admittedly, there is some ambiguity as to whether it is implicit in the everyday linguistic behavior of all societies or merely of modern ones (see chapter 3 above, note 36). However, this point is unimportant for our present purposes.

12. Habermas continues to underscore the importance of formal conceptions of the good society under conditions of postmetaphysical thinking. See J. Habermas, "The Relationship *between Theory and Practice Revisited*," in his *Truth and Justification*, pp. 277–292 (here, p. 279).

13. Honneth, *The Struggle for Recognition*; M. Seel, *Versuch über die Form des Glücks* [Frankfurt am Main: Suhrkamp, 1995], pp. 10–11.

14. Wellmer, "Ethics and Dialogue," in his *The Persistence of Modernity*, pp. 160–168; A. Wellmer, "Truth, Contingency, and Modernity," in his *Endgames*, trans. D. Midgley (Cambridge, Mass.: MIT Press, 1998), pp. 137–154. ("Wahrheit, Kontingenz, und Moderne," *Endspiele* [Frankfurt am Main: Suhrkamp, 1991]); Wellmer, *Sprachphilosophie*, pp. 213–277.

15. The idea of redemption as making good *past* deficiency can be found in the writings of Walter Benjamin (see, for example, his "Theses on the Philosophy of History"). However, the question of whether the idea of redemption should embrace the making good of past as well as present deficiency has no relevance to our present concerns.

16. Wellmer's focus is on claims to truth but he also regards claims to moral and aesthetic validity as context transcending. See Wellmer, *Sprachphilosophie*, esp. pp. 271–277.

17. See, for example, Wellmer, "Reason, Utopia, and the Dialectic of Enlightenment," pp. 34–66.

18. Wellmer's critique of ideas such as the ideal speech situation has been articulated most fully in relation to the work of K.-O. Apel. See, for example, Wellmer, "Ethics and Dialogue"; Wellmer, "Truth, Contingency, and Modernity"; A. Wellmer, "The Debate about Truth: Pragmatism without Regulative Ideas," trans. W. Egginton, in D. Freundlieb, W. Hudson, and J. Rundell, eds., *Critical Theory after Habermas* (Leiden and Boston,: Brill, 2004), pp. 181–211 ("Der Streit um die Wahrheit: Pragmatismus ohne regulative Ideen," in D. Boehler, M. Kettner, and G. Skirbekk, eds., *Reflexion und Verantwortung: Auseinandersetzungen mit K.-O. Apel* [Frankfurt am Main: Suhrkamp, 2003]); and Wellmer, *Sprachphilosophie*, pp. 231–239. However, Wellmer makes clear that his criticisms of Apel also apply to Habermas: see, for example, *Sprachphilosophie*, pp. 227–231.

19. Wellmer mentions this problem explicitly in his "The Debate about Truth," pp. 208–209, but does not elaborate.

20. Wellmer, *Sprachphilosophie*, pp. 247–248.

21. A. Wellmer, "What Is a Pragmatic Theory of Meaning? Variations on the Proposition 'We Understand a Speech Act When We Know What Makes It Acceptable,'" in A. Honneth et al.,

eds., *Philosophical Interventions in the Unfinished Project of Enlightenment*, trans. W. Rehg (Cambridge, Mass.: MIT Press, 1992). ("Was ist eine pragmatische Bedeutungstheorie? Variationen über den Satz 'Wir verstehen einen Sprechakt, wenn wir wissen, was ihn akzeptabel macht,'" in A. Honneth et al., eds., *Zwischenbetrachtungen im Prozess der Aufklärung* [Frankfurt am Main: Suhrkamp, 1989].)

22. Wellmer endorses this component of Habermas's pragmatic theory of meaning, affirming Habermas's view that to know the meaning of linguistic expressions is to know how to use them in utterances in order to reach understanding about something (*sich verständigen*) with another person; moreover, that this entails knowing when the speaker has good grounds to warrant that the conditions for the validity of the asserted proposition are satisfied. See Wellmer, "What Is a Pragmatic Theory of Meaning?" esp. pp. 175, 215.

23. In his summary of Wellmer's contribution to a symposium at which he presented the paper, "Der Streit um die Wahrheit—Pragmatisus ohne regulative Ideen" (an early version of the article "The Debate about Truth"), M. Werner records Wellmer as arguing that "a concept we cannot understand cannot serve as a regulative idea." M. Werner, "Pragmatism without Regulative Ideas? Report of the Symposium in Essen on June 13th and 14th 1997." Http://micha.h.werner.bei.t-online.de/Werner-1997c.htm.

24. Wellmer's agreement with Adorno in this regard is evident throughout his writings. It is especially clear in "Truth, Semblance, Reconciliation," in his *The Persistence of Modernity*. ("Wahrheit, Schein, Versöhnung," in *Zur Dialektik von Moderne und Postmoderne* [Frankfurt am Main: Suhrkamp, 1985].)

25. I do not want to deny that there may sometimes be problems of intelligibility. In the last chapter I made the point that processes of cognitive and social transformation may be necessary before the reasons supporting the validity claims raised for a particular idea of the good society can resonate with the constellations of reasons shaping the subjectivities of those to whom the claim is addressed. This implies that regulative ideas may be temporarily unintelligible. See chapter 6 above, pp. 157–160.

26. See Wellmer, "The Debate about Truth," pp. 200–208; Wellmer, *Sprachphilosophie*, pp. 240–243. In addition to disagreeing with Rorty regarding the need for a context-transcending moment, Wellmer disagrees on the issue of fallibilism. He criticizes Rorty's radical fallibilism, disputing that the behavioral certainties that form the backdrop for practices of making claims and justifying them are fallible. See Wellmer, "The Debate about Truth," pp. 200–208; Wellmer, *Sprachphilosophie*, pp. 238–243, 250–277.

27. Wellmer, "The Debate about Truth," pp. 200–208; Wellmer, *Sprachphilosophie*, pp. 221–225.

28. Wellmer, "The Debate about Truth," pp. 204–208.

29. See note 18 above.

30. As indicated, Wellmer's discussion focuses on claims to truth, however, he makes clear that his argument can be extended to claims to both aesthetic and moral validity (see Wellmer, *Sprachphilosophie*, pp. 271–277).

31. R. Brandom, *Making it Explicit: Reasoning, Representing, and Discursive Commitment* (Cambridge, Mass.: Harvard University Press, 1994), p. 594.

32. Ibid., p. 601.

33. Ibid., p. 595.

34. Ibid., p. 601.

35. Ibid., p. 594.

36. R. Rorty, "Robert Brandom on Social Practices and Representations," in his *Truth and Progress*, pp. 122–137 (here, p. 134).

37. Ibid., p. 135.

38. Wellmer, "The Debate about Truth," pp. 195–200; Wellmer, *Sprachphilosophie*, pp. 245–247. In regarding the truth claims of a second speaker as (subjectively) justified, the first speaker acknowledges that the second speaker has what she regards as good reasons to hold that her claim is true.

39. Wellmer, "The Debate about Truth," pp. 198–200.

40. Ibid.

41. This negative argument echoes his earlier argument against Habermas and Apel in "Ethics and Dialogue." In that essay, he rejects the view that truth or moral validity can be defined as a consensus reached in discourse. He does so on the grounds that the requirements that a proposition must meet in order to be true, or that a norm or principle must meet in order to be morally valid, are not discursive; furthermore, that what matters is not the (procedural) rationality of a consensus reached in argumentation but the soundness of the reasons supporting the judgments. See Wellmer, "Ethics and Dialogue," pp. 160–168.

42. Wellmer, "The Debate about Truth," p. 199.

43. "The Debate about Truth," pp. 187–190; cf. "Ethics and Dialogue," pp. 180–181.

44. I drew attention to Laclau's apparent willingness to accept Žižek's characterization of his idea of political representation as a regulative idea in chapter 5, note 39.

45. It is ironic because Wellmer accuses Adorno of bad utopianism: see Wellmer, "Truth, Semblance, Reconciliation," pp. 11–14; Wellmer, "Reason, Utopia, and the Dialectic of Enlightenment," pp. 50–55.

46. Laclau and Mouffe, *Hegemony and Socialist Strategy*, 2nd edition, p. xvii.

47. Laclau and Mouffe, "Post-Marxism without Apologies," pp. 101–102.

48. S. Benhabib, *Critique, Norm, and Utopia* (New York: Columbia University Press, 1986).

49. Ibid., p. 226.

50. Ibid., p. 225.

51. Ibid., pp. 222–224.

52. For example, she seeks to avoid the pitfalls in his employment of a method of rational reconstruction, for she sees a danger in its reliance on an evolutionary-developmental model of cultural modernization that threatens to make emancipation a theoretical rather than practical project. See Benhabib, *Critique, Norm, and Utopia*, pp. 275–277. A further danger that she discerns in Habermas's methodology is that his reconstruction of universal competences may refer only to

the history and competences of the dominant social group. Against this, Benhabib emphasizes that the subject of emancipation is plural and differentiated. See pp. 331, 351–352.

53. See Habermas, "Discourse Ethics," pp. 63–64.

54. Habermas has shown awareness of this difficulty from the beginning. See his reply to feminist critics in Habermas, "Moral Consciousness and Communicative Action," pp. 116–194 (here, pp. 175–184).

55. Benhabib, *Critique, Norm, and Utopia*, pp. 332–333.

56. Ibid., p. 333.

57. Ibid., p. 336.

58. For instance in Habermas, *Communication and the Evolution of Society*, p. 93. Cited by Benhabib in *Critique, Norm, and Utopia*, p. 333.

59. Benhabib, *Critique, Norm, and Utopia*, pp. 338–339. In the meantime, Habermas has replaced the category of aesthetic-expressive discourses with that of ethical discourses. See his "On the Pragmatic, the Ethical, and the Moral Employments of Practical Reason." However, since the latter, too, are concerned with nonuniversalizable and culturally specific questions (of the good life), Benhabib's basic point remains unaffected.

60. Benhabib, *Situating the Self*, pp. 340–342.

61. Ibid., p. 6.

62. Ibid., pp. 3–8.

63. Ibid., p. 9.

64. Benhabib specifies the regulative idea guiding moral deliberations as the idea of "the general interest." Ibid., p. 9.

65. See M. Cooke, "Habermas and Consensus," *European Journal of Philosophy* 1, no. 3 (1993): 247–267. The context-transcending aspect of her conception remains unclear in the normative model of complex cultural dialogues she proposes in *The Claims of Culture: Equality and Diversity in the Global Era* (Princeton and Oxford: Princeton University Press, 2002).

66. Benhabib, *Situating the Self*, pp. 4–8. Benhabib rejects metaphysical positions that conceive of truth as a property independent of mind. Our discussion in the foregoing has shown the need for Benhabib to adopt a more differentiated position in this regard.

67. Habermas, *Between Facts and Norms*, esp. chapters 7 and 8. In addition to Benhabib, sympathetic critics who have queried his emphasis on reaching agreement include McCarthy, *Ideals and Illusions*; C. Lafont, "Spannungen im Wahrheitsbegriff," *Deutsche Zeitschrift für Philosophie* 42 (1994): 1007–1023 and "Realismus und Konstruktivismus in der kantianischen Moralphilosophie— das Beispiel der Diskursethik,"; Wellmer, "Ethics and Discourse"; and Cooke, "Habermas and Consensus."

68. Here, Habermas distances himself from his earlier position that the presuppositions that constitute the idealized notion of discourse must be approximately satisfied in real discourses. Habermas, "Discourse Ethics," pp. 91–93.

69. Habermas, *Between Facts and Norms*, pp. 323–326.

70. Habermas, "Remarks on Discourse Ethics," p. 51; cf. also p. 55.

71. See Habermas, *Die Nachholende Revolution*, pp. 131–132. Habermas points out that his pragmatic notion of unavoidable presuppositions of communication undermines the classic Kantian distinction between regulative and constitutive ideas.

72. See, for example, Habermas, *Between Facts and Norms*, pp. 164–167.

73. Ibid., p. 151.

74. "Majority rule retains an internal relation to the search for truth inasmuch as the decision reached by the majority only represents a caesura in an ongoing discussion; the decision records, so to speak, the interim result of a discursive opinion-forming process." (For Habermas, opinion formation as opposed to will formation has to do with the generation of valid knowledge.) Ibid., p. 179.

75. As indicated, Habermas continues to defend a constructivist position regarding justice. See especially Habermas, "Rightness versus Truth," pp. 256–275.

76. Habermas, "Rightness versus Truth," pp. 266–271.

77. See Habermas's response to Lafont in his "Rightness versus Truth," pp. 266–269.

78. See M. Cooke, "Avoiding Authoritarianism: On the Problem of Justification in Contemporary Critical Social Theory," *International Journal of Philosophical Studies* 13 (2005), no. 3, pp. 379–404.

79. Habermas, "Rightness versus Truth," p. 260.

80. Ibid., p. 261 (amended translation).

81. Wellmer, "Ethics and Dialogue," esp. pp. 197–199.

Chapter 8

1. N. Fraser, "What's Critical about Critical Theory? The Case of Habermas and Gender," in her *Unruly Practices* (London and New York: Routledge, 1989), pp. 113–143.

2. K. Marx, "A Correspondence of 1843," in D. McLellan, ed., *Karl Marx: Selected Writings* (Oxford: Oxford University Press, 1977), pp. 36–38 (here, p. 38). Part of this quotation is cited by Fraser, "What's Critical about Critical Theory?," p. 113.

3. Of course, it also underscores the need for these descriptions and explanations to resonate with the "struggles and wishes" of those who suffer oppression—a requirement that, as we have seen, finds expression in the Left-Hegelian idea of immanence and that I have identified as central to the idea of situated rationality.

4. K. Marx, "Theses on Feuerbach," in McLellan, ed., *Karl Marx: Selected Writings*, pp. 155–158. ("Thesen über Feuerbach," in Marx, *Frühe Schriften*, Band 2 [Darmstadt: Wissensschaftliche Buchgesellschaft, 1971].)

5. Adorno, *Negative Dialectics*; cf. Honneth, "Eine Soziale Pathologie der Vernunft."

Notes

6. Horkheimer and Adorno, *Dialectic of Enlightenment*, p. 12. Furthermore, the authors claim that the principle of immanence, which the Enlightenment holds up against the mythic imagination, is the principle of myth itself.

7. Ibid., p. 24.

8. Hardt and Negri, *Empire*, p. 187.

9. Ibid., p. 190.

10. Ibid., pp. 326, 332.

11. Ibid., pp. 221, 333–336.

12. Ibid., p. 190; cf. pp. 332–333.

13. Ibid., pp. 221–222, 333–336.

14. The authors repeatedly speak of revolution. See, for example, *Empire*, pp. 321, 324.

15. Ibid., p. 58.

16. Ibid., pp. 330–332.

17. Ibid., p. 217.

18. Ibid., pp. 78–80, 104, 133–134.

19. See chapter 6 above, page 155.

20. A loss of confidence in the regulatory powers of the nation-state, and the apparent lack of an effective supranational equivalent, may increase receptivity to Hardt and Negri's thesis that the negative effects of the global capitalist market cannot be regulated and controlled by democratic political institutions and practices.

21. Before the mid-1840s and, in particular, prior to his account of the materialist method in "The German Ideology", Marx attributed a greater role to (the right kind of) philosophical justification. This does not affect my point here, for his view of philosophical justification, too, was epistemologically authoritarian in its assumption of the inherent rationality of the historical process.

22. Marx, "The German Ideology," p. 160.

23. In the 1840s Marx seems to have held both the view that the validity of the theorist's perspective is guaranteed by the inherent rationality of the process of history and that his premises can be verified empirically. His position, as I understand it, is that the rationality of the historical process is the *source* of the validity of the theorist's perspective; empirical science attests publicly to its validity. Cf. A. Wellmer, *Critical Theory of Society*, trans. J. Cumming (New York: Continuum, 1971), p. 57, 68–69. (*Kritische Theorie und Gesellschaft* [Frankfurt am Main: Suhrkamp, 1969].)

24. Below I suggest that the question of the causes of the identified normative deficits may no longer be a fruitful line of enquiry for critical social theory.

25. Certainly, the theorists themselves present their debate in these terms. Fraser remarks on several occasions that her "conception of Critical Theory differs from Honneth's" (Fraser and Honneth, *Redistribution or Recognition?*, p. 209), while Honneth writes that he and Fraser "seem to

have very different views of the task involved in developing social-theoretical reflections in the present context" (p. 249).

26. Fraser affirms her allegiance to the Left-Hegelian tradition in Fraser and Honneth, *Redistribution or Recognition?*, pp. 198–202.

27. Admittedly, the normative foundations of Fraser's theory are unclear. Her lack of attention to the question of context-transcending validity may well be connected with her concern to downplay the importance of justificatory matters in assessing the critical power of a critical social theory. Honneth comments on the underdeveloped character of this aspect of her theory in Fraser and Honneth, *Redistribution or Recognition?*, pp. 259–262.

28. See chapter 3 above, p. 64.

29. I look critically at this aspect of Honneth's justificatory strategy in chapter 3 above, pp. 66–67.

30. Fraser and Honneth, *Redistribution or Recognition?*, pp. 34–36.

31. Ibid., pp. 229–231. To be sure, Fraser's conceptual argument is insufficient for her purposes. The idea of participatory parity does not follow automatically from a proper understanding of the liberal ideas of equal autonomy and moral worth: the same liberal ideas have formed the basis for theories that project quite different ideas of the good society, for example, Butler's idea of a social condition in which there would be permanent contestation, rearticulation, and reenactment of ideas and identities and Habermas's idea of a communicatively rationalized lifeworld that would exist in a relationship of harmony with the functionally rationalized system. If participatory parity is just one among a number of possible interpretations of these liberal ideas, Fraser has to convince us that it is the best available one.

32. Ibid., pp. 231–233.

33. A paper delivered by Matthias Iser at the Philosophy and the Social Sciences Conference in Prague, May 14, 2002, entitled "Cross-Purposes: The Fraser-Honneth Debate" prompted me to think that an interesting point of disagreement between the two theorists concerns the place of explanation in critical social theory.

34. Honneth, *The Struggle for Recognition*.

35. Fraser and Honneth, *Redistribution or Recognition?*, pp. 249–250.

36. The absence of an explanatory component is a further significant difference between Honneth's and Habermas's critical social theory (see chapter 3 above, pp. 61–66). For, Habermas's theory of formal pragmatics, too, could be seen as a moral grammar. His formal-pragmatic analyses could be described as "grammatical" analyses that reveal the structural features of interaction and provide a normative basis for criticism of actual modes of interaction; in addition, his grammatical reflections make available conceptual tools for describing and classifying certain modes of interaction *as* failures of mutual understanding. However, with his colonization thesis, Habermas, as we have seen, supplements his moral grammar with an explanation of the causes of the pathologies of contemporary social orders.

37. Fraser and Honneth, *Redistribution or Recognition?*, pp. 249–250. In these pages Honneth also clarifies that he did not set out to provide a categorical framework designed to explain the developmental processes of contemporary capitalism.

38. Ibid., p. 249.

39. Ibid., p. 113.

40. We saw in chapter 3 above that Honneth criticizes the functionalist tendencies of Habermas's critical social theory. He discerns a similar tendency in Fraser's perspectival dualist approach, whereby—contrary to her intentions—she ends up attributing the distributive injustice of the contemporary capitalist order to anonymous economic processes. Ibid., pp. 253–255.

41. Ibid., p. 255.

42. Ibid., pp. 255–256.

43. Ibid., p. 4.

44. Ibid., p. 254.

45. Marx, "A Correspondence of 1843," p. 37.

46. See note 23 above.

47. In view of Fraser's emphasis on the need for social explanation, it is not surprising that—unlike Honneth—she shows a concern for questions of transformative political action. Moreover, in congruence with the approach that I have advocated, she is attentive to the importance of context in deliberations about the actions that ought to be undertaken in order to bring about change for the better. Among other things she makes the useful point that actions that appear affirmative rather than transformative may, over time, have a cumulative effect that transforms the basic structures that cause injustice. See Fraser and Honneth, *Redistribution or Recognition?*, pp. 70–86.

48. Ibid., p. 210 (my emphasis).

49. By this Fraser means an approach that insists on the need for a dual perspective on the social order: the perspective of distribution and the perspective of recognition. The need for this kind of double critical perspective on the social order follows from her idea of the good society as one in which the demands of distribution and recognition would be in balance. For Fraser's account of her perspectival dualism, see Fraser and Honneth, *Redistribution or Recognition?*, pp. 60–64.

50. Ibid., p. 218.

51. Ibid., p. 233; cf. p. 206.

52. Ibid., p. 233. Our discussion of the relation between theory and praxis goes some way toward resolving this part of Fraser's and Honneth's dispute. Since, as I have argued, critical social theories do not have to offer an explanation of the normative deficits they describe in order to secure their praxis component, the absence of an explanatory component is not cause for concern from the point of view of practical efficacy. In addition, the force of Fraser's objection that Honneth over-extends the concept of recognition is relativized by my suggestion that contemporary critical theories may be better advised to give up the quest for grand explanations of the causes of dominating power and focus instead on describing the ways in which such power is disseminated and perpetuated.

53. These "others" may be citizens without specialist knowledge, or theorists or scientists with specialist knowledge.

54. Moreover, the authoritarian, Marxist position would be at odds with Fraser's explicit commitment to a nonfoundationalist approach to critical social theory. See Fraser and Honneth, *Redistribution or Recognition?*, pp. 209–211.

55. Ibid., pp. 70–72.

56. Ibid., p. 72. Honneth comments on this aspect of Fraser's approach, pp. 260–262.

57. Ibid., pp. 214–219. In this regard, Honneth's objection, that she "sketches a picture of two different ways of coordinating social action . . . [that] represent different domains of reality," seems pertinent (p. 253).

58. Ibid., pp. 61–62, 216–218.

59. Fraser, "What's Critical about Critical Theory?" At the time of writing this essay, Fraser had not yet given the name "perspectival dualism" to her approach.

60. A similar point can be made about Horkheimer and Adorno's and Hardt and Negri's theories. We may find convincing *Dialectic of Enlightenment*'s account of the ways in which dominating power is disseminated and perpetuated in the culture industry without having to accept their claim that such power can be traced back to the capitalist mode of production—and perhaps even to enlightened thought itself. Equally, we may find convincing *Empire*'s account of the ways in which dominating power shapes subjectivities under the conditions of globalizing capitalism without having to accept their claim that such power has its origins in the capitalist mode of production.

61. Habermas, *Between Facts and Norms*, pp. 445–456 (here, p. 446).

Bibliography

Adorno, T. W. *Aesthetic Theory*. Trans. R. Hullot-Kentor. London: Athlone Press, 1997. (*Ästhetische Theorie*. Frankfurt am Main: Suhrkamp, 1970.)

———. *Metaphysics: Concept and Problems*. Ed. R. Tiedemann, trans. E. Jephcott. Cambridge: Polity, 2000. (*Metaphysik: Begriff und Probleme*. Suhrkamp: Frankfurt am Main, 1965.)

———. *Negative Dialectics*. Trans. E. B. Ashton. London: Routledge and Kegan Paul, 1973. (*Negative Dialektik*. Frankfurt am Main: Suhrkamp, 1966.)

———. *Soziologische Schriften I*. Frankfurt am Main: Suhrkamp, 1972.

Apel, K.-O., ed. *Sprachpragmatik und Philosophie*. Frankfurt am Main: Suhrkamp, 1976.

———. *Towards a Transformation of Philosophy*. Trans. G. Adey and D. Frisby. London: Routledge and Kegan Paul, 1979. (*Transformation der Philosophie*. Frankfurt am Main: Suhrkamp, 1973.)

Apel, K.-O., and M. Kettner, eds. *Diskursive Rationalität*. Frankfurt am Main: Suhrkamp, 1996.

Beck, U., W. Bonss, and C. Lau. "The Theory of Reflexive Modernization." *Theory, Culture, and Society* 20, no. 2 (2003): 1–33.

Benhabib, S. *The Claims of Culture: Equality and Diversity in the Global Era*. Princeton and Oxford: Princeton University Press, 2002.

———. *Critique, Norm, and Utopia*. New York: Columbia University Press, 1986.

———. *Situating the Self*. London and New York: Routledge, 1992.

———, ed. *Democracy and Difference*. Princeton, N.J.: Princeton University Press, 1996.

Benjamin, W. *Illuminations*. Ed. H. Arendt, trans. H. Zorn. London: Pimlico, 1999. (*Illuminationen*. Frankfurt am Main: Suhrkamp, 1955.)

Berlin, I. *Against the Current*. Oxford: Clarendon Press, 1981.

Bernstein, R., ed. *Habermas and Modernity*. Cambridge: Polity Press, 1985.

Berofsky, B. *Liberation from Self: A Theory of Personal Autonomy*. New York and Cambridge: Cambridge University Press, 1995.

Bhabha, H. *The Location of Culture*. New York: Routledge, 1996.

Bloch, E. *The Principle of Hope*. Vol. 1. Trans. N. Plaice, S. Plaice, and P. Knight. Oxford: Blackwell, 1986. (*Das Prinzip Hoffnung*. Frankfurt am Main: Suhrkamp, 1959.)

Boehler, D., M. Kettner, and G. Skirbekk, eds. *Reflexion und Verantwortung: Auseinandersetzungen mit K.-O. Apel*. Frankfurt am Main: Suhrkamp, 2003.

Bohman, J. "'When Water Chokes': Ideology, Communication, and Practical Rationality." *Constellations 7*, no. 3 (2000): 382–391.

Brandom, R. *Making It Explicit: Reasoning, Representing, and Discursive Commitment*. Cambridge, Mass.: Harvard University Press, 1994.

———, ed. *Rorty and His Critics*, Oxford: Blackwell, 2000.

Brockelman, T. "The Failure of the Radical Democratic Imaginary." *Philosophy and Social Criticism* 29, no. 2 (2003): 187–212.

Butler, J. *Antigone's Claim: Kinship between Life and Death*. New York: Columbia University Press, 2000.

———. *Excitable Speech: A Politics of the Performative*. London and New York: Routledge, 1997.

———. *The Psychic Life of Power. Theories in Subjection*. Stanford, Calif.: Stanford University Press, 1997.

———. "Was ist Kritik? Ein Essay über Foucaults Tugend." *Deutsche Zeitschrift für Philosophie* 50, no. 1 (2002): 249–265.

Butler, J., E. Laclau, and S. Žižek. *Contingency, Hegemony, Universality*. London: Verso, 2000.

Butler, J., and J. Scott, eds. *Feminists Theorize the Political*. London and New York: Routledge, 1992.

Castoriadis, C. *The Imaginary Institution of Society*. Cambridge, Mass.: MIT Press, 1987.

Cohen, J. *Regulating Intimacy*. Princeton, N.J.: Princeton University Press, 2002.

Cooke, M. "Are Ethical Conflicts Irreconcilable?" *Philosophy and Social Criticism* 23, no. 2 (1997): 1–19.

———. "Argumentation and Transformation." *Argumentation* 16 (2000): 79–108.

———. "Avoiding Authoritarianism: On the Problem of Justification in Contemporary Critical Social Theory." *International Journal of Philosophical Studies* 13, no. 3 (2005): 379–404.

———. "Between 'Objectivism' and 'Contextualism': The Normative Foundations of Social Philosophy." *Critical Horizons* 1, no. 2 (2000): 93–227.

———. "Five Arguments for Deliberative Democracy." *Political Studies* 48, no. 5 (2000): 947–969.

————. "Habermas, Autonomy, and the Identity of the Self." *Philosophy and Social Criticism* 18, nos. 3–4 (1992): 269–291.

————. "Habermas and Consensus." *European Journal of Philosophy* 1, no. 3 (1993): 247–267.

————. "Habermas, Feminism, and the Question of Autonomy." In *Habermas: A Critical Reader*, ed. P. Dews, pp. 178–210. Oxford: Blackwell, 1999.

————. "Habermas on Meaning and Truth." *European Journal of Philosophy* 9, no. 1 (2001): 1–23.

————. *Language and Reason: A Study of Habermas's Pragmatics*. Cambridge, Mass.: MIT Press, 1994.

————. "Making the Case for Privacy Rights." *Philosophy and Social Criticism* 31, no. 1 (2005): 131–143.

————. "Questioning Autonomy: The Feminist Challenge and the Challenge for Feminism." In *Questioning Ethics*, ed. R. Kearney and M. Dooley, pp. 258–282. London: Routledge, 1998.

————. "Realizing the Post-Conventional Self." *Philosophy and Social Criticism* 20, nos. 1–2 (1994): 87–101.

————. "Review of *Reflective Authenticity: Rethinking the Project of Modernity* by Alessandro Ferrara." *Constellations* 5, no. 4 (1998): 572–575.

————. "Socio-Cultural Learning as a 'Transcendental' Fact: Habermas's Postmetaphysical Perspective." *International Journal of Philosophical Studies* 9, no. 1 (2001): 63–83.

————. "A Space of One's Own: Autonomy, Privacy, Liberty." *Philosophy and Social Criticism* 25, no. 1 (1999): 23–53.

————. "The Weaknesses of Strong Intersubjectivism: Habermas's Conception of Justice." *European Journal of Political Theory* 2, no. 3 (2003): 98–300.

Cornell, D., M. Rosenfeld, and D. G. Carlson, eds. *Deconstruction and the Possibility of Justice*. London and New York: Routledge, 1992.

Couzens Hoy, D., and T. McCarthy. *Critical Theory*. Oxford: Blackwell, 1994.

Derrida, J. *Writing and Difference*. Trans. A. Bass. London: Routledge, 1978. (*L'écriture et la différence*. Paris: Seuil, 1967.)

Dews, P., ed. *Habermas: A Critical Reader*. Oxford: Blackwell, 1999.

Eisenstadt, S. N., ed. *Patterns of Modernity*. Vol. 1. "The West." London: Frances Pinter, 1987.

Fahrenbach, H., ed. *Wirklichkeit und Reflexion*. Pfüllingen: Neske, 1973.

Ferrara, A. *Justice and Judgment*. London: Sage, 1999.

————. *Reflective Authenticity*. London and New York: Routledge, 1998.

Flax, J. *Disputed Subjects*. London and New York: Routledge, 1993.

Foucault, M. *The Archaeology of Knowledge*. Trans. A. M. Sheridan Smith. London: Tavistock, 1972. (*L'Archéologie du savoir*. Paris: Gallimard, 1969.)

Fraser, N. *Unruly Practices*. London and New York: Routledge, 1989.

Fraser, N., and A. Honneth. *Redistribution or Recognition? A Political-Philosophical Exchange*. London: Verso, 2003. (*Umverteilung oder Anerkennung? Eine politisch-philosophische Kontroverse*. Frankfurt am Main: Suhrkamp, 2003.)

Freundlieb, D., W. Hudson, and J. Rundell, eds. *Critical Theory after Habermas*. Leiden and Boston: Brill, 2004.

Gilligan, C. *In a Different Voice: Psychological Theory and Women's Development*. Cambridge, Mass.: Harvard University Press, 1982.

Goodman, R. B., ed. *Pragmatism: A Contemporary Reader*. London and New York: Routledge, 1995.

Habermas, J. *Autonomy and Solidarity: Interviews*. Edited and introduced by P. Dews. London: Verso, 1986.

———. *Between Facts and Norms*. Trans. W. Rehg. Cambridge, Mass.: MIT Press, 1996. (*Faktizität und Geltung*. Frankfurt am Main: Suhrkamp, 1992.)

———. *Communication and the Evolution of Society*. London: Heinemann, 1979.

———. *The Inclusion of the Other*. Ed. C. Cronin and P. de Greiff. Cambridge, Mass.: MIT Press, 2000. (*Die Einbeziehung des Anderen*. Frankfurt am Main: Suhrkamp, 1996.)

———. *Justification and Application*. Trans. C. Cronin. Cambridge, Mass.: MIT Press, 1993. (*Erläuterungen zur Diskursethik*. Frankfurt am Main: Suhrkamp, 1991.)

———. *Moral Consciousness and Communicative Action*. Trans. C. Lenhardt and S. W. Nicholsen. Cambridge, Mass.: MIT Press, 1990. (*Moralbewusstsein und kommunikatives Handeln*. Frankfurt am Main: Suhrkamp, 1983.)

———. *Die Nachholende Revolution*. Frankfurt am Main: Suhrkamp, 1990.

———. *Die Neue Unübersichtlichkeit*. Frankfurt am Main: Suhrkamp, 1985.

———. *The New Conservatism: Cultural Criticism and the Historians' Debate*. Ed. and trans. S. W. Nicholsen. Cambridge, Mass.: MIT Press, 1991.

———. *On the Pragmatics of Communication*. Edited with an introduction by M. Cooke. Cambridge, Mass.: MIT Press, 1998.

———. *The Philosophical Discourse of Modernity*. Trans. F. Lawrence. Cambridge Mass.: MIT Press, 1987. (*Der Philosophische Diskurs der Moderne*. Frankfurt am Main: Suhrkamp, 1985.)

———. *Postmetaphysical Thinking*. Trans. M. W. Hohengarten. Cambridge, Mass.: MIT Press, 1992. (*Nachmetaphysisches Denken*. Frankfurt am Main: Suhrkamp, 1988.)

———. "Reconciliation through the Public Use of Reason: Remarks on John Rawls's Political Liberalism." *Journal of Philosophy* XCll, no. 3 (1995): 109–131.

————. *Technik und Wissenschaft als Ideologie*. Frankfurt am Main: Suhrkamp, 1968.

————. *Texte und Kontexte*. Frankfurt am Main: Suhrkamp, 1991.

————. *The Theory of Communicative Action*. Vol. 1. Trans. T. McCarthy. Boston, Mass.: Beacon Press, 1984. (*Theorie des kommunikativen Handelns*. Vol. 1. Frankfurt am Main: Suhrkamp, 1981.)

————. *The Theory of Communicative Action*. Vol. 2. Trans. T. McCarthy. Boston, Mass.: Beacon Press, 1987. (*Theorie des kommunikativen Handelns*. Vol. 2. Frankfurt am Main: Suhrkamp, 1981.)

————. *Truth and Justification*. Trans. B. Fultner, Cambridge, Mass.: MIT Press, 2003. (*Wahrheit und Rechtfertigung*. Frankfurt am Main: Suhrkamp, 1999.)

————. *Vorstudien und Ergänzungen zur Theorie des kommunikativen Handelns*. Frankfurt am Main: Suhrkamp, 1984.

————. *Zur Rekonstruktion des Historischen Materialismus*. Frankfurt am Main: Suhrkamp, 1976.

Halbig, C., and M. Quante, eds. *Sozialphilosophie zwischen Kritik und Anerkennung*. Münster, Hamburg, Berlin, Wien, and London: LIT Verlag, 2003.

Hardt, M., and A. Negri. *Empire*. Cambridge, Mass.: Harvard University Press, 2000.

Heath, J. "Ideology, Irrationality, and Collectively Self-Defeating Behavior." *Constellations* 7, no. 3 (2000): 363–371.

Honneth, A. *Critique of Power*. Trans. K. Baynes. Cambridge, Mass.: MIT Press, 1991. (*Kritik der Macht*. Frankfurt am Main: Suhrkamp, 1985.)

————. *Das Andere der Gerechtigkeit*. Frankfurt am Main: Suhrkamp, 2001.

————. "Facetten des vorsozialen Selbst. Eine Erwiderung auf Joel Whitebook." *Psyche* 55 (2001): 790–802.

————. *The Fragmented World of the Social*. Ed. C. W. Wright, trans. J. Farrell. New York: State University of New York Press, 1995.

————. "Grounding Recognition: A Rejoinder to Critical Questions." *Inquiry* 45, no. 4 (2002): 499–519.

————. "Invisibility: On the Epistemology of Recognition." *Aristotelian Society* (suppl. vol.) 75 (2001): 111–126.

————, ed. *Pathologien des Sozialen: Die Aufgaben der Sozialphilosophie*. Frankfurt am Main: Fischer, 1994.

————. "The Possibility of a Disclosing Critique of Society: The *Dialectic of Enlightenment* in light of Current Debates in Social Criticism." *Constellations* 7, no. 1 (2000): 116–127.

————. *The Struggle for Recognition: A Moral Grammar of Social Conflict*. Trans. J. Anderson. Cambridge, Mass.: MIT Press, 1995. (*Kampf um Anerkennung. Zur moralischen Grammatik sozialer Konflikte*. Frankfurt am Main: Suhrkamp, 1992.)

————. "The Social Dynamics of Disrespect: On the Location of Critical Theory Today." *Constellations* 1, no. 2 (1994): 255–269.

————. *Suffering from Indeterminacy: An Attempt at a Reactualisation of Hegel's Philosophy of Right*. Spinoza Lectures 5. Assen: Royal Van Gorcum, 2000. (*Leiden an Unbestimmtheit. Eine Reaktualisierung der Hegelschen Rechtsphilosophie*. Stuttgart: Reclam, 2001.)

Honneth, A., and H. Joas. *Communicative Action*. Cambridge, Mass.: MIT Press, 1991. (*Kommunikatives Handeln*. Frankfurt am Main: Suhrkamp, 1986.)

Honneth, A., T. McCarthy, C. Offe, and A. Wellmer, eds. *Philosophical Interventions in the Unfinished Project of Enlightenment*. Trans. W. Rehg. Cambridge, Mass.: MIT Press, 1992. (*Zwischenbetrachtungen im Prozess der Aufklärung*. Frankfurt am Main: Suhrkamp, 1989.)

Horkheimer M., and T. W. Adorno. *Dialectic of Enlightenment*. Trans. J. Cumming. London: Allen Lane, 1973. (*Dialektik der Aufklärung*. Amsterdam: Querido, 1947.)

Iser, W. *The Fictive and the Imaginary: Charting Literary Anthropology*. London and Baltimore: John Hopkins University Press, 1993. (*Das Fiktive und das Imaginäre*. Frankfurt am Main: Suhrkamp, 1991.)

Kant, I. *The Basic Writings of Kant*. Ed. A. Wood. New York: Modern Library Classics, 2001.

————. *The Critique of Pure Reason*. New York: Macmillan, 1956.

Kauppinen, A. "Reason, Recognition, and Internal Critique." *Inquiry* 45, no. 4 (2002): 479–498.

Kearney, R., and M. Dooley, eds. *Questioning Ethics*. London and New York: Routledge, 1998.

Kelly, T. "The Unhappy Liberal: Critical Theory without Cultural Dopes." *Constellations* 7, no. 3 (2000): 372–381.

Kompridis, N. "Heidegger's Challenge and the Future of Critical Theory." In *Habermas: A Critical Reader*, ed. P. Dews, pp. 118–150. Oxford: Blackwell, 1999.

Koselleck, R. *Vergangene Zukunft*. Frankfurt am Main: Suhrkamp, 1979.

Kuhn, T. *The Structure of Scientific Revolutions*. Chicago: University of Chicago Press, 1962.

Laclau, E. "The Death and Resurrection of the Theory of Ideology." *Journal of Political Ideologies* 1, no. 3 (1996): 201–220.

Laclau, E., and C. Mouffe. *Hegemony and Socialist Strategy*. 2nd edition. London: Verso, 2001.

————. "Post-Marxism without Apologies." *New Left Review* 166 (1987): 79–106.

Lafont, C. "Realismus und Konstruktivismus in der kantianischen Moralphilosophie—das Beispiel der Diskursethik." *Deutsche Zeitschrift für Philosophie* 50, no. 1 (2002): 39–52.

————. "Spannungen im Wahrheitsbegriff." *Deutsche Zeitschrift für Philosophie* 42 (1994): 1007–1023.

Landry, D., and G. MacLean, eds. *The Spivak Reader*. New York: Routledge, 1996.

Lara, M.-P., ed. *Rethinking Evil*. Berkeley, Calif.: University of California Press, 2001.

Malachowski, A., ed. *Reading Rorty*. Oxford: Basil Blackwell, 1990.

Mannheim, K. *Ideology and Utopia*. Trans. L. Wirth and E. Shiels. London: Routledge, 1991. (*Ideologie und Utopie*. Frankfurt am Main: Klostermann, 1929.)

Marcuse, H. *Five Lectures: Psychoanalysis, Politics, and Utopia*. Trans. J. Shapiro and S. Weber. London: Penguin Press, 1970.

Marx, K. *Frühe Schriften*. Band 2. Darmstadt: Wissensschaftliche Buchgesellschaft, 1971.

Marx, K., and F. Engels. *Collected Works*, vol. 3. London: Lawrence and Wishart, 1975.

———. *The Communist Manifesto*. Harmondsworth: Penguin Books, 1967. (*Das kommunistische Manifest*. Hamburg: Argument Verlag, 2002.)

———. *Werke*. Band 3. Berlin: Dietz Verlag, 1969.

McCarthy, T. *Ideals and Illusions*. Cambridge, Mass.: MIT Press, 1991.

McLellan, D., ed. *Karl Marx: Selected Writings*. Oxford: Oxford University Press, 1977.

McPherson, C. B. *The Political Theory of Possessive Individualism: Hobbes to Locke*. Oxford: Clarendon Press, 1962.

Menke, C., and M. Seel, eds. *Zur Verteidigung der Vernunft gegen ihre Liebhaber und Verächter*. Frankfurt am Main: Suhrkamp, 1993.

Moi, T., ed. *The Kristeva Reader*. New York: Columbia University Press, 1986.

Munro, A. *The Progress of Love*. London: Chatto and Windus, 1987.

Nicholson, L., ed. *Feminism/Postmodernism*. New York: Routledge, 1990.

Nietzsche, F. *Beyond Good and Evil*. Trans. R. J. Hollingdale. Harmondsworth: Penguin Books, 1973. (*Jenseits von Gut und Böse*. Berlin and New York: De Gruyter, 1988.)

———. *Thus Spake Zarathustra*. Trans. T. Common. London: Allen and Unwin, 1967. (*Also sprach Zarathustra*. Ditzingen: Reclam, 1978.)

Norval, A. "The Things We Do with Words—Contemporary Approaches to the Analysis of Ideology (review essay)." *British Journal of Political Science* 30 (2000): 313–346.

Putnam, H. *Reason, Truth, and History*. Cambridge: Cambridge University Press, 1981.

Rajchman, J., and C. West, eds. *Post-Analytic Philosophy Today*. New York: Columbia University Press, 1985.

Rawls, J. "The Idea of Public Reason Revisited." *University of Chicago Law Review* 64, no. 3 (1997): 765–807.

———. "Kantian Constructivism in Moral Theory." *Journal of Philosophy* 77, no. 9 (1980): 518–519.

———. *The Law of Peoples*. New York: Basic Books, 1993.

———. *Political Liberalism*. New York: Columbia University Press, 1993.

Raz. J., *Morality of Freedom*. Oxford: Clarendon Press, 1986.

Ricoeur, P. *Oneself as Another*. Trans. K. Blaney. Chicago: University of Chicago Press, 1992. (*Soi-même comme un autre*. Paris: Seuil, 1990.)

Rorty, R. *Contingency, Irony, and Solidarity*. Cambridge: Cambridge University Press, 1989.

———. *Essays on Heidegger and Others*. Philosophical Papers 2. Cambridge: Cambridge University Press, 1991.

———. "The Overphilosophication of Politics." *Constellations* 7, no. 1 (2000): 128–131.

———. *Philosophy and the Mirror of Nature*. Princeton, N.J.: Princeton University Press, 1979.

———. "Putnam and the Relativist Menace." *Journal of Philosophy* 90, no. 9 (1993): 443–461.

———. "Sind Aussagen universelle Geltungsansprüche?" *Deutsche Zeitschrift für Philosophie* 40, no. 6 (1994): 975–988.

———. *Truth and Progress*. Philosophical Papers 3. Cambridge: Cambridge University Press, 1998.

Rosen, M. *On Voluntary Servitude*. Cambridge: Polity Press, 1996.

———. "*On Voluntary Servitude* and the Theory of Ideology." *Constellations* 7, no. 3 (2000): 393–407.

Rössler, B., ed. *Privacies: Philosophical Evaluations*. Stanford, Calif.: Stanford University Press, 2004.

Rousseau, J. J. *The Social Contract and Discourses*. Ed. and trans. G. D. H. Cole. London: Dent, 1973.

Sebeok, T. A., ed. *Style in Language*. Cambridge, Mass.: MIT Press, 1960.

Seebaß, G., and R. Tuomela, eds. *Social Action*. Dordrecht: Reidel, 1985.

Seel, M. *Versuch über die Form des Glücks*. Frankfurt am Main: Suhrkamp, 1995.

Smith, G., ed. *Benjamin*. Chicago: University of Chicago Press, 1983.

Smith, N., ed. *Reading McDowell: On Mind and World*. London: Routledge, 2002.

———. *Strong Hermeneutics*. London and New York: Routledge, 1997.

Sorel, G. *Reflections on Violence*. Trans. T. E. Hulme. New York: AMS Press, 1975. (*Réflexions sur la violence*. Paris: Marcel Rivière et Cie, 1972.)

Taylor, C. *Modern Social Imaginaries*. Durham, N.C.: Duke University Press, 2004.

———. *Philosophical Arguments*. Cambridge, Mass.: Harvard University Press, 1995.

———. *Philosophical Papers* 2. Cambridge: Cambridge University Press, 1985.

———. *Sources of the Self*. Cambridge: Cambridge University Press, 1989.

Torfing, J. *New Theories of Discourse: Laclau, Mouffe, and Žižek.* Oxford: Blackwell, 1999.

Tugendhat, E. *Probleme der Ethik.* Stuttgart: Reclam, 1984.

Vaihinger, H. *The Philosophy of "As If."* Trans. C. K. Ogden. London: Routledge and Kegan Paul, 1968. (*Die Philosophie des als ob.* Berlin: Reuther and Reichard, 1911.)

Watson, G., ed. *Free Will.* Oxford: Oxford University Press, 1982.

Wellmer, A. *Critical Theory of Society.* Trans. J. Cumming. New York: Continuum, 1971. (*Kritische Gesellschaftstheorie und Positivismus.* Frankfurt am Main: Suhrkamp, 1969.)

———. *Endgames.* Trans. D. Midgley. Cambridge, Mass.: MIT Press, 1998. (*Endspiele.* Frankfurt am Main: Suhrkamp, 1991.)

———. *Ethik und Dialog.* Frankfurt am Main: Suhrkamp, 1986.

———. *The Persistence of Modernity.* Trans. D. Midgley. Cambridge, Mass.: MIT Press, 1991.

———. *Sprachphilosophie.* Frankfurt am Main: Suhrkamp, 2004.

———. *Zur Dialektik von Moderne und Postmoderne.* Frankfurt am Main: Suhrkamp, 1985.

Werner, M. "Pragmatism without Regulative Ideas? Report of the Symposium in Essen on June 13 and 14, 1997." Http://micha.h.werner.bei.t-online.de/Werner-1997c.htm.

Whitebook, J. *Perversion and Utopia.* Cambridge, Mass.: MIT Press, 1996.

Wittgenstein, L. *On Certainty.* Trans. D. Paul and G. E. M. Anscombe. Oxford: Blackwell, 1969. (*Über Gewissheit.* Frankfurt am Main: Suhrkamp, 1997.)

Wolf, S. *Freedom within Reason.* Oxford and New York: Oxford University Press, 1990.

Žižek, S. *Enjoy Your Symptom: Jacques Lacan in Hollywood and Out.* London and New York: Routledge, 1992.

———. *The Ticklish Subject: The Absent Centre of Political Ontology.* London: Verso, 1999.

Index